REVITALIZING SOCIALIST ENTERPRISE

The collapse of socialism in eastern Europe and the former Soviet Union continues to have profound and far-reaching implications. In the former socialist states, immediate concerns are largely economic, in particular the move to privatization. However, these implications are not restricted to Europe. They have also had a powerful effect on those countries which continue as one-party states under some form of communist government.

In *Revitalizing Socialist Enterprise* the authors place privatization in the wider context of restructuring governments, industries, enterprises and management. The book also examines the similarities and differences between former socialist countries and those which are still socialist but, nevertheless, are also engaged in revitalization. The problems of these two groups are clearly interconnected. While the need for change across most countries has a common origin – an inability to make the communist economic system work well – the 'triggers' for major change have been varied. The book is divided into three parts: Part I introduces the subject; Part II looks at the process in seven of the former socialist states of eastern Europe and the CIS; Part III examines the situation in China, Cuba, North Korea and Vietnam. Each study is discussed by an expert either from that country or closely associated with it. The work also presents valuable conclusions, drawn from looking across all countries by principal topic as well as individual country contributions.

John Heath was Professor of Economics at the London Business School 1970–86 and Director of the Economic Services Division, Board of Trade 1964–70. He was also a board member of the British Airports Authority (now BAA plc) 1980–6. He is the author of *Public Enterprise at the Crossroads* (Routledge, 1990). He is now Chairman of two small companies.

REVITALIZING SOCIALIST ENTERPRISE

A race against time

Edited by
John Heath

ROUTLEDGE

London and New York

First published 1993
by Routledge
11 New Fetter Lane, London EC4P 4EE

Simultaneously published in the USA and Canada
by Routledge
29 West 35th Street, New York, NY 10001

Typeset in 10 on 12 point Monotype Stempel Garamond by
Michael Mepham, Frome, Somerset
Printed and bound in Great Britain by
Mackays of Chatham PLC, Chatham, Kent

British Library Cataloguing in Publication Data
A catalogue record for this book is available from
the British Library

Library of Congress Cataloging in Publication Data
Revitalizing socialist enterprise: a race against
time/edited by John Heath.
p. cm.
Includes bibliographical references.
1. Privatization—Europe, Eastern.
2. Economic conversion—Europe, Eastern.
3. Post-communism—Europe, Eastern.
4. Communist countries—Economic policy.
5. Privatization—Communist countries.
I. Heath, J.B. (John B.), 1924–
HD4140.7.R48 1993
338.947—dc20 92–44128
CIP

ISBN 0–415–09122–5

CONTENTS

Figures and tables vii
Contributors ix
Preface xiii

Part I Introduction

1 SURVEY OF CONTRIBUTIONS
John Heath 3

Part II The former socialist states

2 THE SOVIET SYSTEM AND ITS AFTERMATH IN RUSSIA
Elena Veduta 39

3 REVITALIZING THE RUSSIAN ECONOMY – CATCHING UP
Konstantin Kagalovsky 55

4 RECONSTRUCTION IN CENTRAL ASIA: KAZAKHSTAN
Serik A. Akhanov 76

5 POLAND – THE 'BIG BANG'
Pawel Bozyk 90

6 THE CZECHOSLOVAK 'LARGE PRIVATIZATION'
Michal Mejstrík and James L. Burger 103

7 EAST GERMANY: SCALING DOWN
Robert Bischof, Gottfried von Bismarck and Wendy Carlin 126

8 REFORMING 'SELF-MANAGED' ENTERPRISES IN SLOVENIA
R. Jayashankar 144

9 RESTRUCTURING DURING THE CIVIL WAR IN MOZAMBIQUE
Salomão Munguambe 162

Part III The socialist group of states

10 THE PEOPLE'S REPUBLIC OF CHINA: SOCIALISM WITH A DIFFERENCE
Gu Yang 175

11 VIETNAM: IMAGE AND REALITY
Raymond L. Mallon 204

12 CUBA: CRISIS AND THE ROAD TO RECOVERY
Paul Collins 222

13 NORTH KOREA: 'SCIENTIFIC MANAGEMENT' TO THE RESCUE?
Paul Collins 237

Notes and references 246
Index 255

FIGURES AND TABLES

FIGURES

3.1 The structure of power in the Soviet Union 67
3.2 Governmental structure in Russia after August 1991 68
3.3 The Cabinet in Russia (February 1993) 70
3.4 Structure of the Russian Fund for Federal Property (August 1992) 72
6.1 Privatization information requirements in Czechoslovakia 107
6.2 Timetable for one 'wave' of privatization in Czechoslovakia (including actual dates of the first 'wave') 111
7.1 Stages in the restructuring and privatization of microelectronics in east Germany 142

TABLES

5.1 Structure of industrial output in Poland 1986–91 93
5.2 Changes in enterprise structure in Poland 1989–91 94
6.1 Size of the state sector in eight countries 104
6.2 Czech Republic: privatization projects proposed by the final deadline 113
6.3 Czech Republic: elaborators of privatization projects 114
6.4 Voucher privatization in Czechoslovakia (CSFR) 115
6.5 Approved privatization projects in the Czech Republic (30 June 1992) 116
6.6 Structure of funds in the 'first wave', by size of fund 118
6.7 Czech Republic privatization status, late June 1992 122
6.8 Inter-enterprise debt in Czechoslovakia: involvement of the banks 124

7.1 East Germany: three business strategies for the baukema Kombinat 132

7.2 East Germany: restructuring and privatizing the baukema Kombinat 134

10.1 Structure of Chinese enterprises: end-1989 178

11.1 State enterprise sector in the Vietnamese economy 1987–91 209

11.2 State-owned enterprises in the industrial sector of Vietnam 1987–91 211

13.1 North Korean foreign trade 1986–90 (three largest trading partners) 239

CONTRIBUTORS

John Heath was Professor of Economics at the London Business School 1970–86, Chief Economist at the UK Board of Trade 1964–70 and before that he taught industrial economics at the University of Manchester. He also worked for five years in the paper industry. He was on the board of the British Airports Authority 1980–6, and is Chairman of EXE Ltd.

In 1990 he published *Public Enterprise at the Crossroads* (Routledge).

Elena Veduta studied at Moscow State University, and obtained her PhD in 1980. She is now a Reader in the Plekhanov Russian Economic Academy. Her previous activities included being Senior Scientific Worker at the All-Union Management Research Institute of the State Committee of Science and Engineering.

Konstantin Kagalovsky completed a degree at the Moscow Financial Institute and defended his PhD thesis at the Central Mathematical Institute in Moscow. With the British-based Institute of Economic Affairs, Dr Kagalovsky was a founding director of the Centre for the Study of the Transformation of Communist Economies. Together with Lord Harris of High Cross he has produced several papers on the Russian economy. In November 1991 Dr Kagalovsky was appointed the Plenipotentiary Representative of the Russian Federation for International Financial Institutions and headed the Russian team in negotiations with the International Monetary Fund and the World Bank.

Marjorie Nicholson (Brady) graduated from Hull University in 1987 with a first class honours degree in politics and became assistant editor of the *Soviet Labour Review*. In 1989 her paper on 'The Need for a New Analysis of the Soviet Union' was published by the Russian Research Foundation Trust in London. From 1987 to 1990 Ms Brady was also an adviser to the British Section of the International Society for Human Rights on Soviet Affairs. As a director of Russian Consultancy Ltd, Ms Brady is now involved in advising Western companies of business opportunities in Russia.

George Miller was born in Chile. He graduated from London University in economics and completed his master's degree in Soviet government and politics at Essex University. From 1979 to 1983 he worked as senior research assistant at the Institute for European Defence and Strategic Studies, leaving in 1983 to set up the Russian Research Foundation and publish the *Soviet Labour Review*. Since November 1991 he has been an adviser to the Russian Federation Committee for State Property (privatization ministry).

Serik A. Akhanov is Deputy Director of the Council of Economic Advisors, Office of the President of Kazakhstan, and Associate Professor, Candidate of Science in Economics, Kazakh State Economic University.

His previous post was Head of the Department of Economic Reforms and Structural Policy, Higher Economic Council, in the Office of the President of Kazakhstan. He graduated from the Kazakh State Economic University and for 15 years has been Associate Professor at the same University. He has also a postgraduate degree from the Moscow State University. He is married with two daughters.

Pawel Bozyk is Professor of Economics, Warsaw School of Economics, and Director, Institute of International Relations, Warsaw. He has also been Director, Foreign Trade Research Institute, Warsaw, and a Member of Council and Project Coordinator, United Nations University, Tokyo. His memberships of associations include the European Association of Development, Research and Training Institutes (EADI), International Studies Association (ISA), European Economic Association (EEA), the Club of Rome (Polish section) and the Club of International Relations (Warsaw).

He has published over 20 books and hundreds of articles and papers in Polish, and in English *Global Challenges and East European Responses* (ed., Warsaw–Tokyo 1988), and *Applying Market Mechanisms to the Socialist Economy* (Warsaw 1989). He has been awarded first prizes by the Minister of Higher Education, the Polish Academy of Sciences, the Polish Institute of International Affairs and the Rector of the Warsaw School of Economics.

Michal Mejstrík is acting Director of the Centre for Economic Research and Graduate Education, Faculty of Social Sciences, Charles University, Prague, Czechoslovakia. He has frequently lectured in the United States and in Western Europe (including Oxford, Cambridge and the London School of Economics). He has published over 100 articles on innovation, project assessment and privatization. He is editor-in-chief of the *Privatization Newsletter of Czechoslovakia*.

James L. Burger is a staff researcher at the Centre for Economic Research and Graduate Education, Charles University, Prague, Czechoslovakia. He is also associate editor of the *Privatization Newsletter of Czechoslovakia*. Before coming to CERGE he studied Soviet and East European Studies at Yale University Graduate School.

Robert Bischof served with Treuhand Ansalt from early 1991 as a member of Chancellor Kohl's action team to assist with privatization in east German industry.

A banker by trade, with an honours degree in economics, he has spent 25 years in Britain as managing director of German forktruck-maker Jungheinrich. He is a board member of German Industry Forum and serves as non-executive director on six German and British boards.

Gottfried Count von Bismark was born in Brussels, Belgium. He studied politics, philosophy and economics at Oxford University (BA) and continued his studies at the University of Southern California, Los Angeles, where he graduated in Communications Management (MA). He is currently enrolled in the Freie Universitat, Berlin for a PhD in communications and economics. In addition to his studies, Count von Bismark is working for one of the big institutions set up after reunification of the two Germanys and has been closely involved with east German companies since the beginning of 1991.

Wendy Carlin is lecturer in economics in the Department of Economics at University College, London. Before taking up this position in 1986, she taught for three years in Christ Church College, Oxford University. She is co-author, with David Soskice, of *Macroeconomics and the Wage Bargain* (Oxford University Press 1990). She has published articles on several aspects of the west German economy (including the economics of post-war reconstruction), and more recently on the economics of transition, focusing on east Germany.

Professor R. Jayashankar has a doctoral degree in business administration and is currently Academic Dean of the international MBA programme at the International Centre for Public Enterprises in Ljubljana, Slovenia, in collaboration with the University of Ljubljana.

He has had 17 years of teaching and training experience in various facets of management. He also possesses industrial experience in the port and computer science sectors. He has published extensively in various journals and is the author of four books.

Salomão Munguambe graduated in microeconomics at the Technical University of Lisbon in 1969. From then until 1974 he was Economist at the State Department Research Cabinet which supervised the banks and insurance companies. Then during 1974–5 he was Secretary of Finance during the transition government which led Mozambique to its independence, and during 1975–8 he was Minister of Finance. From 1978 to 1983 he was Minister of Foreign Trade and then became Professor of Economics and Director of the Faculty of Economics in the Eduardo Mondlane University in Maputo. He also teaches economics and accounting. Since 1977 he has been a full member of the People's Assembly, the Mozambique parliament.

Gu Yang was born in Peking and has lived most of her life in China. She was sent to England initially by the government to learn English, and she has stayed in Britain for 12 years. She visits China frequently. She has worked for several British companies and latterly has been teaching business studies.

Raymond Mallon works as an economist with UNDP in Hanoi where he is responsible for planning and supervising UNDP assistance to the economic reform process in Vietnam. He previously served as an economist with the Asian Development Bank (ADB) with responsibility for monitoring and analysing economic developments in Cambodia, Laos, Thailand and Vietnam. Prior to joining ADB, he worked as a consultant economist in Asia, Australia and the South Pacific for private clients, national governments and multilateral institutions. He received his bachelor's degree in agricultural economics (Hons) from the University of New England and a master's degree in economics from the Australian National University.

Paul Collins is principal consultant with RIPA International Ltd (formerly the Royal Institute of Public Administration, International Services Division). Previously he was Principal Adviser, Management Development Programme, United Nations Development Programme, New York. He has led Management Development Programme missions to several countries, including the Democratic People's Republic of Korea and Cuba.

He graduated at the University of Essex and gained his PhD at the University of Sussex. He has held teaching posts in Texas Tech University and the University of Connecticut in the United States, and in Ghana, Nigeria and Tanzania. From January 1993 he will be editor of *Public Administration and Development* (Royal Institute of Public Administration, London).

PREFACE

Since 1989 the world has entered a new era. The disintegration of the Soviet Union, the liberation of eastern Europe from communism and the adoption of democratic processes have brought about new economic thinking and action in these countries. Their impact has been large and widespread.

They have powerfully affected many of those countries which continue as one-party states and which have – or apparently have – communist governments in some form. They are the countries which did not choose the route of political reform but which, to varying degrees, have felt the impact.

In the Soviet Union *perestroika* in 1985, supported by *glasnost*, were important landmarks in the process of change, although many socialist countries had begun their economic reforms even earlier. The truth was that the socialist system could not be made to work well in times of peace and hoped-for prosperity. The subsequent collapse of the Soviet Union and of its special trading system gave these changes greater urgency and momentum (in Cuba, Vietnam and North Korea for example).

China, which started its *perestroika* as early as 1978, is in a different category yet, over a longer period, is going through a very similar transformation.

To consider all such countries – socialist and former socialist – within the same compass widens the possibility of learning and brings to light some insights into the processes of change, and some deeper understanding about the nature of the communist system and the legacies which others have inherited. The changes which are taking place have great importance for the West. Without a broad study of this kind it is difficult to see them in the right perspective.

So much has been written about privatization as an economic process that the focus of this book is both wider (to put privatization where it is occurring within the broader context of economic and political change) and narrower, with some attention to the changing structure of enterprises and the new demands on management.

In putting together this book my thanks are due to all of the authors of individual chapters who have made it what it is. I hope they will think that their hard work has been worthwhile. I am also grateful to Professor John Stopford for his helpful comments on chapter one.

JOHN HEATH
London

Part I

INTRODUCTION

1

SURVEY OF CONTRIBUTIONS

John Heath

INTRODUCTION

What have the following countries in common? China, Cuba, Czechoslovakia, eastern Germany, Kazakhstan, Mozambique, North Korea, Poland, Russia, Slovenia, Vietnam. The answer is that they are all communist states, or recently were communist, which are now trying to revitalize their economies, industries and enterprises through restructuring in one form or another. All reached a point of crisis which required drastic action.

Collectively, and in some countries individually, their future is critically involved with the West. Failure could result in collapsed regimes being replaced by some more hostile to the global interests, and a period of turbulence in their affairs which could be destabilizing and damaging.

They are not of course the only countries in this situation. They have, however, been carefully selected to form a cross-section which will capture the important issues and problems. This chapter summarizes the individual country contributions and then draws general conclusions.

Revitalizing

'Revitalizing' is used here in a broad sense. It stretches out towards what Mikhail Gorbachev called *perestroika*. He described this as 'restructuring' and saw it as 'a revolutionary process...far-reaching, radical, uncompromising, [to] affect the whole of society from top to bottom'.[1] That fits well within the framework of this book and for almost all countries.

But in his vision *perestroika* was 'a jump forward in the realization of socialism...and in its essential characteristics'. He saw it as 'an extension and a development of the main ideas of the Revolution'. While that is not the context of change in most countries in this book, it would find ready acceptance in China, which started its *perestroika* (called *gaige*) seven years before the Soviet Union, and in Cuba.

Three questions come to mind. Firstly, what was the stimulus or trigger that set off programmes of revitalization amongst these countries? Did they come, for example, from a change in political philosophy or from pragmatic responses to events (external or internal)?

Secondly, what were the policies and methods which were used to try to bring about revitalization? Were they broadly common or very different? Are political and economic changes in structure either necessary or sufficient to bring about revitalization?

Thirdly, what can be said at this stage about the results, recognizing that the processes of change may take time even if a country starts with a 'big bang'?

The choice of countries

There are 11 countries in this study through which to find some answers to these questions, and at least five ways of categorizing them which will be significant for 'revitalization'.

As mentioned, the principal division is between those countries that at one time were socialist (in Part II of the book) and those that continue to have socialist governments, in Part III.

The former socialist countries (Russia, Kazakhstan, Poland, Czechoslovakia, East Germany, Mozambique and Slovenia) have all dismantled or are substantially reducing central 'command' planning, abandoned egalitarianism and are heading towards a market economy of some kind, with the privatization of most state-owned enterprises.

Countries which remain socialist (China, Cuba, North Korea and Vietnam, the last of which defies any simple categorization) are, however, also moving in these directions, though partially, more gradually, within a different political framework and (probably) with different goals. Privatization is not on their agenda. Growth of a private sector is, however, permitted and encouraged in China and Vietnam (in Cuba it is limited to one-man businesses). In our list, only North Korea is holding back.

The second categorization is *within* the group of former socialist states. There are those countries which have been communist for more than 70 years, Russia (with the Revolution in 1917) and Kazakhstan (1920), both members of the Commonwealth of Independent States (CIS), and those which came under Soviet domination or influence a generation or more later. These are Czechoslovakia (1948), East Germany (1949), Poland (1947), Slovenia (1945, then part of Yugoslavia) and Mozambique (1975).

The reason for this distinction is that in the 70-year group, experience in depth of modern Western market economies is limited, especially important for the leadership and the bureaucracy. That is a big problem. The European states which became socialist more recently are geographically and culturally closer to the West, and memories of former market economies remain.[2]

Yet we must not underestimate the scale of the problem left even by 45 years of socialism, as Chancellor Kohl did in relation to East Germany (at least DM 140 billion being transferred annually in public money alone). It is against this measure that the problems of Russia and Kazakhstan should be seen.

The third categorization is broadly ethnic and cultural. Russia is largely Slav and Russian Orthodox (with at least 16 distinct ethnic groups), while Kazakhstan has a large Muslim population. Czechoslovakia, Poland and Slovenia are predominantly Roman Catholic. The Chinese culture is very different from the rest. Such fundamentals can be important in understanding differences in behaviour and in the transfer of experience; they should give rise to caution.

Fourthly, there is the question of scale. The countries range from the very small in population, Slovenia (under two million), up to the vastness of China (where two million are added to the population every six to eight weeks) and to the geographical enormity of Russia.

Fifthly, foreign trade is also important, both the share of trade in the Gross Domestic Product (GDP), and the proportion which was within the Soviet trading bloc (called the CMEA or Comecon). Foreign trade is, for example, vital to Cuba (and 85 per cent of it was with CMEA), whereas in China trade has been a much less crucial factor.

Finally, not all chapters have the same focus or purpose. There are two chapters on Russia, symbolizing different points of view of what is a most perplexing situation. There is a chapter which concentrates on the practical details of a voucher privatization scheme (Czechoslovakia). There is a chapter which concentrates on the problem of restructuring the (typically) very large enterprises set up under the Soviet system (two case studies in east Germany), and there are two chapters which focus on the means of introducing modern management methods into socialist economies (Cuba and North Korea), which have wider implications. Poland was the first country to attempt the 'big bang' approach. China is referred to as a possible role model for structural change in many parts of the world, and is of course of global importance.

THE SALIENT FEATURES OF COUNTRY EXPERIENCES

Russia

Of the countries represented, Russia has the largest set of problems and is the most chaotic. To understand why this is so one has to turn to history. The legacy left by the Soviet Union is well described by Elena Veduta in chapter two. Echoes of its system recur throughout the book because its influence was so widespread. What Russia is making of this inheritance is described by Konstantin Kagalovsky in chapter three.

The heart of the communist system was universal state ownership, egalitarianism, central planning and control, in the Soviet Union driven by the State Planning Commission (Gosplan). Although latterly Gosplan was inefficient, its statistics being dubious and equilibrium pricing being infeasible, at least it provided coordination, stability and a system which managers understood. With its collapse, individual government ministries have become the driving force, and the now independent republics, which were an integral part of Soviet planning, are no longer linked to any central economic mechanism. Elena Veduta urges that some form of centralized indicative planning and control should be revived.

The Soviet economy was developed as a single system, dominated by very large-scale enterprises (the 'super-monopolies'). Usually one such enterprise in an industry would be located in Russia, with perhaps two other linked enterprises in separate republics. The average size of all industrial enterprises in Russia was 821 employees in 1987[3] (in East Germany before restructuring it was 893 employees), compared, for example, with 190 in western Germany.[4]

Since interconnected suppliers may now be located in different independent states, centralized coordination has collapsed and international trade between them was until recently at a virtual standstill (all were demanding hard currency and little was available). Bilateral trade agreements are now being negotiated and direct contact is developing.

Elena Veduta describes how the Soviet Union's industry was run as if it were a medium-sized manufacturing company owning its own retail stores. The Supreme Soviet (the Board), Gosplan and state bureaucracies made all business decisions (as would functional managers) and communicated them via 'state orders'. No payments were made between buying and selling enterprises (by analogy, between processes within a plant). The state (the company) paid the wages and procured materials and fixed investment. Retail prices were fixed by the authorities (the company). Retail sales in state shops provided the government's (the company's) revenue.

Much of that system continues, with new problems as enterprises begin to sell to and buy from each other. Most management disciplines have not yet been developed. Credits are accumulated in blocked bank accounts (the 'seller' notifies the state bank what it 'costs' and is credited accordingly, no matter whether the 'buyer' has the cash to make such a 'purchase'). The purpose of this was originally to provide feedback for the planners, although in practice methods did not exist for Gosplan to use this information.

Recently credits have been rising at the speed of light as producers go on producing (and accumulating inventories), and at the time of writing (September 1992) had already reached 3 trillion (3,000 billion) roubles. (It is thought that net of mutual debts, the total may be around 900 billion roubles.) At the same time state-owned enterprises owe the government over 1.5 trillion roubles in credits provided. Konstantin Kagalovsky describes the conflicts and struggles within the top hierarchy of power in Russia about what to do concerning these problems. No satisfactory solution has yet emerged.

Since early 1992 there has also been a cash crisis. To control the money supply (and thus to meet IMF targets) the printing of banknotes has not kept pace with inflation, which in 1992 may exceed 2,000 per cent. In September 1992 the state was said to be owing some 157 billion roubles in unpaid wages and pensions. Republics in the 'rouble area', not under control of the Russian State Bank, have also been expanding credit. The money supply is racing ahead.

Crudely put, the choice is between hyper-inflation and widespread bankruptcy. Balance-of-payments problems add to the difficulties. Economic stabilization is far from being achieved.

Marxist philosophy held that the service sector was non-productive, its activities involving speculation and exploitation. State shops sold all that could be made available. Thus in Russia a competitive service sector did not exist. However, distribution has turned out to be a major problem. Privatization, which is easiest at this level, is providing the opportunity to improve efficiency. The 1992 privatization 'experiment' by selling state shops in Nizhny Novgorod has been successful and was the beginning of a now rapidly expanding small business sell-off (already said to embrace some 20 per cent of the Russian work-force in private-sector cooperatives).[5]

Mass privatization began in Russia on 1 October 1992, as detailed in chapter three. Vouchers worth 10,000 roubles are being issued free to the resident population (some 150 million persons) which, until the end of 1993, can be exchanged for shares in enterprises at auctions, sold for cash or used to purchase land or property. The scheme follows broadly that adopted in Czechoslovakia.

Workers and managers of some 5,000–7,000 enterprises will be able to choose between three options for acquiring shares in their own organizations. Some 200 mutual funds (unit trusts) have been created as financial intermediaries for the general public, enabling voucher holders to spread their risk. However, with continuing high inflation and with no strong attachment to the principle of shareholding, the cash option will be extremely attractive to many people.

There are no specific plans for reorganizing Russian manufacturing before privatization, although complete industries will be considered for restructuring along the lines undertaken by Western consultants in Poland. There seems little time to do this since vouchers are now being distributed (although under one option there are incentives to restructure). Company sales are scheduled to begin in January 1993. The Soviet economy was geared to heavy industry and to the 'military-industrial complex', an orientation which will have to change.

Elena Veduta argues that dismantling the central planning system in Russia was a mistake. She believes that many leading economists in the Russian government are 'theoreticians', and welcomes the arrival near the centre of power of experienced leaders from the state enterprise sector who know how the system actually worked.

But there are difficulties with reviving any form of planning for the CIS as a whole. Politically it would seem to many CIS members as if Russia were trying to take charge. The West would see it as recidivist and would try to prevent it. And events are moving fast in the opposite direction. However, Ukraine retains a central planning system ('state orders' were made compulsory in June 1992), while Kazakhstan positively wants some form of CIS central coordination.

Moreover, Arkady Volsky, head of the Union of Industrialists and Entrepreneurs of Russia and the most influential industrialist, has proposed a Euro-Asiatic Union of six or seven CIS republics which would pursue a slower pace of reform (he has joined with the Union of Works Collectives to form a new political party *Renewal*). There is mention of adopting the Chinese approach.

The present hope is that enterprises can become commercialized and privatized, can quickly behave like proper businesses, and that trade will develop – before the system disintegrates into chaos. Many doubt that this is possible. It will be a race against time.

Konstantin Kagalovsky's chapter shows the fundamental changes in the structure of the Russian government which followed the extinction of the Communist Party's 'parallel hierarchy'. Under that system the Party was all-powerful. Such changes are not merely organizational. In a market system the role of government also changes fundamentally.

At the time of writing the leadership power struggle is intense. The widely different policy conclusions arrived at by Elena Veduta and Konstantin Kagalovsky symbolize Russia's problems. There are no 'obvious' policy directions. Experts are pulled apart by the centrifugal forces of philosophy, belief and hope. Whatever the outcome, severely hard times are ahead for the Russian people.

1 March 1993 A recent visit by the writer to Russia and page-proofing of this book permit a postscript. The political struggle between President Yeltsin, who is unwilling to see his power in any way challenged, and the Supreme Soviet who wish to provide checks and balances, remains unresolved. By Western practice their demands seem reasonable.

Privatization is rushing ahead but with many problems – economic instability, no regulation of Investment Funds, the creation of many private sector monopolies, no concept of 'corporate governance', no requirement for external auditors, concerns about the *mafia* gaining control of enterprises. Many managers of enterprises are however impressive by any standards.

Kazakhstan

Kazakhstan, a republic of the former Soviet Union, had broadly the same inheritance as Russia and was a link in its central planning system. The problems of achieving economic stabilization are similar and hardly less daunting. Inflation is high (the Russian rouble is still their currency, although this may change), output, investment and employment have declined steeply.

Kazakhstan was the first republic of the CIS to pass a law on privatization, and it has made significant progress. Serik Akhanov in chapter four explains that although to mid-1992 only 15 per cent of Kazakh state enterprises had been privatized (1,500 out of 36,000), their target was 50 per cent by the end of that year. Since March 1992 there have been many auctions of shops and other service enterprises. There are two private television stations.

Industrially, Kazakhstan has decided to promote mergers in order to form 10–15 very diversified large industrial groups which would be strong in export markets and would compete with each other domestically (as in Japan, and as planned in Romania).

In Kazakhstan 90 out of the 115 largest enterprises are virtually complete monopolies. The problem of control will be addressed through the formation of an Anti-monopoly Committee, but already a significant part of the recent price inflation has come from price liberalization being applied to these enterprises.

As in Russia, the problem of inter-enterprise credits is severe. The outstanding debt in 1992 was 19 times that at the same time in 1991 and is now 88 billion roubles – and growing fast. Likewise credit from the government is very large. Together they pose a severe threat.

Serik Akhanov reports that Kazakhstan feels the need for the revival of some form of central planning, a combination of 'indicative' and 'directive' within the CIS, and seeks a means of cooperation with the other republics of the former Soviet Union. This echoes the proposals of Elena Veduta.

The programme of reform seems very solidly in the hands of the government, which accepts the responsibility to control it in an orderly way. The Higher Economic Council in the Office of the President, which brings together the heads of the core group of ministries most directly concerned with economic reform, seems to be the driving force.

However, a potential threat exists in that about 40 per cent (6.2 million) of its population are Russian, with also 40 per cent Kazakhs. The integration of Russians into the Kazakh population was never deep (only one per cent of them having learnt to speak Kazakh while 62 per cent of Kazakhs speak Russian). Now Kazakhs are being brought back from China and Mongolia to be resettled along the northern (Russian) border of Kazakhstan where Russians are in a substantial majority.

In spite of their present problems, why does policy in Kazakhstan seem more coherent than in Russia, and to have achieved greater progress? While a longer historical perspective may show otherwise, there seem to be three vital factors. First, President Nursultan Nazarbayev has been in high office since 1984 when he was appointed Chairman of the Council of Ministers of the Republic of Kazakhstan (then elected President by the Supreme Soviet in April 1990 and re-elected by a general ballot of the people in December 1990). The same leadership group which held power when Kazakhstan was in the Soviet Union also continues – indeed, the ruling families in Kazakhstan go back to before the Revolution.

While continuity and stability are important, perhaps more crucial is President Nazarbayev's leadership and style. He has published a personal 12,000-word strategy for Kazakhstan's political, economic and social transformation over a 15–20-year period, with the broad stages and milestones of change clearly described.[6] It identifies the nature and strengths of the Kazakh people and builds upon those perceptions. It gives practical guidance in all aspects of future policy. Its aim could be summarized as a liberal-democratic, multi-ethnic society, a 'social market economy' with about 30–40 per cent of it remaining in the public sector (because of the importance of Kazakhstan's mineral resources). It looks towards both Germany and Turkey as role models (the latter being a Muslim secular state) and seeks to strengthen ties with its CIS neighbours, especially Russia. It is a rather inspiring document.

Secondly, Russia has inherited many of the central problems of the Soviet Union. President Yeltsin has a larger and more complex task than has the leadership in Kazakhstan.

Thirdly, there appears to be significantly less corruption in Kazakhstan than in Russia. This may be a consequence of the longer period of stability in Kazakhstan and their greater sense of national unity.

Finally, Kazakhstan, while a very large country geographically, is much smaller than Russia in population, one tenth of the size, and more highly concentrated. The President can be closer to the action. Russia is large (almost twice the size of the USA) and very spread out (over 8,000 kilometres west to east). And in Russia, regional governments are not under the control of the centre and there is the threat of disintegration.

Poland

With a population of some 38 million, situated strategically between Germany, Czechoslovakia, Ukraine, Belorus, Lithuania and the Baltic Sea, Poland has been subject to many influences and incursions in the past but did not come under communist domination until 1947.

Since January 1990, however, Poland has introduced the most liberal regime of all the central and eastern European former socialist states, and it was the first example of the 'big bang' approach. So Pawel Bozyk's contribution (chapter five) is of special interest.

The Polish political system has resulted in weak coalitions and many Prime

Ministers (five since 1989), but there has been remarkable progress in restructuring their entire economy. Most prices have been liberalized (all agricultural produce, 88 per cent of producer goods and 85 per cent of consumer goods), subsidies have been largely dismantled, public spending has been brought under control, tariff barriers drastically reduced, multiple exchange rates unified, the zloty substantially devalued and the single rate is now on a 'crawling peg' system.

By the end of 1991, approaching 80 per cent of small enterprises, mainly shops and restaurants, were privately owned and 1,260 larger enterprises were in the process of privatization. In the two years since privatization began, private-sector employment has increased to 38 per cent of the total, with joint ventures in which foreign capital played a large part, and private enterprise industrial output has increased to 24 per cent of the total. But there are still over 8,000 state-owned enterprises in industry, some 1,400 in construction, 500 in transport and 600 in trade.

The 'voucher system' proposed earlier for mass privatization, to enable the population as a whole to participate in share ownership, was abandoned by the government of Prime Minister Jan Olszewski in a bid to slow down the hectic pace of change. It may now be revived by the coalition government (since July 1992) of Prime Minister Hanna Suchocka, who is said to be an enthusiast for private enterprise.

One feature of the Polish privatization programme has been its planned restructuring on a sectoral basis, using Western consultants, to accelerate the process. Thus the Boston Consulting Group has been working with a group of 20 construction companies, Bain & Co. with the electronics and industrial gas industries and with detergents, Ernst & Young with the meat industry, Samuel Montague with five power engineering and Kleinwort Benson with four ball-bearing companies, and Hambros with the pulp and paper industry. In the total state sector, however, this has been of limited scope, and there appears to be no government policy on such restructuring.

Some 290 large enterprises (with over 1,000 employees), which grew in size under communism, have been split into 996 smaller ones. Joint ventures have increased substantially, although direct foreign investment has been on a significantly smaller scale than in Czechoslovakia and Hungary, and Polish people living abroad have made a significant contribution.

Commercialization of their remaining state-owned enterprises began at the end of 1991, with supervisory boards comprising representatives of the state, managers and employees replacing the former Employee Councils, which were all-powerful. Pawel Bozyk urges that a Treasury Property Board should be set up, separate from the central administration, to be responsible for all assets owned by the state in order to achieve their better utilization and management. Such a Board would have representation on the boards of all state-owned enterprises. The Industry Ministry would be responsible for government policies concerning these enterprises.

Commercialization of education, health care, research, culture and welfare, to be on a self-supporting basis, has also begun.

The cost has been considerable. The recession has been severe and prices have soared (but are now under control). There are, however, now extremes of wealth (the few) and of poverty (the many). This could have political significance in the future if those who are badly hit by these dramatic events cannot share in the benefits.

Has the Polish 'big bang' experiment succeeded? Pawel Bozyk says that it has proved to be no alternative to an evolutionary process spread over several years. The delay in privatization of the larger enterprises was fortuitous because the substantial degree of economic stabilization already achieved will provide a more suitable environment in which newly privatized businesses can thrive.

Czechoslovakia

In 1988, state-owned enterprises in Czechoslovakia produced 97 per cent of the country's output, the highest share in eastern Europe. The aim of the Czech Republic and of Slovakia, for the purposes of privatization having separate administrations, is to reduce this to 30 per cent as quickly as possible.

Michal Mejstrík and James L. Burger, in chapter six, describe in detail the processes by which the first of two 'waves' of privatization is being conducted. At 30 June 1992, some 2,795 business units had been approved for privatization in the Czech Republic and 500 in Slovakia.

Vouchers were sold to all citizens over 18 (each voucher was 1,000 points of investment 'money') for the equivalent of about one week's average wage. In all, 8.56 million citizens became voucher holders, nearly three-quarters of the entire population. In the first wave of privatization, they were used in connection with the purchase of 1,492 enterprises, employing 1.3 million workers. In the Czech Republic vouchers covered 62 per cent of equity and in Slovakia they covered 74 per cent. The authors explain clearly the advantages and disadvantages of the voucher method.

Several methods of privatization are being employed. While this makes for a wide choice to suit individual and business needs, and thus has the great advantage of flexibility (added to which the privatization authorities have been quickly responsive to the situation where experience differed from their prior expectations), this approach added complexity both for the citizen and for the statistician reporting the results. Presentation is not helped because of the two separate Privatization Ministries in the two republics, and separate but parallel procedures.

Much reliance is placed on the Funds of National Property in the two republics. These Funds temporarily hold the shares in enterprises until they are sold, and they appoint their boards of directors.

There are also 430 privately established Investment Privatization Funds

(IPFs), which are mutual funds (investment trusts). They play a key role by purchasing vouchers from the public for use in exchange for the wide variety of shares on offer. While this system spreads the risk for voucher holders, the IPFs, in strong competition with each other to build their portfolios, have made some rather rash promises which they may come to regret.

An outstanding problem in Czechoslovakia, in common with Russia, Kazakhstan, Poland and other former socialist states, is the large amount of inter-enterprise indebtedness which has arisen from previous practice. Much of this debt in Czechoslovakia is being converted into bonds.

Privatization has made remarkable progress. It is an innovation on a giant scale. There were mistakes, but for the most part they were minor. The most serious fault was one of omission – the failure to establish an early regulatory system for the IPFs. What has been done may not be too late, but if there is big trouble this is likely to be its source.

East Germany

The former German Democratic Republic was in a fundamentally different position from other east European countries following the overthrow of the communist government. It became reunified with the Federal Republic, subject to German and European Community law, and, on a one-for-one basis, it adopted the Deutschmark as its currency (economic and monetary union was in July 1990). The Treuhandanstalt (set up by Hans Modrow under the communist government to commercialize the GDR's state-owned enterprises) was taken over by west Germans and became the centrepiece of the privatization programme.

The work of the Treuhand has been much written about already, and generally it is not a useful role model for other countries. So chapter seven, by Robert Bischof, Gottfried von Bismark and Wendy Carlin, concentrates on two case studies of how the Treuhand went about restructuring the Kombinats – large vertically and horizontally integrated units, many focused on broad industry sectors. The two groups were the baukema Kombinat (employing 16,000 people in over a dozen enterprises in heavy construction machinery, plant engineering and foundries) and the microelectronics Kombinat employing some 36,000 persons. Their findings have a direct relevance to other socialist and former socialist countries engaged in restructuring their industries.

The chapter highlights the need to evaluate expertly each section of each business and to decide its future. The range of strategic options rapidly becomes wide. Many different solutions were adopted according to the circumstances identified. What the Treuhand found itself selling was not 'firms' but rather, as the authors say, 'combinations of physical assets, human capital and cash, in exchange for management/organizational capabilities, technology and markets or market access'. The number of potential buyers internationally for these assets turned out to be rather small.

West Germans became chairmen of the supervisory boards (as they have done of practically all of east Germany's larger enterprises). While this had the advantage that the Treuhand could delegate and decentralize the restructuring task to experienced people, the authors believe that greater care should have been exercised in the choice of such persons because of the potential abuse of power.

There are some illuminating illustrations also about German support for its electronics industry and about the role of the *Länder* in industrial ownership and control.

Slovenia

Formerly part of Yugoslavia, Slovenia became an independent state in January 1992. When Yugoslavia broke with the Soviet Union in 1948 it developed its unique 'worker self-management' system for enterprise control. Enterprises were not owned by the state but by 'all the people'. Dr Jayashankar, in chapter eight, describes this system and considers its legacy for the problems of structural change in the Slovenian economy.

The system had many merits. Those who aspired to be managers had first to undertake manual work and to be sufficiently respected by other employees to be elected to such positions. There were state 'inter-firm' comparisons to assist in achieving high productivity. Enterprises decided their own prices and investment, borrowing from the banks for this purpose, and central planning was more indicative than controlling. There was competition in the marketplace.

But enterprises tended to be dominated by short-term interests, and they were permitted to own their own banks so that obtaining credit was easy, though costly. Managers were not always elected for the right reasons, and their 'term of office' was limited.

One year before independence, in December 1990, the Slovenian government set up the Agency for Privatization, and the associated Development Fund, to supervise, structure and assist in achieving privatization transactions. Revenues from privatization will be used by the Development Fund for national development purposes.

The government cannot force an enterprise to privatize since most enterprises are not owned by it (no one owns them, except 'all of the people'), but the Agency and Fund (the latter negotiates the sales) have been quietly going about their business. Dr Jayashankar gives a useful case study of how they work. This is in spite of the government having not yet passed a law on privatization.

There are several likely reasons for this omission. There is a terrible civil war being fought in other parts of what was Yugoslavia and this has affected

Slovenia considerably, and so this is not the most obvious time for such a fundamental change; there is no final agreement on the restitution of property confiscated by the communists being returned to former owners; there is controversy about which of two proposed privatization systems should be introduced for widespread implementation; and parts of the bureaucracy are against the whole idea. Meanwhile the Agency and the Fund are gaining useful experience.

All former communist states have a problem in valuing their enterprises for privatization. In Slovenia, the Privatization Agency has set up a Valuation Commission of experts which runs training programmes and conducts examinations for persons and agencies which wish to become 'licensed business appraisers'. So far 45 business appraisers have been licensed in this way.

As well as establishing these institutions for privatization, the government of Slovenia has been conducting a series of reforms, including the banking system, taxation, inward investment, introducing a new currency (to insulate Slovenia from the rapidly depreciating dinar), company law, and establishing a capital market and an active stock exchange – much of the legislation and many of the institutions which will be necessary to ensure that privatization, when it does happen on a wide scale, will be successful.

Mozambique

Mozambique was liberated from nearly 500 years of Portuguese rule in 1975. The consequential departure of almost all experienced business owners and skilled workers, graphically described by Salomão Munguambe in chapter nine, left the country in chaos. Private ownership had been an instrument of oppression and so it was not surprising that state ownership, central planning and socialist policies were introduced (aid poured in from Sweden, the Soviet Union, Cuba and East Germany).

From 1975 to 1980 they were at first successful, with major advances in education and health in particular. But then the civil war intensified, with its accompanying dislocation, destruction and the need for further centralization and state control. By 1983 some 70 per cent of Mozambique's industry was in state ownership, as were most of the shops, but by then the impossibility of managing such a centralized system had become apparent.

The period 1983–6 saw the first efforts at restructuring the economy, and 1986 was the major turning point. The new President, Joaquim Chissano, rejected Marxism and introduced the Economic Recovery Programme, assisted by the World Bank and other agencies. Centralization was reversed, private ownership and direct inward investment were encouraged. Enterprises have been progressively sold.

Yet the effects have so far been small. Development has not 'trickled down' the economy to the provincial areas. The majority of the population remain illiterate. Poverty is still widespread. The civil war and the recurring droughts drained the administration and perhaps left too little for anything else.

In August 1992, after long negotiation, agreement was reached between President Chissano and Alfonso Dhlakama, leader of the guerrilla group Renamo, and the cease-fire took effect on 16 October 1992. The structural adaptions to the economy, which were introduced under the Economic Recovery Programme, can begin to have their impact.

There are perhaps two main lessons from the Mozambique experience. First, throughout this whole period since 1975 there has been only one political party in Mozambique's parliament, Frelimo. But a change in leadership (President Chissano took over in 1986 after Samora Machel, the leader who achieved liberation, was killed in an air crash) can, within the same political framework and with the same bureaucracy, transform policy.

The background of President Chissano makes this more understandable. In 1975, during the nine months of transitional government from Portuguese rule to that of Frelimo, he was Prime Minister, and then until 1986 he was Foreign Minister. During this period he both observed the internal socialist policies being pursued and had a window on the world from his international contacts and travels. The international respect which he gained during that period, and his political experience, assured the support of the World Bank and of other agencies when he became President.

Secondly, restructuring on its own will be ineffective. There must be the infrastructure and the systems to make it work. This includes a reasonable level of literacy in government and amongst the people, a regional organization which can take the lead from the centre, and a degree of stability within the country so that people can learn new ways. The war made these impossible to achieve.

China

China is a land of contrasts and contradictions. Gu Yang (chapter ten) brings its achievements and problems to life with a richness of detail and illustrations.

China's reform programme began in 1979. It has involved many experiments, been through many stages, experienced many difficulties – and has achieved much progress in improving the standard of living of the Chinese people.

Deng Xiaoping, the architect of the programme (although Chou En-lai had proposed it earlier) and its constant supporter, based the reforms initially on the introduction of incentives. This worked so well in promoting the growth of collective enterprises ('township' enterprises in rural areas and cooperatives in the towns), which were free of state control and were often subsidized locally, that competition developed and the state-owned enterprises inevitably lost. They were much more rigidly controlled in every way, and had to bear heavy social burdens.

The terms of competitive trading are now changing. 'Reform of the state sector' is a major policy objective. The 'shareholding system' is now becoming widespread, although public authorities must maintain a majority ownership, and is seen as the key to the future.

The success story is in the coastal belt centred upon, but not confined to, Guangdong province. There growth is extremely fast, averaging in excess of 20 per cent per annum over the last 10 years, and it accounts for some 40 per cent of China's exports (Guangdong, with 63 million people, larger than the UK, has only 6 per cent of China's population). There is no single reason for this success.

Firstly, Guangdong was selected as the centre of China's 'open door' policy. Shen Zhen district was endowed with the best administrators, architects and engineers, and a group of communist cadres demonstrated the reality of the freedoms granted. The province was then showered with incentives for growth – 14 cities were designated 'coastal open cities', and 'special economic zones' were created with even greater privileges.

Secondly, the successes were accelerated by inward direct investment by Chinese living in Hong Kong, Taiwan and elsewhere with strong ethnic and family ties in these mainland areas. Wherever Chinese have settled abroad they run successful businesses. They have now brought experience and cash back to the motherland.

Thirdly, controls over collectives, although generally more burdensome to business than under Western capitalism and geared essentially to local interests, are by Chinese standards relatively free. Ethnic Chinese living abroad know how best to exploit these advantages.

Fourthly, Hong Kong sits offshore in the middle of the length of Guangdong; and Fujian Province, hardly less successful than Guangdong, lies along the coast to the north-east, opposite Taiwan (for political reasons this proximity has not so far been fully exploited).

The future of these developments is hard to predict. Reading Gu Yang's chapter, one cannot but feel that the task the government has now set itself, especially in the reforms of July 1992, will be extremely difficult to achieve. A power struggle may arise as the Communist Party *nomenclatura* lose control of state-owned enterprises. Local authorities may not readily relinquish their controls and locally beneficial subsidies. The bureaucracy is being reformed but it will take on many new functions, some not well suited to their traditional role.

Much reliance is placed on the new shareholding system. Public-sector corporate shareholders are likely to invest mainly in related businesses. How significant will be the share price in influencing corporate policies? Will large shareholders intervene in policy and management? Will more monopolies develop (without so far any 'anti-trust' constraints)? In its crucial corporate governance and control functions the system remains untested. Property rights are at the heart of the problem.

China has pursued an incremental and pragmatic path of industrial reform, focused on alternative centres of growth free from state control, with remarkable success. Now – albeit after years of experimentation – it seems set for a leap into the unknown. Transition is the danger period, and this will require the most careful planning.

Unless the July 1992 reforms are quickly consolidated with fundamental change (which may happen since a reformist group was appointed to the Politburo and its inner group the Standing Committee at the 14th Congress of the Communist Party, October 1992), the future will be very clouded when Deng Xiaoping joins his ancestors.

Gu Yang's conclusions are that China is moving towards a new system, with many elements of a market economy whose characteristics are not yet clear. If possible, it must be carried out in a coherent and coordinated way and, because the destination is unclear, she urges a cautious and controlled approach.

She believes that government planning and macro-controls need to be strengthened during the transition period, not weakened. There will be gaps between planning and market systems which the government has to bridge. Until the new system is working well the government should hold the reins.

Because controls over state industries were extensive and created inefficiencies, and because of their social obligations, they need to be helped to reform. They should be supported, not bankrupted.

Private initiatives and incentives are necessary but not sufficient for success. The government must help, too.

Vietnam

Following the expulsion of the French in 1954, North Vietnam adopted a socialist regime of public ownership and central planning, while South Vietnam developed a capitalist economic system. After the military defeat of the South and the departure of US forces in 1975, South Vietnam was integrated into the North's socialist economy. It did not, however, lose its capitalist ethic.

Orthodox central planning was short-lived in Vietnam. Evident weaknesses in its application in the early 1980s permitted growth in the private sector, especially in the south, and lack of effective control over agriculture also gave that sector scope for private enterprise. However, much activity in the 1980s remained under state control, and many prices were fixed on the basis of average costs.

Raymond Mallon, in chapter eleven, describes the way in which, after the Sixth Communist Party Congress in 1986, the economy of the unified Vietnam began to be reformed, with a gradually developing market-orientated economic system. This received greater urgency with the decline of economic assistance from CMEA partners in 1989 and its cessation in 1992. Trade fell to a fraction of its former level, and new markets had to be opened in competition with the West. Petroleum and rice became important export earners. External trade is now almost in balance. Inflation has fallen dramatically. The currency has been stabilized.

Since 1986 the share of output from state-owned enterprises, their number and their total employment have been falling steadily, and with encouragement from the government the private sector has been growing faster. Government and state-owned enterprise employment now accounts for only 12 per cent of the total.

State-owned enterprises still number over 2,500 (one half are locally managed rather than from the centre) but are down from 3,200 in 1987. Their reform has been taking place through commercialization and the gradual reduction of subsidies, through beginning to set them up as companies with shares owned by the government or privately, and through a restructuring of the government control systems (very similar to those measures being pursued in Poland). How far this will be taken is unclear. Agriculture (a most important sector in Vietnam) has also been liberalized with farmers making their own decisions and able to transfer their rights to use land (which remains state-owned). Foreign inward investment has been encouraged through the law of 1987.

However, unlike China, the Vietnamese Constitution of April 1992 has embodied within it the rights of the private sector 'to choose, for their own benefit, the forms of production and business, and have the right to set up businesses without any limitations as to their scope of activity in such branches and trade enterprises that are beneficial to the well-being of the nation'. The government of Prime Minister Vo Van Kiet is looking to the private sector to achieve growth, and it is pledged to privatize all of the small retail state-owned enterprises. Much freedom is being given to state-owned enterprises, with private-sector participation. Earlier uncertainties about the direction of reforms have now been clarified, although some elements of the necessary legal framework for a market economy are still absent.

(In 1986, when there were many changes in the leadership of the government, Vo Van Kiet, who is from the more capitalist south of Vietnam, first became Chairman of the State Planning Commission, although he was hostile to central planning, and soon after First Vice-Chairman of the Council of Ministers, equivalent to deputy Prime Minister.)

Vietnam is still a very poor country. It has received no help from the United States (there are now signs of a thaw in its icy relationships with that country), or from international agencies (that is changing too). Yet it is succeeding in liberalizing its economy to enable it to prosper, with increasingly successful results – within the framework of a proclaimed (reaffirmed in the April 1992 Constitution) Marxist-Leninist regime.

Cuba

Dr Fidel Castro Ruz ousted the Batista regime in 1959 and introduced socialism. The United States (located only 150 km away), on which the Cuban economy had depended, severed relations with Cuba in 1960. The Soviet Union stepped in to fill the void.

In the last 30 years the improvements have been dramatic (especially in education, health and housing). But with rising domestic problems since 1986 and the ending in 1989–90 of very favourable external relationships with the Soviet Union and CMEA countries (which in 1989 accounted for 85 per cent of its external trade), Cuba has had to undertake a radical rethink about how it can survive. The country is presently in a bad way, with severe shortages even of basic essentials, especially fuel and some foodstuffs. Imports have fallen dramatically. International debt is over US $7 billion. Paul Collins, in chapter twelve, describes how Cuba is tackling these many problems.

State ownership will remain, except now for one-man businesses and about 12 per cent of agricultural land which is privately owned. Although there is some 'creeping privatization', as President Castro has said 'for us, socialism cannot question the pre-eminence of social property over private property or the need for planning over the market...our country knew capitalism before the Revolution and does not have kind memories'.[7]

Central planning (in Cuba called Juceplan), although now in the sense of the economy 'being managed rather than intimately controlled', will continue to apply domestically with some decentralization in economic management. The survival package includes a redirection of traditional exports to new markets, export enterprises becoming 'autonomous' and relatively free from central planning, exports and imports freed from all controls, the encouragement of inward investment (even to the extent of foreign ownership), and a focus on restructuring the health care industries for export success – pharmaceuticals, biotechnology and genetic engineering (already export earnings from biotechnology exceed those of tobacco). Tourism is also being heavily developed and promoted, with considerable success (now Cuba's largest earner of foreign exchange). Trade with the CMEA countries is being restructured with bilateral trade agreements and barter deals, though on less favourable terms than before. State-owned enterprises are being commercialized and encouraged to compete with each other.

Paul Collins highlights the adjustments which are needed to switch from an economic system which focused on the internal needs of Cuba, with export operations undertaken by the Ministry of Foreign Trade, to one which can be successful in competitive international markets. The new management skills required are considerable.

As exporting spreads to more sectors, however, the planning system seems likely to become ever more 'indicative' in form or it will become inhibiting. Some materials and products will be used in both the planned domestic economy and the 'autonomous' exporting enterprises. And although the population has become extremely well educated under President Castro, the health care industries are very competitive internationally and high-risk. However, Fidel Castro has said (July 1992) that 'we are willing to be pragmatic in order to find solutions to the problem of development'.[8]

Cuba has had to undertake fundamental readjustment to its economy twice in recent years. Its socialist system is changing under the pressure of circumstances, but Paul Collins sees central planning as necessary to manage those changes efficiently. Cuba has a well-articulated plan for survival and development. The strengths in its work-force, its determination to succeed, its rich mineral reserves (especially in nickel), its strategic position between the United States and South America (which at present it cannot exploit) and its Caribbean climate are advantages which give considerable cause for optimism.

North Korea

From 1905 until 1945 Korea was under Japanese rule. After 1945, and then following the Korean War in 1953, the country became divided. The Democratic People's Republic of Korea (North Korea) was under communist influence, and the same President, Kim Il Sung, has remained in power since 1948. It is a hard-line communist society guided by the philosophy of self-sufficiency.

The country is becoming isolated and is experiencing increasing economic difficulties, as explained by Paul Collins in chapter thirteen. The problems have been triggered by the virtual cessation of trade with the CIS (North Korea's overwhelmingly predominant trading partner), with the *rapprochement* between the Chinese government and the (much more successful) Republic of Korea to the south, and by the realization that technically and managerially the country has become out of date.

Neither political nor economic reforms, however, are being contemplated, except for the interesting policy of attempting to modernize its industry through computerization and automation, and through the encouragement of inward investment. It is felt that modern management and operational methods within the framework of complete state ownership and central planning can be a very efficient combination.

There are also attempts to establish 'special economic zones of free economy and trade', to encourage inward investment and technology transfer. But due to inadequate preparation and a lack of understanding about what would attract foreign enterprises, that policy has not so far been a success.

The key question is whether management development, with modern computer-based methods of analysis, decision-making and control, is likely to be sufficient. The view seems to be taken that management is a strictly technical function. The wider issues of strategic management and direction, risk taking, responsiveness to a rapidly changing environment, motivation and how markets might be used to allocate resources more efficiently are not addressed. The key functions of financial management and control, marketing, etc. remain with the Central Planning Commission and other government bodies.

Paul Collins shows what a programme of updating management and operational techniques on the basis of computerization and automation would consist of. He draws on the aims of the United Nations Development Programme (UNDP) in North Korea in achieving these specific but limited goals.

THE KEY ISSUES

Strategic aims and leadership

What governments are trying to do is usually not very well expressed or clearly thought through. Russia used to make policy by slogans (and then found a justification which fitted). A 'market economy' is the latest rhetoric, although what it means is in many countries – especially those which have experienced 70 years of socialism – not clearly understood.

China is perhaps the most pragmatic. Ideas come from the 'grass roots' and if they seem sensible they are adopted, though usually with imperfect understanding of their likely effect (in spite of many 'experiments'). What China's destination is no one knows. (Gu Yang is cautious about the kind of 'socialist market economy' which will emerge.)

Pragmatically, China has hit upon a most effective strategy. It is to promote a separate geographical focus for growth (in Guangdong province), free from state control, with opportunities for expansion and replication elsewhere in China. These growth points provide competition for the state-owned enterprises (unfair competition as it happens) which then, through the relaxation of central planning and control, will provide the basis for their reform and revitalization. Whether intended or not, the policy has been brilliantly successful.

President Yeltsin has criticized the Soviet planners of *perestroika* for failing to analyse clearly what was wrong with the old system before formulating plans for improvement.[9] The new leaders in Russia may have a vision of their future, but they do not seem to have clearly communicated this to their people, or to have convinced them of its practicability.

At the other extreme, Kazakhstan has a clear statement of national strategy formulated and published by its President, Nursultan Nazarbayev, which is sensitively expressed and realistic in its aims. Cuba, too, has a clearly defined strategy, coherent and well focused.

Neither capitalism nor democracy seem necessary to bring about structural change and economic liberalization. China, Cuba, Mozambique and

Vietnam have the same one-party governments as they had earlier and yet all have now moved away from 'old style' communism.

Indeed, a significant number of the prime movers of change had – or still have – senior positions under avowedly Marxist regimes (Deng Xiaoping, Mikhail Gorbachev, Boris Yeltsin, Joaquim Chissano, Vo Van Kiet, Nursultan Nazarbayev, Fidel Castro). They are pragmatists. Of course there is no guarantee that the policies of communist leaders will change (witness President Kim Il Sung of North Korea and the toppled leaders of eastern Europe), but the evidence provided by those mentioned should dispel any simplistic assumption that all communists must be diehard, unresponsive to changing circumstances or uncaring about their people.

Strategic aims at the national level are best discovered and nurtured by experience, through democratic processes, through a constructive melding of 'bottom–up' aspirations and ideas with 'top–down' proposals and plans. Culture and history will play a large part. Some Russians look to China as a model for change, but their cultures and circumstances are different and copying might not work.

It is unreasonable to expect a people who have lived so long in an alien system to know what would now suit them best. They have been taught that capitalism is evil and does not work (in the early 1990s it is, however, nothing to boast about). Must they now embrace this philosophy? There may be an impression that because so much was wrong with socialism nothing is worth preserving. That surely is too superficial. It will, however, take time for them to realize what they must retain.

There should be no presumption that advanced Western nations necessarily have the right answers *for them*. People in former socialist countries may not be aware of what they will lose in following the prescriptions of foreign advisers.

Gradualism or the 'big bang'?

The main arguments for the 'big bang' – trying to do everything at once – are first that gradualism may not work because it gives time and opportunity for reactionary forces to consolidate their positions and to resist change. Secondly, so much is interdependent that 'all at once' should in principle be more efficient than piecemeal. Thirdly, the need for change may be extremely urgent (the loss of CMEA trade, for example). And finally, the agony will be so great that getting it over quickly has attractions, politically and socially.

However, a 'big bang' may make demands on a government beyond its capability, especially when so much will be unfamiliar and untested in local circumstances. Careful planning and control systems are necessary. The people may need time as well if despair is to be kept at bay.

The 'big bang' in Poland – the earliest example – led to the pragmatic decision to postpone mass privatization until the economy was ready for it.

It proved to be no alternative to progress spread out over many years. Vietnam made more steady progress (a 'little bang' we might say), with results which so far broadly parallel those in Poland.

In Russia, privatization of many larger enterprises commenced only in October 1992, before economic stabilization had been fully achieved, the legal and institutional framework fully prepared, or state-owned enterprises being able to act commercially. Already controversial, it is not difficult to predict this as likely to cause horrendous problems with potentially most serious consequences.

Some other countries have chosen a more measured pace – China, Cuba, Vietnam, although with pressures for acceleration. Czechoslovakia, with a history of stable governments, chose a bold and rapid route. The main lesson is that during the transition process, whether fast or slow, firm control from the centre is necessary to ensure that the transfer from one system to another is well managed.

Strategists and advisers have to look at the circumstances of each country. What can be done speedily in one situation cannot be matched in another. Priorities are different. History plays a significant part, and the cultures which are formed from long experience.

Privatization should come as the final stage. Proper preparation is vital. This includes economic stabilization, business and market law, institutional infrastructure change, commercialization of state-owned enterprises, some restructuring of 'super-monopolies' and widespread management education. Otherwise there is a serious possibility of collapse, disillusionment and political backlash, with dreadful consequences.

Stabilizing the economy

The anxieties of price liberalization, the removal of subsidies, the reduction of budget deficits, the (comparative) freeing of trade and of exchange rate adjustment have all to be gone through. A market system cannot function efficiently as an allocation mechanism unless major distorting factors are first removed.

The question is – how to do it? In the UK most controls were kept in place after the Second World War up to around 1954 (a few remained another year or two),[10] price controls and allocations being relaxed when supply was within sight of demand. With hindsight, nine years was too long, but removing controls overnight when there are fundamental changes to be made in the real economy (reorganizing industry, re-equipping, retraining, new product design), and when an economy is dominated by monopolies, cannot be sensible. A better way would be to remove most general subsidies, to introduce some very specific subsidies for modernization on the basis of approved business plans and to retain price controls on monopolists – three years might be a sensible target for their removal.

Economic stabilization can be directed and managed largely from the top, but it will be very demanding and difficult. Macroeconomics will become more important as socialist and former socialist economies enter world markets and central planning is dismantled. It cannot be ignored altogether in socialist economies (in North Korea incomes were increased 40–50 per cent to celebrate the birthday of the President's son early in 1992, with economic consequences which have yet to unfold).

Inter-enterprise indebtedness has reached vast proportions in Russia, and is reportedly significant in Czechoslovakia, Kazakhstan and Vietnam. Cancellation of mutual debts between trading enterprises solves part of the problem. Because they are a relic of the former system now abandoned and the product of transition, they should be irrelevant to the future. They might be released in small tranches, to assist enterprises with working capital for example, be converted into government bonds to relieve the burden of bad debts, be exchanged for promissory notes or – as a last resort – simply be cancelled.

Foreign trade and the collapse of CMEA (Comecon)

The Council of Mutual Economic Assistance had ten full members (the Soviet Union, Bulgaria, Czechoslovakia, Hungary, Poland, Romania, the GDR [East Germany], Cuba, Mongolia and Vietnam). Yugoslavia (including Slovenia) was a 'limited participant', and other socialist countries had observer status, including China, Mozambique and North Korea. It was set up in 1949 as a political response to the US Marshall Plan for the reconstruction of Europe. Counter-trading was at its centre (barter, counter-purchase, 'buy-back' and 'switch trading'), enshrined in bilateral trade agreements between its member governments and incorporated within their central planning.[11]

The CMEA came under strain as attempts were made to extend its activities (into multilateralism, long-term economic cooperation in joint investment projects). In 1984 a summit of Party leaders failed to resolve the growing conflicts, and its collapse in 1991 left the Soviet bloc system of trading in shreds. Those hardest hit were Russia itself, and countries such as Cuba, Vietnam and Mongolia which had benefited from favourable terms of trade and other assistance. The members of CMEA which lost their trade found that many of their manufactured products were uncompetitive with the West. As the case studies in East Germany revealed, switching markets was not easy. Finding 'core businesses' with prospects for survival was like looking for the proverbial needle in a haystack.

Attempts in 1991 to form a 'free trade area' out of the membership of the CMEA came to nothing because of conflicts of interest. Most central and eastern European members saw their future as members of the European Community, and they objected to the inclusion of Cuba, Mongolia and Vietnam (this was before they had appreciated that the EC would block the very items in which they had most export potential – agricultural produce). So a network of bilateral agreements has come into being, some based on the former barter system with prices set in US dollars but without cash payments. Most countries have also introduced tariffs on imports.

Notwithstanding the earlier problems, the case for a free trade area in the CIS seems strong (with a bank for international settlements). Membership of such an area would be no barrier to joining the EC (witness EFTA). The interdependent structure of industry in the CIS, the still common use of the rouble, and the open borders in many areas point in this direction.

Managing the privatization process

All former socialist countries have very large numbers of state-owned enterprises (some owned centrally, others locally). Small enterprise privatization presents comparatively little problem. It is the many medium-sized and larger enterprises that create the difficulty.

For 'mass privatization', especially where the people with money are the former Party *nomenclatura*, other bureaucrats and the black-marketeers, a national voucher scheme seems most fair and appropriate. Such a scheme has been adopted on a large scale only in Czechoslovakia, Mongolia and recently Russia. Kazakhstan's scheme relates largely to the housing market (the Kapchagai Porcelain Plant has, however, been bought by its employees using vouchers). Poland abandoned its scheme (which differed in concept from that in Czechoslovakia) although may now revive it.

Mass privatization is not easy. In spite of the meticulous preparation in Czechoslovakia, several things were misjudged. In particular, legislation for regulating mutual funds (the 'Investment Privatization Funds') was not in place soon enough.

The practice in Poland of scrutinizing whole industries for privatization, which has attracted the attention of the Russian government, was rejected by the Treuhand in East Germany because it was seen as being essentially a political matter and thus beyond their jurisdiction. However, the boundary is a fine one, and the idea is sensible.

The range of strategic choices from such an approach will be very wide (as the East German case studies showed). Russia will need a central organization to assist with this process, one which could also check the capability and reliability of Western consultants who may wish to be involved.

Most ex-socialist countries in this book have made a start in privatization (Slovenia without even having the necessary legislation). Czechoslovakia and eastern Germany are in the lead. For larger enterprises (not on the present agenda in some countries) thorough preparation is essential, and assistance from the private sector is most desirable (as in Czechoslovakia, eastern Germany, Poland and Slovenia).

Firm control by the state of privatization policies (and of transition processes more generally) are essential if the desired outcome is to be achieved, and if fairness and honesty are to prevail. This does not of course exclude the possibility of some delegation to the private sector, but it has to be within a carefully controlled framework.

The case of east Germany is exceptional in many ways and is not a role model. Political reunification, economic and monetary union and the dominance of west German experienced businessmen at the top of east German enterprises, put it in a different class. While this take-over by the Federal Republic will speed the adjustment process, its adverse psychological impact should not be underestimated.

The two case studies were very illuminating in highlighting the problems of strategy formation, identifying the core businesses with a chance of survival, giving practical expression to the need to preserve as much employment as possible (through subsidies), and showing – if it is to be done well – how complex the task is. In part, what was being sold had to be created from the resources which existed in another form.

Company valuation is a problem in all socialist or former socialist countries, because their accounting systems were not based on Western principles of business, stewardship or probity, and transactions were not conducted on the same basis as in the West. Slovenia has its Valuation Commission and 'licensed business appraisers' who have to pass examinations. In Poland, companies being leased to their workers (in 'liquidations') are valued by consultants hired by management and workers and approved by the Ministry of Ownership Changes. In Russia, company valuations appear to be undertaken by a branch of government. In east Germany there was a team of 80 top west German managers which spent three to four months analysing balance sheets and restructuring plans.[12]

Privatization should not mean a total withdrawal by government. Industrial strategy, especially early in economic transformation, will continue to be important. Basic infrastructure will need priority, plant re-development and location (especially steel works, chemicals, airports) will have national implications, environmental protection legislation may not be sufficient. Support may be needed initially for start-ups. Subsidies may be involved initially (east Germany).

Management

In general, education under communism has been given high priority. Their technical education has enabled Russia to be first in manned spacecraft and Cuba to major on pharmaceuticals, biotechnology and genetic engineering in the drive for export earnings. Engineers have a high reputation.

But in the context of introducing a market economy, education under communism has been seriously misleading, irrelevant (the focus on Marxist economics) or non-existent, because business management subjects were not necessary under a system dominated by central planning.

Indeed, it removed the need for practically all functional management in enterprises except production (although usually even production schedules were decided centrally). Accounting was part of the information system for national planning. Finance as practised in the West did not exist in enterprises, nor of course strategic management, investment decision-making, management information systems, depreciation – and everything else required in a modern business, including even commercial negotiation. Teaching functional management to people for whom the very concepts are unknown may seem difficult, but they have the advantage of good standards of education.

The problem is not simply that such subjects were not taught in the socialist education system but also that currently there are few teachers in those countries who themselves understand what needs to be taught and are capable of doing so. (Russia has applied to the IMF and the World Bank to fund the training of some two million accountants.) But that is not the end of the road – just the end of the beginning, and the easy part at that. The problem is strategic management, organizing for success, high-level *policies* of all kinds.

The role of management education in revitalizing socialist enterprises is crucial. The approach in Cuba (chapter twelve) illustrates the desired scope of education for business. The emphasis in North Korea is more narrowly on 'scientific management', computerization and automation. Functional management is a basic building block. But then what makes a business successful is much harder to convey, and more controversial.

How a medium-sized or a large business in Russia should be managed to achieve success is not something that most Western consultants or managers will find easy to prescribe. China is very different again, because of its culture and habits.

One may have to start with practices which are known to work in the country concerned and only then to progress in stages and at a pace which can be absorbed and practised. Delegated authorities and 'empowerment' at lower levels may or may not create motivation and a sense of responsibility in say Tajikistan (which looks towards Iran as a role model). And in North Korea, where strategic and leadership functions remain with the Central Planning Commission, they may be infeasible.

The most urgent need in Russia is a massive programme of business education. Privatization is no good without it. The hoped-for results would not be forthcoming. Bankruptcies would be the quick result, creating yet more chaos.

The simplest way would be through television (an equivalent to the British 'Open University'), as already widely used in China. Several groups in the UK are conducting negotiations with Russia to generate a series of programmes there.

East Germany is in the most fortunate position, with experienced businessmen from west Germany at the top of their supervisory boards. Other countries do not have this opportunity.

Large enterprises and monopoly power

The Soviet Union's policy of large-scale enterprise was at two interconnected levels. First was the distribution of 'super-monopolies' throughout the Soviet Union and its satellites, in which Russia was predominant. This comprised a total system of production, and hence brought about the need for coordination – the issue about which Elena Veduta was particularly concerned, and was seen also by Serik Akhanov in Kazakhstan.

At the other level was the policy of large scale within individual republics, reported in Czechoslovakia, East Germany, Kazakhstan and Poland, which was the counterpart and consequence of the Soviet Union's policy.

That policy came about it would seem because 'economies of scale' were thought to be limitless. But also large scale made control through central planning more practicable (fewer enterprises to incorporate into the system), enhanced the power of bureaucrats at the centre and bound the Soviet Union and its satellites together through economic interdependence.

Now many large enterprises are being dismantled. In Poland 290 large enterprises were split into 996 smaller ones, and in east Germany, 18 months after currency union, 8,000 enterprises had grown to 11,000 as a result of splitting. In Czechoslovakia restructuring is left to the new owners to undertake, and although many competing proposals for privatization involved breaking up existing large enterprises many were technologically infeasible.

In Kazakhstan, however, large enterprises are being re-bundled into a small number of diversified groups. And in China, although Gu Yang writes that the economy is very fragmented, there are many gigantic enterprises (she quotes the Nanjing Chemical Complex with 390,000 workers), and in the automobile industry a series of 494 mergers have reduced the number of enterprises down to four. A single plant to make video-recorders for the whole of China is currently under construction. The contrast in policy with many former socialist states is striking.

The arguments for and against large-scale enterprise are well known and need not be rehearsed here. The 'small is beautiful' approach, popularized by E.F. Schumacher in 1973, had become familiar much earlier as 'dis-economies of scale'. It has clearly won widespread support in the West.

Large enterprises under socialism also had (and some still have) social obligations (housing, health care, education, pensions) which in the West would be provided partly or wholly by the state or in separate organizations privately. In many countries in this study such obligations create confusion in assessing the profitability of enterprises, and when they are removed the state will have some responsibility for their provision.

The important issues are efficiency, market responsiveness, long-term viability and the control of monopoly power. Disintegration into smaller though viable enterprises before privatization seems most desirable, otherwise much reliance has to be placed on 'anti-trust' policies. In Russia, Kazakhstan and Poland Anti-monopoly Committees have been set up but functionally they appear to be weak. Until competition becomes effective, price regulation is desirable.

Corporate governance

In Poland and Czechoslovakia there is a policy of two-tier boards (supervisory and management), in Slovenia some 'social boards' are to consist of representatives of the state, creditors (probably bankers) and employees. In Czechoslovakia, initially boards will be appointed by the Funds of National Property (the temporary owners of privatized companies). In China boards will be appointed by shareholders.

In general, however, very little thought has been given to the structure and role of boards of enterprises, whether state-owned or privatized. The appointment of non-executive directors and their role, and of such devices as 'audit committees', have not been addressed. This is a serious weakness in policy.

Shareholding through voucher schemes will be widely dispersed (at least initially) and therefore corporate governance from that source will be weak. Where mutual funds have been established as important intermediaries, their role will be crucial. If they act like institutional shareholders in the West there will be a problem. The behaviour of public-sector shareholders in China is untested.

This issue is especially important because anti-monopoly policy generally seems weak. Much reliance – perhaps too much reliance – is being placed on the effectiveness of competition.

State-owned enterprises

Whether enterprises are to remain state-owned or not, they need to be well managed. Commercialization is a top priority (removing them from the central planning system, distancing them from government, earning revenues sufficient to cover costs and managing them as far as possible like well-run businesses in the private sector).

Those enterprises which will remain state-owned need also to establish effective long-term working relationships with their government departments which will distinguish clearly between the duties, responsibilities and powers of the enterprise and those of the government. The previous book by the present author (Heath 1990) was addressed partly to that problem.

There it was argued that informal written contracts between government ministers and the chairmen of enterprises, negotiated and agreed willingly by both sides, covering perhaps 3–5 years ahead, would be very desirable. Contracts should preferably be short documents; their length and scope would reflect the degree of trust between the two parties and would crystallize the nature of the relationship between them. That will change over time and with experience. Such a document, agreed separately for each enterprise, would provide a framework for management to act within the powers granted to it, in order to achieve the agreed strategic aims, goals and targets.

This issue does not appear to have been addressed by any country in this book except China and Kazakhstan. But in China the 'contract' system does not work well. There are perhaps too many publicly owned enterprises (over seven million) for the system to be sufficiently refined (although it could apply better to very large enterprises), poor performance has not been penalized, contracts tend to be extremely detailed and there is too much corruption. Rules are issued – and then largely ignored.

The Chinese will rely on granting greater autonomy to state-owned enterprises, on achieving fair competition between them and those owned by local authorities, and on the recently tested system of shareholding. Public enterprises and the state itself will be the principal shareholders. There is no hint that their role is to exert pressure on management to improve performance, although this may emerge.

Pawel Bozyk argues that the first stage is commercialization and that Poland needs to have a Treasury Property Board to represent the interests of the state as owner, and to have a representative on the supervisory board of each enterprise, while the Industry Ministry would be responsible for policy. A similar idea is put forward by Raymond Mallon for Vietnam.

However, a state-owned enterprise with two powerful masters will be in difficulty if there is conflict between them. Other ministries may also have strong interests. It might be better if all government policies were to be channelled through a single 'sponsoring' ministry and to make it responsible for policy coordination.

If a contract existed between the 'sponsoring' ministry and the enterprise it would be unnecessary to have a representative from the Treasury on the board. To have such a person implies a lack of trust, and opens the door to contradictory policies.[13] There could be government appointed auditors.

Corruption and crime

A worrying aspect of the reform process in some countries is the rise in criminal activity. This has been most widely reported in the Guangdong province of China and in Russia. Poland and other countries are not free of the problem. Speculators, black-marketeers, bureaucrats and especially the former Party *nomenclatura* have been referred to many times as a source of trouble. In Russia they could buy up vouchers (which can be sold for cash) and if shareholders become entitled to vote could gain control of many enterprises. That would be a bleak prospect.

In part the rise in crime reflects a rise in opportunity – the inevitable dislocations of rapid change, sudden new freedoms and cash easily earned by those who know how. Where the controlling institutions of a market economy are not in position before these changes take place, criminals will step in. Gu Yang referred to the gaps between a centrally planned and a market system and the need for more government control, not less, during the period of transition. That has a direct relevance to this problem.

The role and structure of government

Once a state ceases to control in detail the economy and the lives of its citizens, or embarks on that route, the role of government must change. Old ways of thinking and working become redundant. New skills and attitudes will have to be acquired. The machinery of government may be no smaller but it will certainly be different.

In former socialist states the 'parallel hierarchy' of control by the Communist Party would be abolished. Russia and the eastern European countries in this study have done so. Mozambique has reached the point. China has not yet faced the challenge.

During the transition control is essential if chaos is to be avoided. This means strong government and an efficient bureaucracy responsive to it. After the transition the balance of power in government is most likely to change, depending upon the final resting place. The key words for government may become not controlling but enabling, promoting and providing, protecting and regulating (and legislating for such matters). Such a change heralds a major transformation in style, and hence in the need for reorganization and training.

In formulating policies, and in balancing between those which may conflict, a government and its people should decide. After a generation or more of over-riding state control the pendulum may swing too far. Changing the structure of government is relatively easy (in the sense of lines on an organization chart), but it is what people do within the new structure which matters. That will take time to develop.

The centralization of policy in the Soviet Union meant that when the whole system collapsed, the newly independent republics had to create their own government institutions for policy formation. As in Kazakhstan, many countries went for an 'Office of the President' to provide the expertise and new thinking.

CONCLUSIONS

The communist economic system – central planning and control, state ownership, large-scale enterprise, egalitarianism – pervaded the Soviet Union and its satellites. However, most countries within the system began turning away from its strict application long before any major break came about. The truth is that it did not work well even in the Soviet Union, nor did it transplant well to other countries. The problem was not one of scale; much smaller countries than the Soviet Union – Cuba, Mozambique and Vietnam – also found great difficulties. The reasons were both technical and cultural.

What emerges in this book is that each country experienced a chain of events, commonly starting with difficulties over 'command' central planning. There was then a 'trigger' for major change at some point (the overthrow of political regimes in eastern Europe, the disintegration of the Soviet Union and the collapse of its trading system, new leadership in Mozambique and Vietnam). One picks up the story at that point, but it is easy to misinterpret unless one traces back the origins.

When these events took place the economic responses were varied and with different emphasis, but the general direction was remarkably similar. They can be summarized as attempted economic stabilization (control of inflation, budgets, foreign currency/exchange rate), reduction of controls and subsidies, freer markets, commercialization of state enterprises, privatization, more open international trade, inward foreign investment, better management, more incentives. North Korea is making the least change and revitalization is seen in a very narrow context.

This list fits remarkably well with the evolution of policy in China since 1978 (though for 'privatization' read 'encouragement of the private sector'). Deng Xiaoping was looking for a way of revitalizing the Chinese economy. He had seen that incentives worked, he favoured market forces and a degree of private ownership. With his return to power he was able to take action.

Such policies have a very broadly based appeal and a degree of universality. But even if the general direction of change is similar the ultimate destination is most likely not common. In many countries, especially those which are the most pragmatic, the destination is simply not known. 'Role models' vary. The journey seems to matter most, because it is here and now, and urgent. The rhetoric may reflect times gone by and the need to placate internal opposition. What countries actually do may be quite different and is what matters. If the outcomes are diverse and do not accord with Western preconceptions, as seem likely, so be it. Culture and history vary widely between countries and peoples. No single 'solution' can therefore be sensible or desirable.

Revitalization is helped by the support of successful ethnic *diaspora* from abroad (China is the best example, and to some degree Poland). They bring cash, experience and an intimate understanding of society and of what is possible within it. They know how to get things done. They may also have a clearer view of what lies ahead in the chosen path.

Inward investment by foreigners is also widely encouraged as a means of bringing capital and know-how, and to accelerate the process of change. But it is not always easy to handle, especially for countries in the '70-year' category, and often cultures are alien.

External help can be a blessing or a curse. Its absence may cause slower change, but that may be desirable in any event. Aid should be earmarked, but conditions should be minimized – experience suggests that they are unlikely to be well judged in relation to the specific circumstances of each situation. Unconditional, technical, 'enabling' aid perceived to be useful by the recipient, such as management development, is near the 'blessing' end of the spectrum. Large-scale projects often turn out to be the opposite.

Some stabilization aid may however be necessary. The problem is this. Economic stabilization if achieved cannot be sustained unless the economy both earns its way externally and satisfies the people. This means that manufacturing enterprises, whether state or private, must act commercially (revenues covering full costs, borrowing at commercial rates, shedding social obligations). If their productivity is low and product designs out of date then they cannot compete against imports except at 'give-away' exchange rates (and perhaps not even then). But such rates will inhibit imports of modernizing machinery.

Because revitalization of manufacturing industry will take time (even in east Germany), one solution is to earn hard currency through non-manufactures where product design is less relevant (though quality may be) – primary energy (coal, oil, natural gas), minerals, agricultural products and services (especially tourism). Technical aid and inward investment may be specially useful in these sectors.

Another solution, as China discovered, is to promote an alternative focus for growth (supported by the *diaspora*, which seems a crucial element) while the commercialization and modernization of the state-owned sector takes place through freedom to compete and in other ways.

A third solution is to use foreign aid to modernize manufacturing. But clearly this may not be a necessary condition for revitalization if the right strategic policies are pursued domestically.

Private ownership of a substantial part of an economy is *probably* a condition for successful revitalization because of the difficulty of commercializing state-owned enterprises in the short time available (before any achieved economic stabilization is undermined), and because of the well-known long-run problems with managing the relationships between the government and such enterprises efficiently and sensibly. In China the true extent of the private sector is unclear and it is not the fundamental basis of its policy. Cuba may also be a contrary indication (and their race against time is being jeopardized by renewed outward migration).

The success of privatization, the key element of revitalization policy in some countries, is jeopardized if it is undertaken before economic stabilization has been substantially achieved, before the legal and institutional changes necessary for an efficient operation of a market economy are in place, and before widespread business and management education have been undertaken.

Governments should handle the transitions firmly, bridging the gaps between central planning and a market economy (even if privatization is not on the agenda) and between state and private ownership.

A 'pure' market economy is most likely to be inefficient (because short-term interests are likely to prevail and because of externalities) and uncaring. So the problem is the role of the state. Under communist ideology this was clear. In a market economy the choice is more open. Most countries in this study are too preoccupied with the short term to consider the need for strategic policies in, for example, energy, transport and R & D, but there is recognition of the need for social policies.

Leadership is the key to revitalization, both of the nation and in business – leadership however with the support of the led and in tune with culture and society. It is more than mouthing the right words and charisma. It consists of a series of appropriate actions which motivate and inspire people.

Some reformers have held high office under communism, having (like Boris Yeltsin) fought their way to the top through sheer guts. To have served the communist system is no disqualification for success. The experience of office, even under a regime that is antagonistic to one's instincts, is training for top leadership. One learns political skills, and how to get things done.

Such people introducing market economies (and pursuing the measures listed above) appear then to be the pragmatists, but all they needed was the opportunity. Others are the 'genuine' pragmatists, like Fidel Castro, responding to serious events using their accumulated wisdom and common sense and putting aside dogma. Pragmatism is not, however, within everyone's grasp.

Democracy does not seem essential for economic revitalization – Cuba, Mozambique and Vietnam remain one-party states. Indeed, as mentioned earlier, the parallels are striking between Poland with multi-party democracy, and Vietnam with a single party. The firm central control that is needed for a successful transition may perhaps come more easily from a socialist background – or from the experience of war.

Many countries are in a race against time. In different ways, in Russia, China and Cuba reform is not yet secure – and time is short. Kazakhstan too has serious problems. Poland is having a pause which it can ill afford. North Korea has barely begun to meet its difficulties. Czechoslovakia is well on the way.

So this book is by way of an 'interim report'. Deng Xiaoping reckons on a 30-year transition period, but in the context of 5,000 years of Chinese history and culture that is short. If it were not for human mortality one would say that they have plenty of time. Twenty years in the CIS and ten years or even less in some eastern European countries might not be unreasonable expectations, because what they are moving towards accords more closely with their recent past (and in east Germany because of massive support). A successful overnight 'big bang' is not feasible.

Part II

THE FORMER SOCIALIST STATES

2

THE SOVIET SYSTEM AND ITS AFTERMATH IN RUSSIA

Elena Veduta

The most fundamental economic policy of the Russian government under President Boris Yeltsin is privatization. It is a continuation and development of *perestroika*, an idea borrowed from the West and the most internationally approved policy introduced over recent years.

Russia has achieved much in the past, thanks to the Soviet Union's centralized system of government. Now Russia is an independent state which rejects centralized government and prefers a market economy based upon private ownership. Why is privatization being introduced, and what is its future?

During the Sixth Congress of Deputies of the Russian Parliament in April 1992 there was a noisy debate on whether to continue the radical reforms proposed by the Russian government for the acceleration of privatization. Which path should Russia choose? This is a very serious question for all republics of the former Soviet Union because they depend on Russia for many of their supplies of principal products.

THE SOVIET ECONOMIC SYSTEM

It is not possible to understand the problems faced by Russia today, or the problems of the other republics of the CIS, without appreciating how the Soviet industrial system really worked. To Westerners the Soviet system, which substantially remains in existence today although with a higher degree of anarchy, seems utterly crazy. Western advisers, who do not take the trouble to understand it, reject it in favour of a model which they do understand – the 'free-market economy'.

There are two structural features of the Soviet system which are fundamental to this understanding: the centralized system of government (sometimes known as the 'command economy'), and the existence of 'super-monopolies'.

The centralized system of government, introduced in all its complexity by Joseph Stalin, changed its characteristics somewhat over time with different leaders, up to and including the present day. There was no single standardized model for its application either in the Soviet Union or in its satellite countries, although broadly the system was common. The general principles can be explained by analogy with a model familiar in the West.

A model based on Western experience

Imagine that there exists a rather centralized, medium-sized manufacturing company which makes a range of consumer goods, and which sells them direct to the public in many cities and towns through its own retail shops.

Within this company there is a strategic five-year plan decided by the board, together with annual plans and budgets, and monthly, weekly and daily plans and work schedules.

Budget proposals for the next planning period are submitted to the centre from divisions and departments. Through an iterative process, agreement is reached with the chief executive. The budget is approved (or not, subject to further revision) by the board. Divisional and departmental managers, who will have contributed to this process, will then know what has to be achieved.

Material and semi-finished goods move in a regular flow between different production departments for further processing. There are no cash transfers between these production departments, and no free-market trading.

The different stages of manufacture are planned and coordinated from the central production department so as to achieve the overall planned rate of production.

Capital investment proposals come up from divisional and departmental managers and are considered at the centre in the context of the approved strategic plans for the company, both in aggregate and in detail. When agreed, the finance for investment expenditure is paid from the company's bank account, as required.

Wages and salaries in the company are all decided at the centre, with some delegation of authority, and are paid weekly or monthly by the company from its bank account. Managers and shop-floor workers receive bonuses according to the achievement of their targets.

To supply its many shops, the company has several warehouses at strategic locations, but again these warehouses simply receive the goods sent from the factory, which are then 'called-off' by the retailers as required.

When sales are made to final consumers the revenue is paid into the company's bank account, which then finances all of the above.

Such was the Soviet system. The whole vast endeavour was managed as if it were a centralized, medium-sized, multi-product manufacturing company. In the above example, the board was the Supreme Soviet, the chief executive was the Prime Minister, head of the government, the planning department was the Gosplan.

Decisions on aggregate output and aggregate investment were taken arbitrarily by the political leadership and were executed through 'state orders'. Plant and equipment for investment was obtained from the suppliers without cash, according to the state plan, again through 'state orders'. Output was not connected with any clear idea of the needs of consumers. Heavy industry was the priority.

Transfers of intermediate products between state enterprises were made without payment, while information about the movements of goods between these enterprises was concentrated in the state bank.

Wages and salaries were determined by state 'tariffs' or norms and the cash was paid by the state bank (though distributed by the enterprise).

Regional warehouses were Soviet wholesalers, who likewise transferred goods when 'called-off' by retailers without payment. The wholesale transfer prices of goods were given by producers; they reflected only the 'cost' of production, without profit, although wholesalers did not pay for these goods. Retail prices were controlled by the state, the region and the municipality (the Leningrad City Council decided some 22,000 prices) on the basis of cost, with turnover tax and subsidies (for some foods retail prices were lower than wholesale 'costs'). The bank was the Soviet state bank, which paid all wages, salaries and bonuses and which received the cash paid by final consumers.

So this system was not so crazy after all.

How did the system of centralized planning really work?

The task of each level in the hierarchy of the stages in production and distribution was to coordinate the linkages between organizations which were within its authority in order to achieve the purposes of the next higher level. The highest level was the Supreme Soviet of the USSR, which defined the main purposes of economic policy. The highest executive power which must implement this policy was the government.

The idea of centralized government was realized in practice, as in the hypothetical example above, by the method of iteration. The State Committee of Plans, Gosplan, worked out the proposals for the state plan of the whole of the Soviet Union. This was based on past information, and originated from the purposes agreed by the Supreme Soviet for that period, taking into account social, economic and technological forecasts.

According to this proposed plan, from the top down, assignments were given to each organization within the hierarchy about externally sourced inputs and the outputs of final products. Taking into account these assignments, each organization worked out their own proposals for themselves, and defined their necessary resources. Therefore these requirements for resources reflected the real situation in each industry, from the bottom up. They could challenge and correct the previous top–down assignments. This coordination of the plan took place within each level of the hierarchy. We can describe this process as a typical programme:

1 Each organization defined the assignments of the final output and exter-

nally sourced inputs for subordinated organizations. These originated from the purposes of the next higher level.

2 Subordinated organizations then defined their needs in productive investment for the achievement of these assignments, and the necessary materials, labour and financial resources for current output.
3 If the requirement for external resources was different from the assignment limits set by the next level above, their requests returned to that level, and calculations in this process were repeated.

The coordination of the plan calculation continued until the final structure of the state plan could be completed in a form which began to satisfy the original purposes. Because this process was limited by the assignment period, the results could only approximate those purposes. The iterative process generally had to be repeated more than once. For example, each one-year state plan might take approximately eight iterations to achieve this coordination, and to determine prices for one enterprise might take five or six iterations. Taking into account that Gosplan could do only 1½ iterations in one year and that wholesale prices in the Soviet Union changed only once in five years, it would take more than five years to find the correct state plan and in principle more than 30 years to find the prices for the enterprises which would satisfy the chosen conception of how prices should be formed.

The Soviet Union used the ability of its centralized government to concentrate the resources where needed in time and place. This was especially important and was successful in the forced development of heavy industry before the Second World War, during this war, and after the war for reconstruction. But then after the 1950s, it experienced many problems of transition from these needs towards improving the living standards of the people.

Enterprises were out of touch with the needs of consumers. There was no marketing analysis undertaken. The indices for planning concentrated on intermediate products.

An early problem for the state planners was that statistical information was not coordinated and was on many different bases. Gosplan worked with one set of statistics which was essentially different from those used by the other centralized state bodies, including the Ministry of Finance, which was different again from the State Committee of Supply and the State Committee of Prices – and so on. It was thought that the most accurate information was in the state bank, but methods did not exist to enable Gosplan to make use of it.

In the West, money is taken for granted as conferring purchasing power and as being a tough discipline on enterprise and personal behaviour. In the Soviet Union after Khrushchev, people were paid whether they worked hard or not. Physical resources (within the plan) were provided by the state, and the factors of production were paid for by the state whether the final products had a market or not. The role of money during the processes of production and distribution was completely unimportant.

The 'super-monopolies'

The second major structural problem in the Soviet Union was that enterprises had their own unique technologies, were situated in different republics as 'super-monopolies', and were created under the state plan as parts of a complete system.

The reasons were said to be solely economic, based on notions of 'economies of scale', and were not political in origin. They included the transport cost implications, and the location of available labour and of social infrastructure. In fact, of course, the policy also suited the politicians, for it helped to develop all the republics of the Soviet Union, and it bound the USSR together in a tightly knit economic interdependence. It suited also the government bureaucrats, since the birth of these large enterprises necessitated centralized government coordination and as a result they assumed commanding positions of power. Also it was easier to plan with only a few enterprises than with many. But these political and administrative issues were not seen to be important at the time. Economic reasons were predominant.

The supplies of materials to these 'super-monopolies' located throughout the Soviet Union, and the delivery of finished products, were all conducted without the need for cash payments between enterprises. What the system did require, however, was a nationwide and efficient system of transport, at freight rates which reflected the real costs involved. Roads generally were inadequate, and so the railways played the largest part. Both rail and air travel were, however, heavily subsidized, through the same divorcement of 'costs' and prices described earlier.

The legacy of this widespread distribution of super-monopolies and the problems created can be imagined now that the Soviet Union has disintegrated into the independent states of the CIS, each country requiring hard currency for its sales between republics within the former Soviet Union.

THE EVOLUTION OF SOVIET POLICY

The first attack of the leading economists on the centralized government system began in 1965 under the new leader of the country, Leonid Brezhnev. It was decided to begin to use profit as the basis of planning in enterprises, as had been observed in the West. Financial resources for investment, for paying wages, for buying materials and for social needs, which previously had been wholly centralized, were divided arbitrarily into two parts. One part remained centralized and controlled as to its use, while enterprises had more freedom to use the other part although with strict norms set from the top.

As the bonuses of all workers in enterprises became more dependent on profit after 1965, these enterprises increased their producer prices after agreement with the pricing authorities, which was not difficult to achieve if accompanied by suitable means of persuasion, though without any consumer market information. Increasing prices to earn bonuses was easier than to earn profits through improved efficiency and new technology.

The system became the 'theatre of the absurd'. On the one hand, enterprises were required to implement the state plan and to produce products whatever their theoretical 'profitability'; on the other hand, the enterprises tended to use increasingly scarce resources to produce expensive products at high prices which were not in the state plan, though without reference to consumer market information. Enterprises would receive money from the state banks whether or not they sold these products.

There was in recent years also a problem in using modern computers for the more accurate coordination of plan calculations because industry linkages had become more and more complicated. A new economic thinking was needed for the solution of this problem, but who could undertake it? It was easier for the ruling economists to say 'yes' to the whims of political leaders than to construct a new economic system. From the 1950s, all economic reforms made life worse and worse for the people. Inevitably the mechanism became somewhat decentralized, but basically it remained as it was before. Maintaining industrial ties between producers was continued only with the greatest difficulty.

The Soviet Union began to lag more and more behind the market economy of the West. It was decided that the old centralized system of government was bad, and that a transition would have to be made to a new economic system. *Perestroika* began in 1985 without any constructive plan, and then from August 1991 began *post-perestroika*. The republics became independent and chose their own separate ways forward.

There were, in effect, three related problems facing the government of the Soviet Union in considering strategies for change. The first and most obvious was economic. The system was incapable of maintaining the stability of the existing regime, let alone producing the goods and services which would raise the standard of living of ordinary people. The second problem concerned the role of the state. It was being overwhelmed by the technical difficulties of planning and required fundamental rethinking. The third problem was psychological – the behaviour and responsiveness of the people. They were becoming extremely fed up. Their attitudes were deep and intractable and in the end will determine the pace and effectiveness of change. This problem, however, is still hardly recognized.

All the innovations of the leading economists from 1965 to 1985, which were intended to promote technological progress, were restricted by the reforms of 1965 and by the lack of consultation with enterprise managers, who themselves knew that the system was unworkable. So the economic situation did not improve. In 1985 Gorbachev believed that the 1965 policies of reform were correct but that they had been inhibited by the bureaucracy in the enterprises.

In this period 1965–85, from Brezhnev to *perestroika*, the profits of producers and their wages and salaries were increasing without any growth in productivity. Coordination in supply became ever more difficult. Output stagnated. Retail prices were fixed for long periods. The outcome was a sharp increase in shortages in the retail trade. The system of distribution with such shortages led to an increase in the privileged supply to political leaders and to an increase in corruption.

By 1985 it had become clear that the situation was worsening and that it could not be improved through the existing methods of government. It was necessary for the new leader of the country, Mikhail Sergeyevich Gorbachev, to introduce currency reform in order to stabilize the rouble, to relate wages to productivity and to introduce stability in consumer markets in order to balance the demand and supply of goods. It was also necessary to clarify the reasons for the failure of the previous economic reforms, and to put forward proposals for a more workable economic system. Unfortunately Gorbachev did not do this. Today it is even more urgent.

Gorbachev, the architect of *perestroika*, preferred to take a risk with another route. Influenced at first by the experiences of Yugoslavia and China, his ideas were in practice closer to the 'achievements' of the reforms of 1965 and the so-called 'period of stagnation' which followed.

Gorbachev's many attempts from 1985 to 1990 to introduce reforms were, however, all thwarted to a greater or lesser degree by the pressure groups of managers of state enterprises. In the opinion of Gorbachev and his advisers (some of whom were advisers from the Brezhnev period), the fault was not the use of profit in monopolistic enterprises but was a failure of the centralized mechanism of government.

Why did they conclude this? As the leading economists had no clear vision of how the economic system could work successfully to achieve stability and growth, it was easier for them to look superficially towards the West, which had profit and private property without a centralized mechanism of government. And the 'children of stagnation' – the speculators (those who bought at state prices and then sold at higher prices) – aspired to legalize their illegal incomes.

In truth it was not a failure of the idea of a centralized mechanism of government but of the way in which it was implemented.

However, in this general situation, privatization began to be seen as an attractive solution. They decided that reform of the existing system was not feasible. This decision was profitable for the leaders who managed the system as it promoted corruption. Many of those who gained from this system had become very rich and now hold important positions in many republics, including Russia. Many of the former leaders of the Communist Party became leaders of 'democratic' parties, and they preferred to be in private business and to have a government suitable for their new purposes.

Ordinary people also wanted change because they were tired of shortages, they resented the privileged position of their leaders, they perceived the gap between the fine words of these people and their actual deeds, and on television they saw that the West was prosperous.

What were the main differences which they saw between the economic mechanism of the West and that in the Soviet Union? The West has private properties, a free market and enterprise managers who could make their own decisions. So the slogans of 'privatization', 'market' and 'economic freedom' became popular in the Soviet Union during the period of *perestroika*. The Soviet people, however, did not see that these freedoms were constrained by legislation, by competition and by the discipline of money.

WHY MOSCOW PREFERRED PRIVATIZATION

In the past, as well as today, political leaders are always right. Each political leader wants to make good changes for the better life of the people, and has his own ideas how to do it. These ideas depend upon his knowledge, his culture and the suggestions of his closest advisers. Each leader puts forward his own slogans, such as 'development socialism' (Brezhnev), 'market socialism' (Gorbachev) and 'market economy' (Yeltsin). The ruling economists help these leaders to find new slogans, and to provide theoretical explanations for them, and they will put forward reforms on that basis. We can call this a 'personality cult' system.

The fact that these reforms may have the result opposite to what was intended is not important in this system. The ruling personalities have no responsibilities towards their constituencies for their decisions. So they can introduce reforms in the country, as if they were experimenting with rabbits.

To solve the problem of coordination of industrial linkages for efficient production and distribution, which in part arose from these location decisions, required the effective use of computers. Even when they became available in Nikita Khrushchev's time, from 1956, they were not correctly used, either then or subsequently. As the leading economists did not know how to resolve this problem, they tended to make reforms which artificially reduced the flows of information between the different levels of government, in order to reduce the work at the top of the system, and under the current 'market economy' slogan to give more independence to enterprises to make their own decisions. As the reforms became deeper, anarchy became more widespread. To an increasing extent after the collapse of the Soviet Union and the demise of the Gosplan planning system, 'state orders' were made by the Ministry of Economics and other ministries independently of what other producers and ordinary consumers needed or thought necessary.

Moreover, many transfers between enterprises which formerly had been undertaken without cash have now, following the collapse of the Soviet Union and the formation of independent states, become international trade. Hard currencies are now demanded for such trade.

With the collapse of the single centralized planning system and with the formation of the CIS, the integration of supply within the Soviet Union has been all but destroyed. To many people, especially Russian economic theoreticians and political leaders, as well as Western advisers and political leaders, privatization was the only solution.

STAGES IN THE INTRODUCTION OF PRIVATIZATION

By the time the Soviet Union burst apart in December 1991 and the CIS was formed, the Soviet economic system was in total confusion. The issue of privatization became more popular within the wider chaos in which Russia and the other republics found themselves after wresting their independence. The subject cannot therefore be treated in isolation from its surrounding events.

It is possible for public enterprises to behave to some extent as if they were private. Thus anticipated profit can be used as a means of deciding what to produce. It can be claimed therefore that an element of privatization in the Soviet Union began in 1965 under Brezhnev.

The next stage began in 1987, under Gorbachev, with the adoption of new laws which introduced 'radical economic reforms'. The essence of these reforms was gradually to relax the vertical ties between the government and individual enterprises, and also to free horizontal ties between enterprises. It was decided (in Nikolai Ryzhkov's period as Prime Minister) to replace the former state plan with 'state orders' – in the sense of 'commands' – from Gosplan, though increasingly from the Ministry of Economics and individual production ministries. These represented only a part, though the largest part, of the former plan. The state was obliged to provide enterprises receiving these 'orders' with resources, while giving them freedom for the remainder of their output – similar to the Brezhnev system. But it was necessary to produce these 'order' resources within the state, and also to include them in other 'state orders' – and so on. Hence the original problems of industrial coordination continued, with the same unsatisfactory methods of decision-making.

Simultaneously with the relaxation of vertical ties between government and individual enterprises, in 1987 Gorbachev and the Soviet government proposed to create competition and a 'market economy' through cooperatives, joint ventures, small enterprises and joint-stock companies.

State enterprises began to behave more and more like private enterprises, making some of their own decisions. Gosplan ceased to give 'state orders' in December 1991 and the Ministry of Economics began to implement its functions.

The role of a government ministry, however, was quite different from that in the West. It was not, for example, the Ministry of Health which ordered drugs for hospitals but the Ministry of Medical Industries. They decided what drugs hospitals could have because they were dependent on the production potential of the drug manufacturers. The Ministry of Medical Industries placed 'state orders' on these manufacturers. Therefore hospitals received only what they were given. Other production ministries decided in a similar manner what 'state orders' to give.

The increase of freedoms within enterprises to produce profitably resulted in yet higher producer prices, the weakening of the former coordination between enterprises, the reduction of output, and hence the reinforcement of their monopolistic interests. At that time the incomes of the workers were increased with higher profits, but retail prices were unchanged until 1991. Thus during *perestroika*, the shortages had become more serious, and simultaneously privileges, speculation, corruption and criminality increased. Valentin Pavlov, the new (and the last) Prime Minister of the Soviet Union (now in jail for his part in the failed coup) could only increase retail prices, which were still controlled, and continue this process.

The government of the Soviet Union issued many decrees which had the effect of increasing the gap between rich and poor in society. Speculation, which had been a natural result of the economic reforms of 1965, in spite of legislation to the contrary, started to prosper on a legal basis in the period of *perestroika*. Unrestrained printing of money made a contribution to this process.

Workers increasingly bought goods in cooperative shops because the state shops were empty, and so the state lost some of the revenues to pay the wages of workers. Where could the state find the money after all? How could it implement the socialist and ecological programmes? There was nothing left but to print money. So the printing press has been working at full strength, and the shortages have been growing and life has become more and more intolerable.

This spiral – higher prices, printing of money, shortages, ration cards, privileges, speculation, corruption, criminality – was growing ever faster during *perestroika*. The process was accompanied by a deterioration in output. As the leaders talked more about competition, the state 'super-monopolies' were becoming stronger. But competition in the sphere of distribution increased. In Russia, in the first half of 1991, profits in state enterprises increased by 70 per cent compared with the same period in the previous year. Simultaneously, shortages of goods in consumer markets became more serious. The population received in this period 15 per cent less meat, 10 per cent less milk, 25 per cent less margarine, 30–8 per cent less cotton, wool and silk goods, and so on.

Centralized government in the Soviet Union was completely destroyed after August 1991. This was the beginning of the third stage of privatization.

Each republic of the former Soviet Union decided to paddle its own canoe in this stormy ocean. The most confident of survival was Russia, the biggest and richest of them all, which also took the rights of the former Soviet Union.

President Boris Nikolayevich Yeltsin, who had the support of the largest part of Russia, continued the policy of *perestroika* after August 1991 with great determination. In his report on 28 October 1991, in the Fifth Congress of the Deputies of Russia, he emphasized the necessity of the development of economic reforms to overcome the crisis. He considered that commands from the top and 'state orders' could not help to overcome the crisis, though they continued to be used. He wanted to introduce privatization through the command system. He rejected the problem of coordination as though it did not exist. He planned to give full freedom by privatization. The main direction of the economic reforms were therefore strict financial and credit policies, liberalization of prices and privatization.

For the stabilization of the rouble, and to eliminate the budget deficit for 1992, it was decided also to reduce expenditure on defence, on the government bureaucracy and on the support of social needs. It was also decided to reduce subsidies to so-called 'loss-making enterprises'. In Russia all prices are to some degree 'wrong', so it is impossible to define 'loss-making enterprises'. In this system, all enterprises are needed because they are interconnected. To reduce subsidies to them is to reduce output.

It was proposed to privatize more than 50 per cent of small and medium-sized enterprises, to split the large industrial enterprises into smaller competing units and to convert them into joint-stock companies. It was also decided to privatize the supply of materials and the distribution of manufactured goods, as in the Western example of transfers within a manufacturing enterprise mentioned earlier. But because of the existence of super-monopolies, customers for intermediate supplies today have no choice.

Also loss-making collective farms were to be privatized. President Yeltsin wished to permit the sale and purchase of land, but this has not been adopted. Evidently the railways and road transport were to remain in the state.

At that time (October 1991), the statistics showed that more than 55 per cent of the population lived in poverty. There were many difficulties with the supply of basic necessities, and inflation reached a critical point. Boris Yeltsin understood that the destruction of the linkages between industries – and hence the reduction of output – would continue. He asked the people to be patient during the worsening situation until September 1992. He was sure that after this time the situation would improve. Like the legacies of previous leaders, the results of Yeltsin's policies were contrary to what he wished.

In the Soviet Union there were 88 government ministries, and 44 in the former Russian Socialist Republic. These have been united in the new ministries of Russia. The number of ministries in Russia, however, is now less than it was in the former Soviet Union, but the process of bureaucratization is continuing under a new name. The number of buildings occupied by the administration is increasing. This is also true of some municipalities – for example the city of Moscow now has more bureaucrats than when it was in the USSR. Moreover, many of these bureaucrats take part in private businesses, and so they can ensure that materials are supplied to those businesses. Some bureaucrats have large bank accounts abroad. There are many new privileges, and more bureaucrats now take bribes, almost openly.

The reduction of output in 1991 was 10 per cent. After the formation of the CIS in December 1991, from 2 January 1992 the government of Russia began to introduce the recommendations of the Fifth Congress and of the advisers from the West, especially Jeffrey Sachs from Harvard, to liberalize most prices. Prices were increased many-fold, and the proportion of those living in poverty increased to 80 per cent.

The structure of the Supreme Soviet of Russia is the same as the structure of the former Central Committee of the Communist Party of the Soviet Union. However, the Russian government consists of former pupils with excellent results in their studies of the faulty economic theory of socialism. As specialists in this theory they cannot easily change the trend from collapse, but they may strengthen it. They have an insoluble task trying to stabilize the chaotic economy by destroying the previous system. Trying to achieve economic and financial stability, they increase prices more and more. The Russian government is sure that there is no alternative to this process, so they have the immense task to achieve macroeconomic stability by interrupting the spiral of inflation and shortages. The government is sure that the West will help them to continue this process, and US $24 billion have been promised for this purpose.

New waves of indignation in the beginning of 1992 forced the parliament to break their adopted budget on 24 January 1992. Parliament reduced VAT twice, increased pensions and student grants and military expenditure. Moreover, the Parliamentary Commission made a list of company monopolists and set limits on their profits (the 2,000 or so enterprises which produced 70 per cent of industrial production). This fact is considered by many specialists to be the real threat to the conduct of radical economic reforms.

As the government wanted to eliminate the budget deficit by every means, they could do this only by increasing debt to the workers. In January 1992 the debt of the government to these workers was 19 billion roubles. The situation became worse on 1 March. The reduction in the output of the food industry was 25 per cent, and the government debt increased. In the coal-producing Kemerov Region, near Kazakhstan, the government debt was still 2 billion roubles, in the oil and gas region of Tumen it was 4.3 billion roubles and in the Moscow Region it was 12 billion roubles.

As both the system of the supply of resources and the financial system were destroyed, enterprises began to trade by barter. At the same time 80–90 per cent of enterprises in different regions began to use credits as 'payment' for goods received. This has escalated greatly and will pose the Russian government with a serious problem. The potential money supply has been increased.

The gap between rich and poor is increasing. Taking into account the possibility of social unrest, the Sixth Congress of Russia in April 1992 greatly criticized the activities of the government. The main wish of the Sixth Congress was not to reduce the standards of living of the people. Deputies wanted to see in the government more people who understood how the system really works. President Yeltsin agreed to do this, and since June 1992 more industrial managers have been recruited into government. Since the parliament has no effective strong political opposition with a constructive economic programme to overcome the crisis, it allowed the Russian government to continue its economic reforms until 1 December 1992, with a continuing spiral of inflation and reducing output. The command system remained the same, but with more anarchy. On 8 October 1992 the Russian parliament appraised the situation as a crisis, and the activities of the government as unsatisfactory. It is to be hoped that this move towards the abyss will now be halted. But, like former Soviet governments, this government will not resign.

A WORKABLE WAY OUT OF THE CRISIS FOR RUSSIA

The lessons of history teach us many things, but sometimes people forget them. As the former Soviet Union represented a single economic complex, only a new powerful federal economic system based on the former Soviet republics can serve people's interests and their freedoms. What is needed now is a new system of centralized government with the efficient management of enterprises, and with free consumer markets. The popular idea of privatization has spread to the newly independent territories. The destruction of the single coordinating centre, and the near destruction of linkages between producers, will lead to a deepening of the economic crisis and perhaps to the expansion of local wars. The West, which does not understand that the economic system of CIS differs from Western economies as a car from a horse, is helping in this destructive process.

The proposal here is to revert to the previous system of centralized government, as described above, but to improve it in a number of ways which will ensure that it will work efficiently. The principal features are summarized as follows:

1 Retail prices should be free of all state control.
2 All producers should study their markets and should plan their output and investment accordingly.
3 These output and investment plans should then be submitted on a regular basis to the relevant government authorities (the central government,

individual ministries, municipalities, etc.) in terms of aggregate values, for transmission to the centralized coordinating body.

4 This centralized body will coordinate all of these proposals in order to satisfy final consumer needs identified by producers, wholesalers and retailers, and the education, health and defence, etc. needs of the government. Coordination is achieved through the manipulation of a matrix of inputs and outputs and a similar method of iteration to that used previously in the Soviet Union, using a large inter connected computer system. It would, however, be significantly more flexible and responsive to final demand.
5 Government priorities for industrial policy would be fed into this coordinating process.
6 Transfers between producers, and from producers to wholesalers and to retailers, would continue to be made without payment.
7 Revenues from retailers would continue to be paid into the state bank.
8 In its turn, the state bank would continue to pay wages and salaries according to the 'tariffs' set by the state, and all bonuses would be dependent upon real increases in output. It would also pay enterprises for approved expenditures, such as market research and advertising.
9 All privatized enterprises, except for the very smallest, should therefore be brought back into state ownership, or at least should be required to participate in the above system. A substantial private sector outside of the system would create great complications.
10 Enterprise taxes would be of two kinds. The first would be a tax on wages (i.e. income tax), effectively deducted at source, as at present. The second, also as at present, would be an annual tax on industrial investment (which would be provided free by the government) for a specific number of years of use. This could be considered as being like leasing payments, or as the equivalent of interest on borrowing and the repayment of capital.

The essence of this proposal is to maintain the existing connections between state enterprises in ways which are familiar to all concerned. Currency reforms, however, would also be required. There could be two ways of doing this.

First, the state could establish limits on the number of roubles which it will exchange for new money – 'one for one'. Let us call them 'new roubles'. For the remaining part, the state should issue obligations which will be liquidated in terms of the new money over some years. Old roubles would no longer be legal currency. All wages would be paid in the new currency.

An alternative method would be to have two internal currencies, as in Ukraine and Belorus. The state would pay wages to employees in state enterprises in the new roubles, which in turn would be provided by consumer sales in state shops. Old roubles could then only be used in the private shops and manufacturing enterprises. (In practice private shops would most likely be willing to accept either currency.) Currency dealers no doubt would exchange one currency for another at a rate determined by supply and demand. Russia may be forced to follow this system because of the surplus of roubles from other republics, and their uncontrolled creation of credit.

Foreign exchange from exports would be returned to the state. Foreign exchange for imports would be obtained from the state bank, on application to prove necessity.

The state would hold stocks of consumer goods so that fluctuations in prices could be smoothed.

State banks would be permitted to lend to individuals (e.g. for large purchases, such as a car), but should not – indeed they would not need to – lend to producers.

The specific structure of the means of satisfying non-industrial and consumer needs within the limits of state budgets would be determined by the appropriate managers in health services, education, housing, etc. For example, the structure of products required by the Ministry of Health would be decided jointly by hospital managers and by the Ministry, which will establish priorities.

The West may reject the creation of new coordination centres because they think that it will mean a return to Stalin's political system, which had total control over the behaviour of people. Moreover, how can a new coordination centre be created since the republics of the Soviet Union have become independent states? Where is the freedom of managers in decision-making, where is competition and the market in this system?

The formation of a single coordination centre is necessary for the development of industry in the whole of the CIS because enterprises were created under the previous state plans not as a result of market forces. The new leaders have rejected the coordinating mechanism because it was seen by the West as 'Stalinism', and because they lacked the ability to make it work. They needed also to be able to justify 'democracy' in the country.

Centralized government became a victim of the political approach to finding a solution. The destruction of this mechanism and its catastrophic consequences demonstrate that the solution of the economic problem by voluntaristic means can only make the situation worse. Who is losing from the destruction of the mechanism? Enterprises and ordinary people are the losers, through the reduction of living standards.

Between enterprises within Russia, and between enterprises which are situated in different states of the CIS, there has been a spontaneous creation of cooperation. This has been achieved partly by the enterprises themselves and partly by new committees of industry, such as the Ministry of Economy. These associations try to undertake the functions of planning of the former state organizations. The final stage is most likely to be the creation of a new coordination centre.

The two main reasons why Russia should continue with a system of centralized government, though very different from what went before, are firstly, enterprises in Russia are totally unfamiliar with the free market mechanisms which are taken for granted in the West. Enterprise managers have never had to do any of the strategic management, marketing, selling, pricing, raising capital, investment appraisal, wage negotiation and so on which would be required of them in a free market system. They are used to a planned system in which market coordination was done for them, materials were provided by order from the state, in which money played an unimportant role. To teach managers throughout the economy how to manage efficiently and competitively in a free market system would take many years because of the fundamental difference between centralized government and such a system.

Secondly, production is still dominated by 'super-monopolies', geographically dispersed throughout the former Soviet Union. Monopolies on this scale need to be controlled, both as to prices and as to where their supplies should go. Many such enterprises will want to sell their goods to the West to earn foreign currency, and if taken too far will leave the CIS starved of supplies. It will take very many years for alternative suppliers to develop on a sufficient scale, even with Western help, in order to create effective competition. Meanwhile, Russia and the other CIS republics cannot be left to starve.

3

REVITALIZING THE RUSSIAN ECONOMY – CATCHING UP[1]

Konstantin Kagalovksy

Of all the former communist states attempting to transform their economies, Russia is in perhaps the best and the worst position. It is in the best position because its young economists leading the transformation have had the opportunity to observe the process in other former communist states which embarked upon this road earlier: the worst, because the problems facing the Russian economy are more serious than elsewhere and the psychological barriers towards transition to a free market economy are more deep-seated due to decades of ideological indoctrination.

THE SCOPE OF ECONOMIC REFORM

Before the restructuring of political and economic decision-making processes could take place it was necessary to develop the basic principles of the reform package. It was believed that once these were established, the necessary restructuring could proceed more logically and in response to the demands of the programme. While both have evolved together in practice, I shall deal with the reform package first and then discuss the structural changes that have taken place in order to implement it.

The main aspects of reform were major trade liberalization, stabilization of the economy and radical reform of the public sector.

Liberalization

The liberalization of trade was a major concern. During 1990–1 the constituent republics of the USSR had already begun to bypass the central economic ministries, including Gosplan (the central planning body), responsible for determining what would be produced, who would produce, and organizing the transfer of goods and raw materials from one republic to another. Acutely aware that the rapidly declining economic situation was leading to severe shortages of goods in one area and gluts in another, republics were refusing to trade in those goods in which they were suffering a shortage despite orders to do so from the centre. A series of bilateral treaties was signed between republics, ranging from the simple recognition of their economic autonomy (or independence in the case of the Baltic states) to agreements on the trade (usually through barter arrangements) of goods and services. The break-up of the Soviet Union following the attempted coup in August 1991 saw the threat of tariffs and restrictions being placed upon the free flow of goods between the republics.

It was for this reason that President Yeltsin passed a decree on 31 January 1992 lifting all tariffs and quotas limiting trade with the outside world. Until 1 August 1992, when tariffs were again placed on imports, Western goods were brought into the country without the Russian government obtaining revenues for them. This resulted in a flood of Western goods in all of Russia's major cities alleviating the worst of the shortages, and boosting internal trade with these imported goods being sold, and re-sold, on the streets. The tariffs are now, at the time of writing, being formalized and differ from product to product, with the main burden falling on luxury items and some agricultural produce.

The relationships with other countries of the former USSR have been in flux, and are only now slowly being formalized in bilateral trade agreements. Russia has signed agreements with all five central Asian republics, Belorus, Ukraine and the three Baltic states, as well as Armenia. At CIS summits the members have managed to reach agreements on the price of goods to be sold between them. This meant, in essence, that Russia was subsidizing the other republics with cheap energy prices, a practice which continues even after the doubling of oil prices in September 1992.

At the beginning of 1992 trade between the CIS republics had shrunk practically to zero. In the case of trade between Russia and Ukraine, the Russian authorities refused to deliver products which were necessary for the upkeep of Ukrainian mines, and Ukraine stopped the flow of sugar to Russia. By the end of 1992 disagreements on the balance of trade between the two republics had still not been fully resolved.

The three Baltic republics, Moldova and Ukraine are proceeding with the issue of their own currency, with Estonia and Lithuania already having their own notes. The IMF has put pressure on the states, including Russia, for this process to be coordinated, and has stressed that the Baltic example needs to be followed by other nations. Once these countries have introduced their own currencies, and the exchange rate against the Russian rouble has been established, the Russian government will be free to set world prices for sale to the old republics of the USSR, which it has hitherto been unable to do because of the common use of the rouble and a reluctance to raise prices to them.

The disintegration of Comecon, which began prior to the attempted coup, and demands from the former USSR that payment for goods be met in hard currency, required a further realignment of trading relations. In most instances countries were not able to meet the hard currency requirement, let alone at world prices which the USSR demanded. A similar problem arose when these countries also began to demand payment from the USSR in hard currency and at world prices. Given that Russian factories were now no longer receiving hard currency reserves from the central funds and that most hard currency funds of Russian companies were frozen in the foreign trade bank in the aftermath of the attempted coup, trade between Russia and eastern European countries virtually ceased. The temporary removal of tariffs on imported goods also applied to these countries and succeeded in reviving trade until new trading agreements could be negotiated.

Relationships with former close allies of the USSR, such as Cuba, deteriorated sharply following the attempted coup as Russia cut their subsidies. In part, the shortage of sugar in the Russian Federation can be explained by the worsening relationship between Russia and Cuba. In an attempt to retrieve the money owed by these countries to Russia, the Russian government is now negotiating the possibility of debt-equity transfer deals.

Stabilization

Stabilization of the economy has proved a more difficult task, not least because of the hardship caused to the populace. It has been necessary to reduce the fiscal deficit, establish real effective interest rates and de-control prices.

To reduce the fiscal deficit it was necessary to prune investment in public enterprises where they were financed by the Treasury, and only allow them to be financed by a commercial credit system through the Russian Central Bank. Through this system enterprises were able to obtain credits at very cheap rates, usually lower than the rate of inflation (averaging about 20 per cent per month), to ensure that they could continue production. While this removed the incentive on factories to carry out the necessary restructuring of their operations, a result soon realized by the Russian government and the Central Bank, it nevertheless delayed the expected mass unemployment should these factories fail to remain in business.

In an effort to counter the lack of incentive to restructure and commence the establishment of real interest rates, Giorgi Matyukhin, the Chairman of the Russian Central Bank until August 1992, increased the Russian base rate above the rate of inflation following pressure from the Prime Minister's office. He was then forced to resign by the Supreme Soviet under whose jurisdiction the position of chairman of the Russian Central Bank fell. The appointment of Viktor Gerashenko, the former chairman of the USSR Central Bank, sent shudders through the reformist cabinet which, although horrified, was not surprised when the first act of the new chairman was to cancel all debts owed by the factories. This decision was later reversed under threats of resignation from the Prime Minister, Yegor Gaidar, and his economic team.

With the proposed capital injection of 500 billion roubles into the heavy industry sector, particularly the military-industrial complex, at the beginning of September 1992, it is unlikely that the commercial credit system will continue in its present form. For those enterprises outside this sector who require further financial assistance, there will be greater emphasis placed upon restructuring, especially those ear-marked for privatization, and future moneys will depend on this taking place.

The Economics Minister, Andrei Nechayev, has stressed several times that factories have to either sink or swim by themselves, and that money will be available only as a temporary measure and directed at enterprises which will take the necessary measures to move into the free market.

The de-control of prices has had to be graduated for pragmatic reasons to reduce the impact on the populace as they become accustomed to 'real' prices which reflect the actual costs of production, as opposed to the heavily subsidized prices that had existed under central planning.

It has been in this area that the Russian government has faced the greatest criticism, even though its ability to introduce these policies has been limited because of its lack of control over the Russian Central Bank (due to the powers of the Supreme Soviet to appoint the chairman and reject his policies). The Supreme Soviet as a whole, and a special committee within it, closely monitor the actions of the Russian Central Bank, and the chairman of the bank is required to report regularly to the Plenum of the Supreme Soviet. Moreover, the Supreme Soviet committee which monitors its activities has the right to request and examine any of its files and correspondence.

The full impact of unemployment that will result from inefficient state enterprises failing to find funding and having to cut the labour force or go out of business has yet to be felt. The hardship encountered following the liberalization of prices was only short-term, the greatest sufferers being on fixed incomes. However, within two months of the price liberalization there was a noticeable increase in the amount of goods available, particularly foodstuffs, and since April 1992 state prices have fallen in real terms.

Despite these difficulties, the stabilization of the economy is fundamental to the reform process. Without the restoration of price stability and a sustainable balance between available resources and demand in the economy it will be impossible to correct the imbalances that have arisen as a result of the centrally planned system. Moreover, the failure to enable the economy to develop according to supply and demand for goods, and the artificial setting of prices with accompanying subsidies, has proved an impediment to managerial discretion, innovation, entrepreneurial initiative, and generally discriminated against the private sector by limiting new entrants. Instead, it protected privilege, monopolies and oligopolies, and gave rise to overmanning and the inefficient use of resources.

Radical reform of the public sector

The third aspect – reform of the public sector – is vital for the Russian economy. The objectives here are to eliminate special access to the budget to cover operating losses and to place public enterprises in a competitive framework. In addition to this, the administrative offices involved in many control procedures must be restructured or abolished since, without redeployment of such staff, the tendency to return to the old policy remains strong, as is the tendency to revert to government controls in case of difficulty.

Calculating the level of operating losses in the public sector is extremely difficult given that the accounting procedure that has existed is radically different from that in the West. Under the Soviet system the purpose of accounting was to provide the central planners of Gosplan with the information they required to achieve centralized control of the economy. The 'fixing' of accounts was common practice to hide involvement in the black market or lax practices which resulted in heavy losses or failure to fulfil the plan. The calculation of profit was not considered important. The profit/loss accounts that did exist included all administration fees and expenses rather than the actual costs of making the product. Thus, it was extremely difficult to calculate actual trading profit. Moreover, little consideration was given to the depreciation of equipment.

Further complications arise from the fact that many companies have borrowed from banks against their assets. The poor monitoring system has further hampered the ability to ascertain the true level of losses. In addition, the barter trade that has developed between large enterprises has meant that large amounts of money are owed by enterprises to each other but there is no system by which they can be paid. The debt is currently estimated by the Russian government to be over 3 trillion roubles.

PRIVATIZATION

Privatization is a fundamental element in restructuring the whole economy. Early privatizations involved the auctioning of flats and household premises, shops, and public catering enterprises in the cities. Resistance from trade unions and employees required some adaptation of this policy, and a system of contracting out the retail shops, public catering and public consumer services was adopted instead. The most successful areas of privatization have been in farms which began in 1990, and in 1992 the privatization of 250 shops in Nizhny Novgorod. Other towns have also begun the privatization of small retail outlets but as yet, with the exception of Nizhny Novgorod, no one has privatized more than 50 per cent of the municipal retail sector.

However, on 1 October 1992 the mass privatization of some 5,000–7,000 manufacturing enterprises began (out of more than 25,000 larger enterprises), incorporating the free distribution of vouchers, each valued at 10,000 roubles.

This marks a fundamental turning-point in the ownership and management of Russian industry, and a political event of historic significance.

Privatization goals

The basis for the Russian privatization programme was set out in the law on 'Privatization of Government and Municipal Enterprises of the RSFSR' (the Russian Federation) of 3 July 1991. By 23 January 1992 Boris Yeltsin was ready to introduce instructions to Russia's regional governors on how to implement the privatization programme.

This 30-page document, which was fully approved by the government in January 1992, confirmed the main idea of the government's policy. It was to transfer into private hands as soon as possible enterprises which could provide competition. The programme was also designed to stem the rise in prices which, under monopoly conditions, could rise almost without limit.

To support this policy, an Anti-monopoly Committee has been set up to regulate the degree of control which a single enterprise, or a few enterprises acting together, may have in a given market. The aim is to prevent any of the newly privatized companies from controlling more than 30 per cent of its market.

The Committee comes under the jurisdiction of the Supreme Soviet of the Russian Republic and reports directly to this legislative body. At present its powers are limited only to making recommendations to the Supreme Soviet, which in turn will make recommendations to the government on what action to take. The chairman of the Committee is appointed by the Russian President but must be ratified by the Supreme Soviet. The Committee, therefore, has only advisory powers and is not an administrative tribunal, nor can it enforce decisions.

The privatization programme itself consists of a number of phases. The first phase ran from 2 January 1992 to the third quarter of 1992; the second, from the middle of 1992 to early 1993.

In the first phase, which became delayed, it was planned to privatize 50–70 per cent of all industrial enterprises. This included 60 per cent of the food industry (estimated to be worth 23 billion roubles at December 1991 prices); 70 per cent of the construction industry (32 billion roubles); 70 per cent of light industry (10.6 billion roubles); 60 per cent of retail shops (10 billion roubles); and 20 per cent of unfinished construction projects (7 billion roubles). The total revenue expected to be generated eventually from this phase of the privatization programme is 92 billion roubles.

The second phase would see the extension of this programme both in existing sectors being privatized and in new areas, with an estimated revenue of 300 billion roubles in 1993. A planned third phase for 1994, after the completion of phases one and two, is expected to produce a revenue of 270 billion roubles.

Initially, there will be a list of sectors and companies excluded from privatization (detailed below). These will range from the territorial waters of the country to the main transport services, through to platinum and gold mining, as well as television and radio sectors.

Certain key areas will require government permission, in the guise of the Committee for State Property, to be privatized. These include oil and gas production, pharmaceuticals, and enterprises employing more than 10,000 workers or with assets valued at over 200 million roubles as of 1 January 1992. No government authorization is required for the privatization of enterprises below the above limits except where they fall into one of the categories that has been excluded from privatization. The methods and procedures for privatization are described below.

The mechanisms of privatization

The privatization programme was devised following close examination of experiences in other former communist countries and after taking into account the practicalities of privatization in Russia. Recognizing that the issue of social justice had to be addressed, the Russian government decided that workers and managers (the work 'collective') of some 5,000–7,000 enterprises (about 70 per cent of Russia's productive capacity) can choose between three options.

1. The collective can purchase 51 per cent of the shares at 1.7 per cent of book value (as assigned by state auditors). Or –
2. Accept the free distribution of 25 per cent of shares to the collective, plus (1) 10 per cent extra available to workers, at 0.7 per cent of book value, less 30 per cent discount, and (2) 5 per cent extra to managers at 0.7 per cent of book value. Or –
3. The free distribution of 20 per cent of shares to workers and managers who agree to group together to restructure the company, plus a further 20 per cent sold to the collective at 0.7 per cent of book value.

In collectives, vouchers may account for no more than 35 per cent of a company's shares, with cash paid for the remainder. The shares issued to collectives are not intended to bestow voting rights.

A minimum of 10 per cent of shares must be made available to the general public for purchase by voucher, and there will be some share auctions. Some 200 mutual funds have been created as financial intermediaries, thereby enabling ordinary voucher holders to spread their risk. Voucher holders may, however, sell them for cash as an alternative or use them for the purchase of land or property. But vouchers will no longer be valid after the end of 1993. This creates pressure for the administrative procedures to be speedily completed.

Given the size of the industries in the Russian Federation, other methods are also being discussed by the Russian government. The first, known as the sectorial approach, is to privatize whole sectors of the economy at the same time. This was developed in Poland as a way of accelerating the process.

In that country Western consultants were hired to study particular industries and suggest a privatization strategy for all enterprises within it as a package. Thirty-five branches of industries were ear-marked by the Polish ministry for this form of privatization.

A similar approach is considered to have major benefits for Russia, especially as the initial study would provide a strategic view of each industry and would suggest tactics for the viability of the companies within it. In addition, the ministerial structure of Russian industry further complements this approach given that the ministries have been organized on an industry basis and a method of communication already established. Even though the economic and political decision-making processes have been separated to prevent a conflict of interest (as shown in Figure 3.4 below), there is no reason for this to hamper the process. Indeed, it could be enhanced because the whole purpose of separation was to ensure that the country's interest was placed above that of individuals.

By analysing whole industries in the first instance to determine whether they may be privatized as a unit, it also allows for the possibility of a multi-methodological approach to the implementation of privatization, and as a result the forms and methods of privatization may vary even within a sector with perhaps some companies being sold to Western firms by competitive tender, others being more suited to management buy-outs, and some told to restructure or be put into a general group for mass privatization.

This approach also helps to counter the argument that Russia is being sold to foreigners. As each industry is being analysed as a whole, only certain parts will be recommended for sale to investment capital from abroad, while others could be backed by domestic capital investment. Indeed, a variety of different forms of ownership may even exist within a company: Western shareholders, Russian shareholders – either employers or private individuals – and even the state maintaining a share.

Two other methods of privatization have been considered: 'privatization from above' and 'privatization from grass roots'.

Privatization from above was adopted in Hungary, and was used in Russia in the early privatizations, primarily because of the lack of necessary institutions to carry out the process. This approach envisages an establishment or specialized state body possessing the rights of ownership and disposal over public property and charged with the task of privatization. A prime function of this body is to transform public enterprises into joint-stock companies and then to sell their shares either directly or through specially established investment funds which would be subordinate to it. Shares would be sold according to a plan approved by a higher legislative or executive authority, and within a stipulated time schedule. A simpler procedure of bypassing the joint-stock stage may be employed in the case of small and medium enterprises to be sold or leased to a private owner.

This option envisages the sale of state property to individuals and organizations willing to buy it for cash. It is here that the main danger lies in the probability of negative social implications if the populace lack sufficient funds to participate. According to various estimates, no more than 10 per cent of the residual value of state assets could be purchased by Russian citizens at present from their own savings. Those entrepreneurs able to use the funds of state enterprises through banks and holding companies controlled by them, as well as interested foreign companies and joint ventures that possess considerable funds in roubles and hard currency, would be given an unfair advantage.

A further problem with this method is that it envisages a high degree of centralization of the management of state property within a state department responsible for privatization. Such a concentration of executive authority in a single state body may result in privatization escaping control by the legislative authority and undermine the new structures which have sought to separate economic and political control. The whole purpose of the separation of powers under the new structure has been to reduce the corruption which had arisen in the former Soviet Union, whereas this method could enhance it if not managed correctly.

'Privatization from the grass roots' is the means whereby property is distributed equally among the population with the help of specially issued vouchers, and was the system adopted in Czechoslovakia. It is a version of this system which has now been introduced in Russia for about one third of the medium-sized and larger enterprises, as just described.

The privatization plan for sectors and industries

The programme divides state and municipal objects for privatization into five groups:

1 *Objects liable to privatization according to obligatory tasks* – retail trade shops and consumer services, building trade and building materials industry, enterprises of agricultural goods processing, enterprises of technical provision to agriculture, food processing and light industry enterprises, unprofitable enterprises, unfinished enterprises.
2 *Objects not liable to privatization* include – underground mineral reserves, water and timber reserves, objects of natural heritage and art objects, state treasury, military equipment not liable for industrial processing, property of the Home Affairs Ministry, as well as the property of other budget institutions, energy enterprises and pipe lines, communications, motorways and other roads.
3 *Property and assets liable to privatization only after permission* has been

granted by the Russian Federation government – enterprises which prove to be irremovable monopolists, the largest enterprises (average assets of more than 200 million roubles at January 1992 prices or more than 10,000 employees), enterprises producing arms, extracting industry (except local raw materials), oil-gas complexes, rail and roads, aviation, sea and river transport. The government has the right to take decisions retaining the ownership of these enterprises for a period of up to three years.

4 *Assets liable for privatization only with the agreement of local authorities* – urban transport and its repair services, pawnshops, public baths, laundries, hotels, pharmaceuticals, garbage processing plants, unfinished socio-cultural objects, cinemas and distribution outlets at local level.

5 *Assets liable for privatization, but not included in obligatory tasks* – these include enterprises that can be privatized in accordance with the Russian Federation 'Law on the Privatization of State and Municipal Enterprises'. Such claims can be made by the administration leader of an enterprise or by its employees' association if more than 50 per cent of its members wish, or by other juridical persons.

Areas in which privatization is prohibited until the appropriate laws are adopted include public health and education institutes, cultural centres and sports complexes (including the facilities of enterprises).

Problems of privatization

The first problem to be overcome in order to set a privatization programme in motion is the valuation of the state enterprises and, accordingly, their shares. As explained above, a number of factors make this task difficult, as does the absence of a capital market. Secondly, there are no mechanisms providing for the circulation of securities, in particular there is no stock exchange. Thirdly, there are no organizations capable of performing the tasks of stock placement and other privatization procedures. Finally, the population has limited funds to enable it to participate in the purchase of shares in privatized concerns.

At present, the only means available to assess a value on enterprises are the written down value of assets based on their original purchase price with a coefficient for inflation being added. On top of this, prices are calculated in roubles and then converted at a market rate which often makes Russian enterprises ridiculously cheap.

The technical difficulties are supplemented by considerable social problems, namely that state property is the common heritage of all the people and that it belongs to all members of society. Thus, the issue of social justice must be addressed in determining how privatization is to take place, and the psychological barriers to personal ownership of property overcome. Giving away state property free of charge will fail to address properly the social justice issue as not all enterprises may be privatized, or will be done so at different speeds. The sense of responsibility and pride that comes in owning property and investing one's own capital in the process, would be omitted.

Privatization legislation

No mass privatizations have taken place in Russia until now, partly because of the immense task in assessing and trying to calculate a value of the enterprises or whole industries, and partly because of the logistical problems in carrying out the privatization. As detailed above, there is a shortage of funds available among Russian citizens and an immense need for Western input – both financial and technical – to make the enterprises/industries economically viable.

In an effort to hasten the process (a little) and gain wider support from the populace, Boris Yeltsin announced plans for every Russian citizen to become a property owner in the course of his 19 August 1992 speech on the anniversary of the attempted coup. He said that 'every man, woman and child is to be given 10,000 roubles' worth of coupons free on 1 October through their local savings bank'. This would mean that from that date every Russian citizen will have the right to purchase state assets up to that amount irrespective of whether he is five or fifty-five years of age, or whether he wants to buy in Vladivostok or in Moscow. Russian citizens will also have the option to entrust their vouchers to funds which would buy shares on their behalf – the Western equivalent of a mutual fund or unit trust.

For privatization to proceed on a realistic scale and with the necessary injection of capital funds and know-how, Western investors are needed.

During the course of 1992 the Russian government has put in place the necessary legislation setting out the rights and obligations of the parties involved, and the procedure which must be followed. The most important items of legislation are the 'Law on Privatization of State and Municipal Enterprises in Russia' (adopted in July 1991, with amendments in June 1992), the 'State Programme of State and Municipal Enterprises Privatization in the Russian Federation' in 1992 (adopted on 11 June 1992) and the Russian Federation Presidential Decree on 'Organizational Measures on State Enterprises and Voluntary Amalgamations of State Enterprises Transfer to Joint-Stock Companies' (adopted in 1992).

The privatized enterprise must ensure that it complies with the Russian Federation Law on 'Protection of the Environment' of 19 December 1991, and all legislation relating to the ownership of land, including the various regulations on ownership rights for land, order of reserve land use, methods of compensation for damage and order for land conservation.

One of the major pitfalls in the privatization process is the lack of clarity about the ownership of land. Although there are large amounts of legislation on the privatization process, neither Russian nor Western banks are able legally to accept land as collateral to lend money for the development of a business. This is the major failing of the Russian legislation and of the whole privatization process.

In theory the legislation has been prepared, the structure to oversee the privatization of industries and enterprises is in place, and the voucher system of privatization will provide the minimal capital needed and also deal with the social arguments against privatization. Interest has already been shown by a number of Western companies in either investing in or purchasing outright various enterprises, and obviously these areas are being given priority. Major privatizations, however, are not expected to commence until well into 1993.

RESTRUCTURING THE POLITICAL AND ECONOMIC PROCESSES

A major challenge for the young Russian economists and the Russian government has been to separate the political and economic structures of the country. Privatization, which is at the core of the Russian programme for transformation, is motivated by pragmatism rather than ideology, although it is necessary to recognize that the political will must exist for the policy to be successful.

Boris Yeltsin, in announcing the radical new economic package on 28 October 1991, stated that 'privatization of industry will be a crucial part of the reform package'. This message has been repeated in subsequent speeches and despite opposition being raised to the proposals, most notably at the Congress of People's Deputies in June 1992, it is recognized that for the Russian economy to be revived this policy must be followed. Opposition to the proposals has not so much been concerned with their substance, but rather with the mechanism and means of implementation, and the psychological difficulties in coming to terms with the need to transfer decision-making away from the centre.

The separation and restructuring of the political and economic decision-making processes were completed in the first six months of 1992.

Figure 3.1 below explains the degree of integration between the political and economic decision-making processes which used to exist, and the extent to which the Communist Party dominated both. Figure 3.2 shows the new structures that have been created, and how they interact.

The most striking change is the removal of the Party structure which permeated every aspect of Soviet life and all economic and political processes of decision-making. The new structure clearly separates the government from the legislature, with the President appointing the Cabinet and his ministers. A Security Council is retained, with the Supreme Soviet at its head (this is a smaller version of the Congress of People's Deputies and comprises Deputies elected from this body), and the President now maintains his own team of

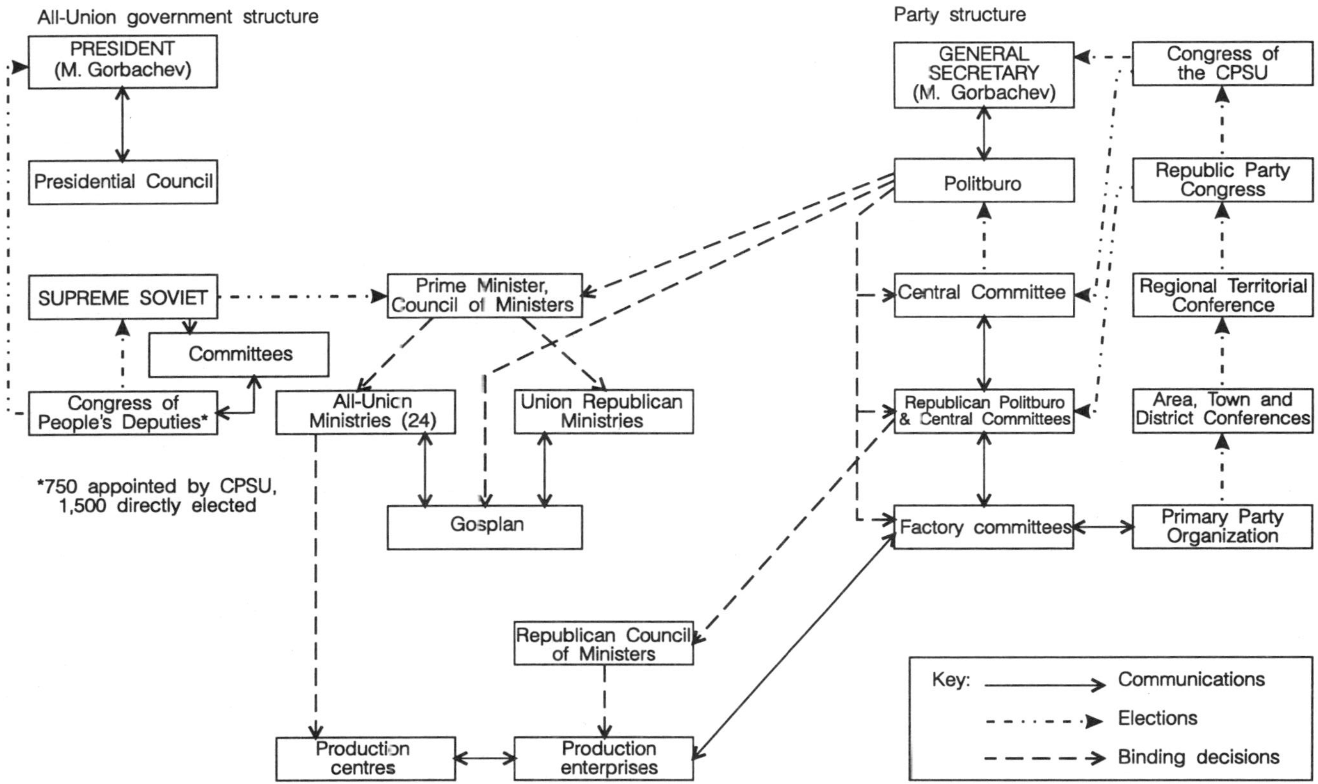

Figure 3.1 The structure of power in the Soviet Union
Source: Russian Consultancy Ltd.

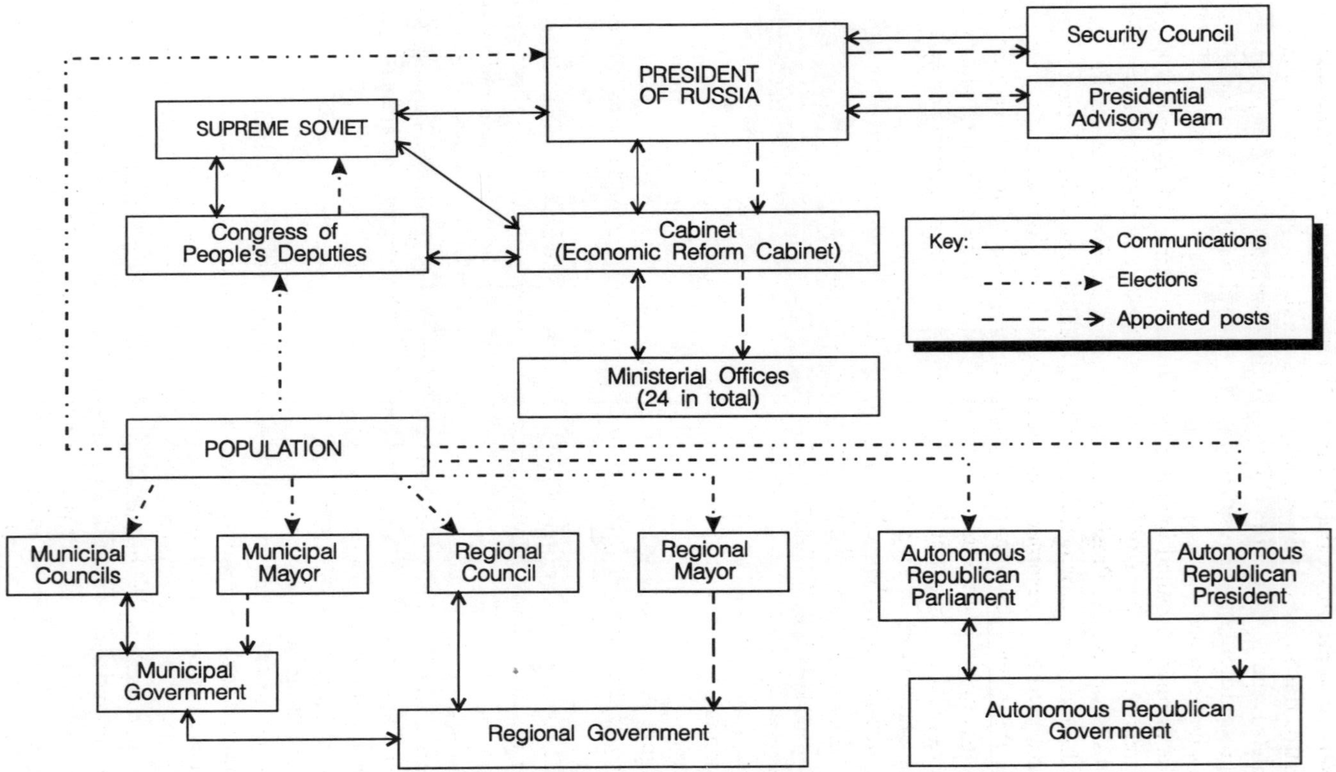

Figure 3.2 Governmental structure in Russia after August 1991
Source: Russian Consultancy Ltd.

advisers in addition to the Cabinet. The Cabinet and the President must report to the Supreme Soviet and are answerable in law to the Congress of People's Deputies. As in the US system, they should carry the support of the Congress although the President does have the power to over-ride them if he deems it necessary.

The Security Council includes the Prime Minister, Minister of Defence, ministers for the security services, First Deputy to the Government and whomsoever else the President wishes to include. Within the Cabinet there is an Economics Reform Cabinet which includes the Prime Minister, First Deputy to the Government and ministers for employment, the economy, finance, foreign economic relations, Committee for State Property and the Anti-monopoly Committee. No member of the Supreme Soviet is allowed to serve as a Cabinet minister or official of the government, thereby completing the separation of powers at this level.

A further radical change has taken place in the relationship between central government and regional governments. There is no longer any direct control over the regional governments, of which there are 86, and the autonomous republican governments, of which there are currently 16. Beneath the regional governments are municipal governments (of which there are thousands), which would be comparable to local councils in the British system.

Figure 3.3 sets out the current organization of the Cabinet and the 24 ministries that now exist, with their current ministers (updated to February 1993).

The Committee for State Property, in effect the Privatization Ministry, under the direction of deputy prime minister Anatoly Chubais, has overall responsibility for organizing the privatization of the public sector, drawing upon the expertise of Western companies experienced in privatization methods and analysis of industries and companies within them. The size of Russia – covering one-sixth of the world's area, and the former means of central control, require that some body exists which is capable of coordinating and devolving power to local level.

The Committee for State Property has split its functions into three tiers: the property and assets to be distributed at the federal level; the assets to be distributed at the autonomous republic and regional level; and those properties that are to be privatized at the municipal and city levels. While the Russian Federation Committee for State Property is responsible for the privatization of state property, appropriate committees have been established at local levels to deal with the privatization of property under their jurisdiction. As soon as the ownership of property is determined, it will be allocated to one of these three levels for valuation and assessment, and for the means by which it will be privatized to be decided.

The number of representatives on each of the 86 regional committees will depend upon the size of the region, but will at minimum include a

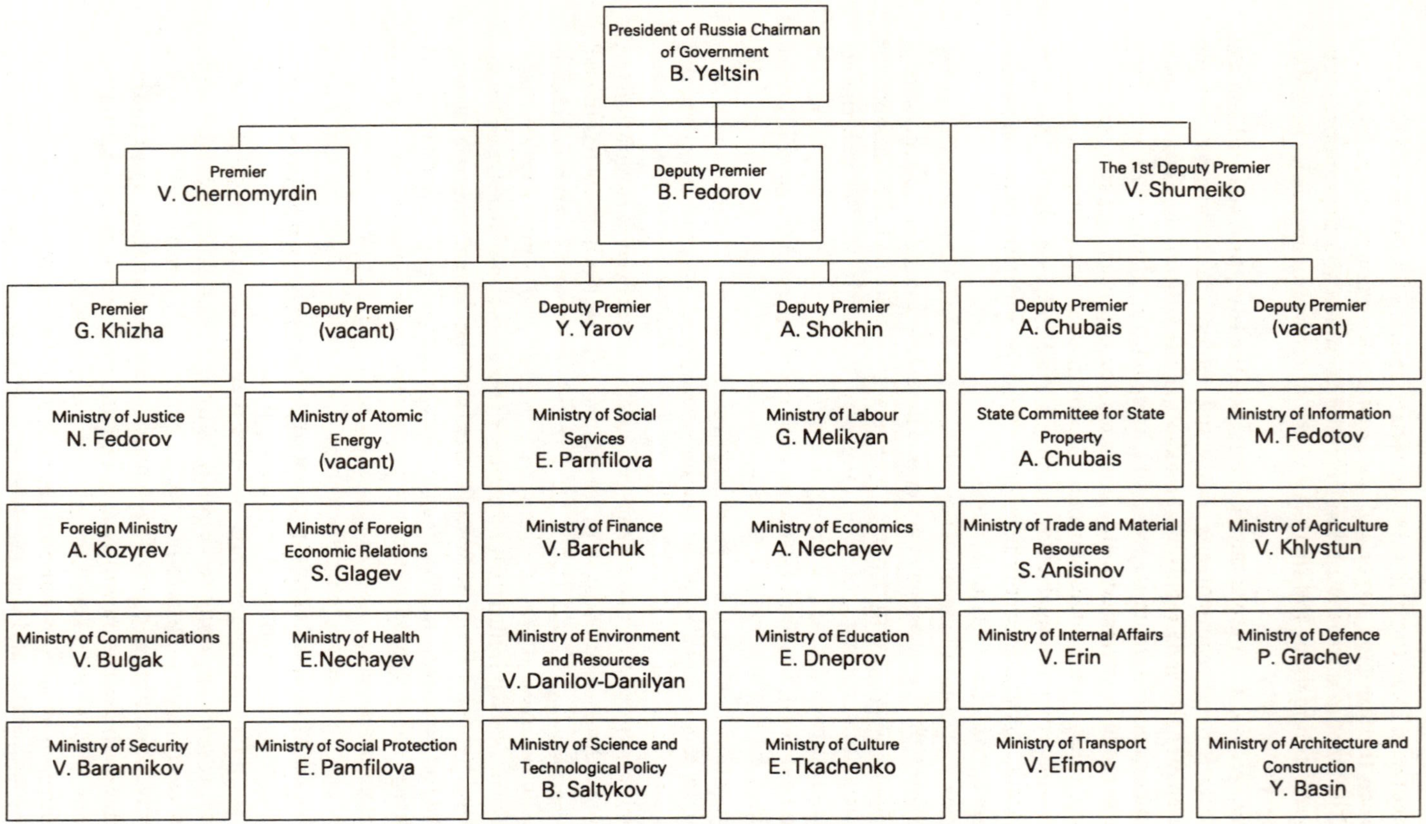

Figure 3.3 The Cabinet in Russia (February 1993)
Source: Russian Consultancy Ltd.

representative from the Federal Committee for State Property, one regional representative from the mayor's office, one from the regional council and one from the executive of the region. This representation is repeated for the municipal committees, and there is a direct link of communication between the two levels.

A similar system of representation exists on the 16 autonomous republican committees: one representative from the Federal Committee for State Property, one from the republic's presidential office, one from the republic's parliament and one from its executive body. Again, the number of representatives may be increased if this is considered necessary and appropriate.

Within these committees, commissions are created to deal with the actual privatization of individual enterprises, take decisions on their method of privatization, reorganize enterprises and transfer certificates of ownership to the appropriate property funds for sale.

Figure 3.4 shows the structure of the Russian Fund for Federal Property, which is a structure mirrored at regional, autonomous republic and municipal level. The function of these Funds is to conduct the sale and hold the proceeds of sale once the committees have completed their work on what and how industries/enterprises will be privatized.

Only the Russian Federal Property Fund and its representatives are to be the sellers of privatized federal enterprises and of the appropriate shares. The main function of the Russian Federal Property Fund is to hold temporarily federal ownership certificates or shares of joint-stock companies. It, and the Funds established at the lower levels, have the authority to sell shares, issue ownership certificates and establish joint-stock companies, as well as to execute the power of the Russian government as the coordinator at general meetings of shareholders. While the Russian government has a degree of control in the initial stages, it is limited by the fact that a Fund may only hold 20 per cent of each joint-stock company's shares and that these shares have no voting rights.

Thus the privatization process is initiated and coordinated by the various committees for state property, but implemented by the representatives of the Property Funds.

RESTRUCTURING INDUSTRIES AND ENTERPRISES

While the political and economic decision-making structure has largely been changed, alterations in the relationship between these structures, individual industries and enterprises are still taking place.

Firstly, it has been necessary to decide at what level operational decisions, such as the purchase of raw materials, production levels and similar business decisions, should be taken. Government enterprises have now been given autonomy, or what is commonly described as 'financial independence', to buy and sell goods and organize the internal manufacturing process. The

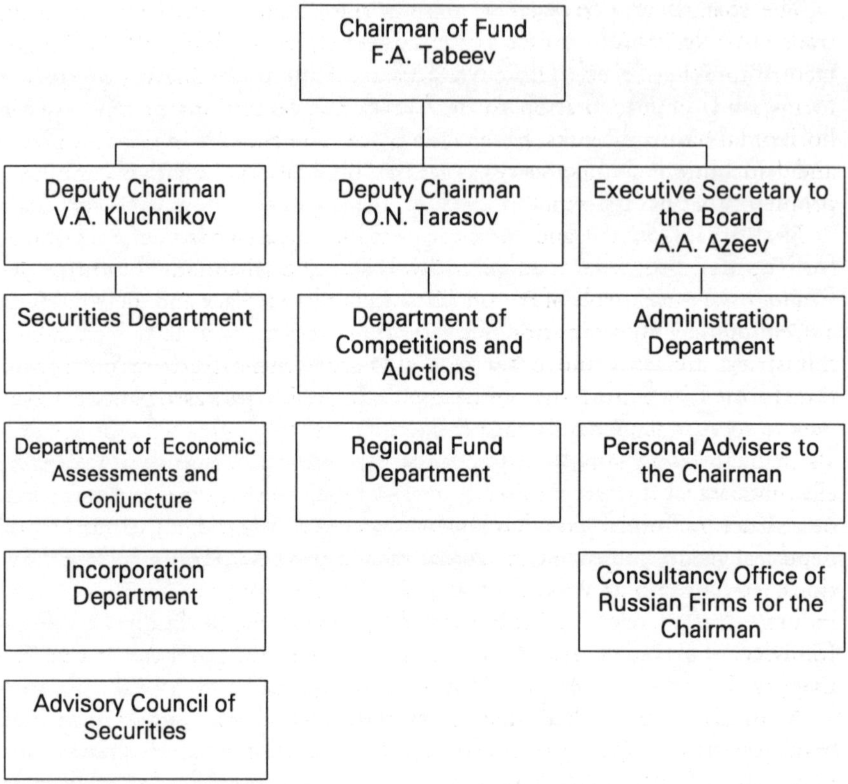

Figure 3.4 Structure of the Russian Fund for Federal Property (August 1992)
Source: Russian Consultancy Ltd.

Communist Party has been removed and so no instructions now come through the First Party Secretary of the region. The factory director now has to decide the 'what and where, when and how' of his factory's operations and must take full responsibility for them. Unfortunately, because the factories are not yet in private hands, the goods produced can still be directed by state authorities.

For example, when the Kazan Helicopter Factory has ten helicopters for sale the government, knowing that the Tyumin oil fields need three for the transportation of oil workers and that another two are needed in Vladivostok, still has the power to order these helicopters to be sent there.

In addition to overcoming the psychological barriers to taking responsibility, the directors of factories must also learn how to manage them effectively, and adjust to the new distinction of roles by the state authorities and the factory management.

The changes that have taken place at the political level have led to the transfer of decision-making on organizational, legal, social and production factors to other levels. The development of more flexible organizational forms, and their adaptation to new economic conditions on the basis of horizontal industrial links, have taken place. The changes in the production and distribution of vodka serves as a useful illustration of this process and the problems that have arisen.

Real organizational and juridical decision-making has been transferred from upper power level to medium level (i.e. regional administration), significant growth in the role of regional bodies has taken place and there has been a strengthening of the position of directors of every factory. The former union ministries, divisions and other central management structures have been transformed into concerns, joint-stock companies and associations which seek to solve independently the production tasks beginning with raw materials through to the supply of goods for sale. In addition to this, within the existing central Russian ministries, departments and regional power bodies, new structural subdivisions have been created, e.g. committees, commissions, deputies' groups, departments, guiding associations, concerns, trade institutions, etc. Examples of such new organizations found within the vodka industry could be the Committee on Processing in the Ministry of the Food Industry, the Department of Food in the Moscow government and the Deputy Group at the Moscow Liquors and Vodka Plant 'Crystal'.

A negative result of these changes has been a rise in corruption at industrial management levels, the use of semi-legal methods of activity to obtain raw materials and other necessary products which in turn has led to a sharp increase in the influence of the black economy.

As a result of this reorganization, and despite the problems concerning corruption, the way has been opened for foreign investors to enter the vodka industry. This has been further enabled by the recently issued 'permission' acts concerning alcohol pricing and the growth of productive independence of enterprises in this industry. These allow for decision-making to take place at local and middle level rather than only at the upper levels of power.

Attempts at this type of reorganization (despite the pitfalls) have taken place across most industries, but the success and depth of change has depended upon the management of the individual factories within the industry and whether they belong to the reformist or reactionary wing of Russian political spectrum.

The internal restructuring of individual enterprises has been even more limited and is not expected to happen on any large scale until the process of privatizing them actually begins.

CONCLUSIONS

While the first phase goals of privatization have not been realized in full, it is considered that the mechanisms and legislation are now in place for this process to proceed rapidly in 1993–4. A start has been made on 'mass privatization', through the use of vouchers. Increasing Western interest in investing in Russia will greatly assist this process, and an advertising campaign by the Federal Committee for State Property is hoped to accelerate it.

We must remember, however, that industrial output fell by about 15 per cent during the first six months of 1992 over the same period in 1991. Government sources suggest that the metallurgical industry in Russia will have a net output fall of 27 per cent in 1992, while light engineering and food processing will drop by 33 per cent and 28 per cent respectively. Moreover, given that investment has totally collapsed and is only 56 per cent of what it was in 1991, enterprises are in a worse state than ever. This explains why banks have been compelled to lend them money just to survive.

On the beneficial side, enterprise profits are rising. In 1990 total profits for Russian industry were 154 billion roubles, or 25 per cent of GDP; in 1991 they doubled to 320 billion roubles, or 27 per cent of GDP; and in the first six months of 1992 rose to 979 billion roubles, or 33 per cent of GDP.

The foreign currency reserves and deposits of the Russian companies have also shown marked improvements. Between the months of January and May 1992 these reserves more than doubled, from US $1.8 billion to US $4 billion, largely thanks to booming exports. The extent of the illegal foreign currency reserves is not known, but some observers suggest that it is as high as US $20 billion.

There has been steadily growing pressure from the industrialists to slow the pace of reform. Pressure has increased especially since they have established a political body called the Russian Union of Industrialists, led by Arkady Volsky. They have also called for the reintroduction of subsidies to state enterprises and have expressed disagreement with the privatization policy.

By joining an organization called Civic Unity, which includes Vice-President Rutskoy as a member and which unites the Russian Democratic Party, led by Vladimir Travkin, and the Smena faction of deputies in the Russian Congress of People's Deputies, they now have the opportunity to exert political pressure from within the government and legislature.

Their support for Gerashenko in his proposal to write off 1.5 trillion roubles of debt that enterprises owe to the government, knowing that this would cause hyper-inflation, illustrates how serious a challenge they could present to the government's economic policy. If they succeed in slowing down the reform process this would not only undermine the government's strategy but also the confidence that Western financial institutions have shown in the government led by Yegor Gaidar. It would, for example, mean that the US $24 billion aid package from the IMF would be suspended.

The importance of these views, and their potential power, lies in the growing support they are attracting both from within and outside the government. Representatives of this group are already present in the government and include V. Shumeko, first Deputy Prime Minister, Deputy Chairman of the Government Giorgi Khizha and Deputy Chairman V. Chernomyrdin, responsible for energy and fuels.

If this group succeeds in having debts to the central government written off, it will also succeed in postponing the next crucial stage of industrial reform. Any substantial injection of new credit will give significant buoyance to the production of unnecessary goods, finance further stockpiling of production and maintain artificially high prices. It will mean that in the not too distant future more cash injections will be needed to maintain consumer demand, inflation will accelerate, real interest rates will again fall, and this ruinous cycle will continue until the economy collapses totally. The Gaidar government argues that no credit bale-out should be given to enterprises. In my opinion, all hope for reform depends on whether the Gaidar government prevails.

4

RECONSTRUCTION IN CENTRAL ASIA: KAZAKHSTAN

Serik A. Akhanov

KAZAKHSTAN TODAY

Kazakhstan became – almost reluctantly – an independent country in December 1991, following the disintegration of the Soviet Union and the setting up of the CIS. It has a very long border with Russia to the north, and to the south and east with Turkmenistan, Uzbekistan, Kirghizia and the People's Republic of China. Its huge land mass of 2.7 million sq km is about five times the size of France. The population is in excess of 16 million, some 40 per cent ethnic Kazakhs and 40 per cent Russians, with a significant number of Muslims. While it retains strong ties with Russia and is a keen supporter of the CIS, it also has an orientation towards Turkey as a possible role model.

In 1990 Kazakhstan's GDP was about US $57 billion (1985 prices), and GDP per capita was US $3,433. Its radical economic reform programme, aimed at the revival of the country and improved prosperity within a social market economy, is, however, being conducted under conditions of severe economic crisis.

The period 1976–80 was one of fast growth. (Generated National Income rose at an annual average rate of 4.4 per cent, capital investment for production rose by 7 per cent per annum, national income used for consumption and savings rose by 4.5 per cent per annum.) However, 1981–5 was a time of recession. Generated National Income rose by only 0.9 per cent annually, and the rate of investment, consumption and savings also fell. The recovery in 1986–90 was very slow, and in the 'post-planning' economy of 1991 was soon followed by a sharp decline in demand, output, investment and in the standard of living. Unemployment, the money supply, inflation and the budget deficit all increased.

In the first five months of 1992 (at the time of writing the latest statistics) the situation has worsened considerably. Gross Public Product (a concept which involves some double counting) decreased by 21 per cent over the same period in 1991, Generated National Income fell by 26 per cent, and the output of consumer goods by 16 per cent. Consumer goods are now very scarce and the market is unstable. The decline in production seems uncontrollable.

In 1991 the money supply of roubles in Kazakhstan increased 14 times. In the first five months of 1992 it rose by a further 10 times compared with the previous year, while the prices of consumer goods and services rose by 623 per cent during this period. Investment is down by one-third. The budget deficit in 1991 was 6.2 per cent of GDP, although this is forecast to fall during 1992.

Kazakhstan has taken responsibility for 3.87 per cent of the debt of the former Soviet Union. The government has also signed a treaty with the creditor countries of the 'Group of Seven' most advanced industrial nations and has undertaken certain commitments – including the commitment not to interrupt the servicing of foreign debt.

The economic dislocation between enterprises, however, is worsening, and their outstanding debts between themselves (in blocked bank accounts) have reached 88 billion roubles (May 1992), 19 times greater than in 1991 which, if they were released, would be very significant in terms of the total money supply. Some 940 state enterprises (17.8 per cent of the total) are making losses.

As the Kazakhstan economy moves towards hyper-inflation, constructive and drastic measures are urgently needed to eliminate the crisis.

ECONOMIC AND INDUSTRIAL POLICIES

The transformation of the economic system

The government of Kazakhstan is aware of what is needed. Policies for economic stabilization must include the liberalization of prices and of external economic relations and economic ties, a reduction of the trade and budget deficits, and a dramatic decrease in inflation. A restrictive credit policy will be necessary, with income controls, privatization, the promotion of competition, the implementation of land reform, the attraction of foreign capital and the widening of interstate economic ties. Also of fundamental importance will be the transition from a command economy to one based upon markets, the retention of strong management structures and the abandonment of running enterprises on the basis of their expenditures. Preventing mass bankruptcies and encouraging the efficient operation of enterprises will also be crucial. This is a vast and complex programme on which it is now embarked.

External relations have become a major problem. The economy of the former Soviet Union had a high level of economic integration between the republics. In 1991 the share of inter-republican turnover in Kazakhstan's GDP was 32 per cent (higher than the 25 per cent in Russia itself). Kazakhstan receives up to 40 per cent of materials and equipment (used mainly in making machinery) and up to 68 per cent of consumer goods from these countries. More than three-quarters of Kazakhstan's exports to other republics (62 per cent of which is to Russia) consists of the products of the extractive industries and of agriculture.

The disruption of this trade has become one of the main factors that has caused the steep decline in Kazakhstan's industrial production and its shortage of consumer goods. Great importance is now attached to increasing the share of processing industries in Kazakhstan's exports, to decreasing its dependence on imports of equipment and of consumer goods, and to creating conditions for the development of technology-intensive industries.

When the normalization of economic ties between member states of the CIS occurs it will have a positive impact on enterprise performance in Kazakhstan. Enhancing mechanisms for the clearing of payments and progressively lifting all quantitative restrictions on the exports and imports of goods will help economic reforms. It will also be important to create a system of quoting and licensing products for promoting their distribution in domestic, inter-republic and other external markets. This is a means of having a controlled growth in exports where formerly sales were either all domestic (within the Soviet Union as part of 'state orders'), or externally through Comecon inter-government agreements.

Moreover, in order to simplify the contradictory procedures of coordination it will be necessary to reduce the list of 'state orders' issuing from the government and attempts at centralized industrial coordination. But it will still be necessary to ensure that the volume of deliveries between enterprises is nevertheless properly coordinated, and to establish financial penalties for failures to reach promised commitments.

To achieve the more normal performance of enterprises it will be necessary to coordinate the economic policies of all CIS member states and to create the institutions to achieve this, with systems of management and regulation. The government in Kazakhstan will encourage domestic enterprises to establish direct contacts with enterprises abroad, and to create inter-state, joint-stock and transnational companies.

Privatization and the private sector

Three categories of enterprise are envisaged:

1 Enterprises which will remain state-owned and under direct state control;
2 Enterprises which will remain state-owned, acting on a commercial basis and within the sphere of state regulation; and
3 Enterprises in private or collective ownership (i.e. with many shareholders) outside of the system of state management and regulation.

By 1 May 1992, out of a total of 30,761 state-owned enterprises, the government had privatized 1,539. Of these, 63 per cent are collectively owned with shareholders, and 24 per cent are in private ownership.

As a result the non-state sector now includes 35 joint-stock companies, 76 intersectoral and external economic associations (joint ventures), 230 medium-sized industrial companies, 120 commercial banks, 60 exchanges (including 22 universal exchanges, 10 commodity exchanges, three commodity and fund exchanges, seven commodity and raw material exchanges and five exchanges for intellectual property), 40 insurance and 20 leasing companies, two auditing centres, 11,000 cooperatives, 5,500 small enterprises and 6,000 farms. These enterprises employ about 500,000 persons, 15 per cent of all employees in Kazakhstan.

Exchanges are being liberalized. This is partly to eliminate distortions in the development of new exchange markets, but also to lift regional restrictions on the export of goods, to increase quotas for the unrestricted sale of raw materials and to de-monopolize trade processes so as to render better services to production enterprises.

Currently the state owns some 80 per cent of the national economy. The present plan is to privatize 50 per cent of the assets of industry during 1992, together with 40 per cent of agriculture and all housing construction. Privatization will cover many kinds of property, in consumer services, trade, social amenities, public utilities, housing (on which see below), small industrial enterprises, construction, agriculture and autotransport. Large industrial and agro-industrial enterprises will become joint-stock companies (details of which are also given below).

Large state monopolies are typical of a command economy. For technological and organizational reasons it is not possible to privatize these in the short term. They will be transformed initially into independent productive structures (category 2 above), to encourage efficiency and higher quality in production.

The division of state property into republic and municipal components has given additional impetus to the privatization programme. It has resulted in a diversity of forms and methods of implementation suited to local circumstances. These include both purchasing for cash and for non-cash through coupons. However, for historical, social and psychological reasons, land is retained as the exclusive property of the state. It will be leased on a life-long inherited basis, in which foreign citizens may participate.

At present 68 per cent of all housing is state-owned or in cooperatives, and 32 per cent is individually owned. Housing reforms are in the process of implementation, and a housing market is coming into being. A coupon mechanism has been developed to assist in the privatization of housing, based on ensuring equal starting opportunities for all citizens during the transition, adherence to the voluntary principle, recognition of the length of work of their inhabitants and the protection of people in need. Rent for state housing is being introduced.

Joint-stock companies

In industry it is planned to create 10–15 parallel financial and industrial groups, competing between themselves, and in foreign markets. This form of restructuring should lead to the creation of competitive firms with efficient production and management.

Horizontal integration of production and distribution in industry and agriculture is being carried out, requiring the merger of firms producing homogeneous products. Vertical integration is also developing, with firms merging which serve different stages in one technological process.

A high level of industrial concentration, with the monopolization of sectoral markets by state concerns, was brought about through the state planning system. While at present there is in reality little difference between a ministry or government department and state-owned business concerns, it is planned to transform the latter into joint-stock companies. The creation of such large intersectoral holding companies with a wide distribution of share ownership is becoming more important. It is planned to incorporate in these companies economic activities of many different kinds and holding different forms of property.

Within these companies there will be provided all necessary scientific, informational, technical and engineering services, as well as foreign economic and commercial activity. This economic independence will permit the best use of material, financial and labour resources, and the creation of new subdivisions for particular tasks. At present, however, due to the under-development of the market infrastructure and of services to enterprises, and because of the predominance of the 'state order' system, it is more difficult for private firms than for state enterprises to obtain equipment, raw materials and credit.

This approach will constitute a fundamental restructuring of work and of responsibilities from the time when the bureaucracy in the state made all important business decisions, procured all resources, undertook all research and development, negotiated foreign sales agreements, etc.

In addition to these 'mixed' joint-stock companies where all of these activities will take place, there will also be a few 'net' portfolio holders exercising only the general financial management of enterprises.

Management and control over the activities of enterprises

Enterprise control should develop as follows. The highest control body will be the meeting of shareholders. This will determine the main direction for the development of a business and will elect the board of directors or governors, who will hold the real power. Representatives of the workers and employees are also to be included on the board. The board will elect its chairman (president) and the vice-presidents. The president or the vice-presidents appoint the heads of departments, divisions, sectors and shops. Depending on the size of the enterprise, there will be a two-, three- or four-level system of management.

A new procedure for the appointment of the directors of enterprises is being developed, on the basis of a contract with the government for state enterprises stating their powers and obligations. Managers should have the right to make decisions independently of the government and to be responsible for the final results. Directors of enterprises should be able to manage effectively the factors of production, the production processes and sales.

A functional system of management is predominant. The management functions of supervising different divisions (sales, planning, supplies, research and science) are brought together. The role of planning in the activity of enterprises is becoming more important. It will involve major changes in the work of such subdivisions as accounting and finance. The general results of enterprises should be carefully monitored and proper records kept.

Pricing policy and the efficiency of enterprise performance

As a first step in price reform, the prices of about 90 per cent of retail items and 80 per cent of wholesale items have been liberalized. Prices for only 14 items of foodstuffs, fuel, transport tariffs and certain services are retained within state regulation.

During the first five months of 1992, retail prices and tariffs for consumer goods and services have increased 6.2 times compared with the corresponding period in 1991. Wholesale prices in industry have grown 15.6 times. Especially high was the increase in prices of ferrous metal (31.4 times), chemicals (29.1 times), nonferrous metals (25.1 times) and electrical energy (17.2 times).

The main reason for these huge price increases is the monopoly position of producers, the abolition of price controls and the slow formation of competitive market structures.

Artificial restraints on price increases cause 'hidden' forms of inflation. The liberalization of prices has a negative impact on the raw material export potential of Kazakhstan and creates financial complexities for the extractive industries, for agriculture and for other sectors. The non-payment by enterprises to each other, and the growth of 'blocked accounts' mentioned earlier, do not necessarily imply bankruptcy. However, even highly efficient enterprises are in danger of closure because of these huge price increases. There is at present no law on bankruptcy in Kazakhstan and one is required, as a result of the enhanced economic independence and responsibility of individual enterprises.

For exporting industries, at present the existence of an efficient system of 'state orders', and the determination of previously established prices are important. Internal and inter-republic prices for fuel will be regulated with the export tax. Subsidies for certain enterprises will have to be maintained in order to sustain their low controlled prices.

Price regulation is aimed at reducing inflation, encouraging scientific and technical progress and the increase in profits through the reduction in cost. Also, price controls on a few basic items remain for the time being for social reasons.

Social issues

The costs of production of state-owned enterprises currently include social commitments to employees concerning the provision of their housing, which is controlled by the state, expenses for the education of their children and the training and retraining of their employees and the members of their families.

Environmental and health protection undertaken by enterprises is controlled by the state. The Ministry of Environment and Bioresources is participating in the development of appropriate legislation for the regulation of environmental protection, and undertakes training and the financing of research and development. The state renders many kinds of assistance to enterprises, including the development of new technology, the provision of credit and tax concessions.

Kazakhstan is contemplating the lifting of restrictions on wage increases in production enterprises. At 1 May 1992 the average monthly wage in material production was 1,747 roubles. This was 6.2 times greater than in 1991 and was therefore in line with the rate of inflation. The present minimum wage is 600 roubles/month, but it is planned to increase this to 900 roubles/month from 1 October 1992.

The largest part of wage payments, some 70–80 per cent, consists of the tariff set by the government, with increments on top. Additional wages include payment for idle time, extra hours and bonuses. Payment by time period is predominant. In practice there are differences in wages depending upon the size of the enterprise and the qualification of employees. Agreements between the administration and the unions determine the terms of working, rest periods, hiring and firing, the level of wages within the tariffs, social insurance and working hours.

There are methods of collective motivation, such as profit-sharing, the acquisition of shares and dividends.

The Ministry of Labour and the Ministry of Social Welfare analyse the structure of the labour market and regulate employment, public works and the professional training of employees.

Early in 1992 there were only 20,000 unemployed in Kazakhstan, although by the end of 1992 this is expected to rise to 300,000–350,000. Such an increase will require enhancing the Labour Code, adopting a law on labour conflicts and improvement of systems for the conclusion of labour agreements.

Reduction of the budget deficit requires the reorientation of social programmes to benefit only those in need, the reduction of subsidies and support for low-income families. A fund for the social protection of the population is therefore being created to provide for the means of social insurance and the payment of all kinds of pensions, allowances and compensations. Enterprises and trade unions will also contribute to this fund.

Measures are also planned for the regulation of employment, the level and rate of change of wages, social insurance and the pensions of employees of state-owned enterprises. Also, to provide incentives, it will be important to provide employees with the possibility of obtaining long-term consumer credit for the acquisition of capital goods, the expansion of private education and of private medical services.

Management training under transition to a market economy

The government is paying great attention to the need for personnel training in a market economy. The training and retraining of specialists in management, marketing, banking, finance and insurance has already started in Kazakhstan. Technical assistance from the IMF, the World Bank and from foreign states and companies is very important. An indicative programme of technical assistance has been signed with the Commission of the European Communities.

For example, market analysis is not yet undertaken in all enterprises – under the former command economy, marketing decisions were taken by the bureaucracy in government, and international trade was largely arranged through inter-government agreements within Comecon. There is only one institute in Kazakhstan for the 'Investigation of Demand and Market Conditions'. It is in the Ministry of Trade and is a relic of the former system within the Soviet Union. Consulting firms offering services in investigating markets, prices, competition and the technical characteristics of goods are now emerging. The investigation of foreign experience in the organization and management of enterprises is just starting in economic institutions and universities. Enterprises will quickly have to undertake their own marketing analysis.

The 'Institute for the Improvement of Qualifications' is training high-ranking officials and specialists of the Cabinet of Ministers. The 'Kazakhstan Institute of Management, Economics and Forecasting', under the President of the Republic, has started its work. It will train specialists in modern economics and business, and its graduates will receive international diplomas. Several groups of young specialists from enterprises are receiving training abroad, in the United States, Turkey, the Republic of Korea and elsewhere.

ANTI-MONOPOLY POLICY AND ENTERPRISE ACTIVITY

Kazakhstan's economy is highly monopolized. Many sectors have only one enterprise. The result is dictatorship of producers, low quality, lack of competitiveness of products and price increases.

Out of the 115 largest enterprises in Kazakhstan, 90 are virtual monopolies, producing some 104 industrial items. One enterprise in electronics and instrument making produces 11 out of 12 items in this sector (92 per cent). One enterprise producing tractors and agricultural machinery makes 85 per cent of items; one enterprise in chemicals makes 80 per cent of products; forestry is the same; metallurgy is 85 per cent and machine tool construction is 100 per cent. Conditions are now being created for reducing this high degree of monopolization in machine building, energy and metallurgy.

The Anti-monopoly Committee has concentrated on the prevention of new monopolies; the divestment of existing ones is not taking place. The Committee is fighting against monopolization during privatization and the concentration of economic power, and has been concerned with the issue of quotas and licences for export, the prevention of unjustified price increases and the encouragement of scientific and technical progress.

The degree of market monopolization, anti-competitive mergers of enterprises, price agreements, price discrimination and other uncompetitive trade practices are subject to state regulation. The main thrust of its policy is control over the mechanisms of determining the prices of monopolists, the limitation of agreements between enterprises and the elimination of regional barriers for the free exchange of goods.

FORMS AND METHODS OF INDIRECT STATE INFLUENCE ON THE ACTIVITIES OF ENTERPRISES

The system of relationships between the state and enterprises in Kazakhstan is changing as a result of the developing market economy. The transition is being carried out from directives and plans of the state bodies concerned, especially the Department of Economic Reforms and Structural Policy (of which the present author was previously head) supported by state orders and contracts.

The state still acts as the main customer for the products of enterprises, and is the main investor (although investment in state enterprise is now falling). However, decisions on investment are often taken irrespective of commercial criteria. It is important to make it worthwhile for enterprises to receive 'state orders', guaranteeing the supply of materials and technical products, and a system of incentives for their fulfilment. To solve the contradictions of the present contractual system it is also necessary to maintain direct ties between enterprises, producers and consumers, and an orderly market.

The state can influence enterprises through short-term 'state orders', and in the long term through the preferential financing of investment. It can therefore prevent monopoly in the production of specific commodities, and promote competition.

With privatization and the growth of the market economy, directive management by the state, and the regulation of enterprise performance have been weakened. Kazakhstan is now moving towards a combination of directive and indicative planning principles for organizational change and for the outputs of enterprises. Indicative planning, in the short, medium and long term, is to be accompanied by forecasting. Some enterprises are offered direct grants, targeted credits and the freezing or writing off of debts. Many enterprises now function on the basis of leasing their assets from the state. And in mining the government may grant concessions.

Industrial policies being implemented in this way include – satisfying the market for foodstuffs and consumer goods, building up the construction industry, less orientation of the economy towards the production of raw materials, the development of technology-intensive industries, diversification and the conversion of defence industries, the formation of a modern transport infrastructure, improved communications, the development of the nation's energy resources (in July 1992 deals were signed with British Gas and Agip from Italy to develop oil and gas fields in north-western Kazakhstan, and with the Turkish company Birlesmis Muhendisler Burosu to increase oil output and to build a gas-fired power station). Also there is a developing hotel network for tourism and business. To achieve all of these goals, state sectoral programmes are being developed.

To support such developments, a standard system of amortization is planned, to include accelerated amortization, credit concessions for enterprises successful in their conversion, reorientation or divestment of activities. In the former Soviet system there was no such concept as 'amortization', because investment goods were simply supplied under 'state orders' and the acquiring enterprise did not have to pay for them.

It will be necessary at every stage from scientific research, product development and production to achieve economic motivation through tax concessions, and financing credits. At present, the state acts as the customer for the products of enterprises, undertakes research and development, and places 'state orders' through the Ministry of Science. This will gradually change as the market develops and as enterprises become privatized.

Financial policies

Outstanding credit in Kazakhstan on 1 May 1992 had reached 141 billion roubles, 4.8 times larger than at the same time in 1991, and within this short-term loans – by far the largest element – had increased six times. This excessive growth of credit has caused a great increase in demand. The growth in circulation of the means of payment has now slowed down, and is causing severe economic problems in enterprises.

The government of Kazakhstan stands for the preservation of a single rouble area, and the coordination of its credit policy with that in the Russian Federation. There should be the same reserve requirements for all deposits and tax rates for loans.

While it is important to ensure the stability of the rouble in order to eliminate the crisis, taking into account the complicated political situation in the CIS, it is necessary to continue efforts aimed at the introduction of a national currency in Kazakhstan. The costs and benefits are being considered. At present the republic is not able to pursue an independent monetary policy. A new money system should contribute to stabilization in the economy and increase efficiency in production.

To decrease the rate of inflation and of credit expansion, the scale of internal financing is being limited, and the control of the National State Bank over reserve requirements and over credit to commercial banks is being strengthened.

Since the interest rate should be the main instrument for the allocation of credit, it is necessary to eliminate subsidies of that rate. The government should have a list of sectors and enterprises enjoying interest rate concessions while receiving credit. The National State Bank could then implement selective credit policy, give significant privileges to investment programmes and promote structural transformation in the economy.

Taxation policies

The tax system is currently being reformed. The most important new measure is the introduction of a Value Added Tax (VAT). An analysis of its current application shows that more work is needed to improve revenue estimates, the determination of the compensation system and the limitation of tax exemptions and concessions.

The government expects to receive additional revenues through the expansion of the tax base and the introduction of VAT on imports, natural resources and excise revenues, and through consolidation of control over tax collection.

The 1992 forecasted revenue from VAT is 40.9 billion roubles, from corporate income tax 31.7, from personal income tax 14.5 and from excise duties 10.6 billion roubles.

Practical experience indicates that it is important to reduce the VAT rate for businesses, because of their performance, especially for the extraction industries and for agriculture. Tax concessions and credits should be tied to structural policy, and support to priority sectors and enterprises. As business performance improves, new taxes may be introduced, and tax rates and tax concessions will be regularly reviewed.

Inward investment and trade policy

In the former command economy, many technologies and commodities became obsolete and uncompetitive with the corresponding commodities produced in the West. The reconstruction of industries and enterprises requires significant internal and external investment.

A National Agency of Foreign Investments has been created to attract foreign investment, and a law has been passed on inward investment which provides for the concessions available to foreign investors.

Foreign investment is permitted in all spheres of economic and other activity, except for production with military purposes. Property imported into the republic as investment by foreign enterprises, not designed for sale, is not subject to customs duties. Foreign enterprises wholly owned abroad are permitted. Foreign investors are exempt from corporate income tax for five years from commencement, and for five subsequent years they would pay 50 per cent less if their share of ownership exceeds 30 per cent and if they are involved in certain industries (consumer goods, electronics, construction materials, biotechnology, medical equipment, medicines or processing the industrial wastes of mining, metallurgical output and other secondary resources). The tax regime should then be uniform for both foreign and local enterprises.

To accelerate the development of rich mineral and raw materials in Kazakhstan, concessions are encouraged. Concession agreements may be for not less than five years and not greater than 40 years, with the right of buy-out. The state guarantees protection of the invested property from groundless nationalization, as well as providing compensation for losses incurred because of the violation of an agreement on behalf of the government, central or local administrations, and ensures the independence of administrative and economic activity. The elimination of double taxation agreements is under consideration. The republic guarantees to foreign investors exemption of customs duties on the imports of equipment and on raw materials for the production of export goods, and the free transfer abroad of the proceeds from their activity. An agreement on guarantees for investment protection has been signed between Kazakhstan and the US government.

On trade policy, it has been mentioned already that it will be necessary to coordinate the economic policies of all member states of the CIS, with the development of mutually beneficial trade, and that domestic enterprises are being encouraged to make direct trade contacts with enterprises in other countries. Quantitative restrictions on imports are being lifted.

In Kazakhstan there are over 1,100 participants in exporting and external economic relations registered in the republic, including 116 joint ventures (225 joint ventures have so far been registered, 13 per cent with US companies, 12 per cent with German, 10 per cent with Turkish and 8 per cent with Chinese companies), and there are 21 external economic associations. There are more than 290 items in the export goods list. The contribution of foreign partners to the foreign currency earnings of Kazakhstan is more than US $140 million.

At present fuel and energy resources account for over 32 per cent of Kazakhstan's exports, with the chemical industry 23 per cent, and the agro-industrial complex only 3 per cent. Russia takes 62 per cent, China takes 20 per cent and the United States 18 per cent.

One problem in knowing what is happening in international trade between the republics of the CIS is that there are no border checks. Exports to and imports from Russia move freely across open borders, and the currency on both sides is the same – roubles. This type of international trade is therefore in a sort of twilight zone.

GOVERNMENT INSTITUTIONS FOR RADICAL RECONSTRUCTION

The existing institutional structure in Kazakhstan is a legacy of the former highly centralized command economy. Republican bodies were 'affiliations' of the Soviet Union administrative structures and did not develop their own policies.

The implementation of radical changes in Kazakhstan, the transformation of the institutions of state property, the commercialization of enterprise activities, price liberalization and the maintenance of financial disciplines have led to the need for, and the creation of, a compact and stable administrative system which will possess real power and influence.

Administrative structures have had to be re-created, with direct subordination of lower-level bodies to higher ones. The structure of economic management should be clear-cut, with the division of powers among its different levels, and as between the state and business management. Duplication of functions amongst economic departments should be eliminated and the implementation of policies of a specific kind entrusted to one administrative body. The main economic levers should be concentrated at the highest level of government. It is important to form a core group of key ministries concerned with the realization of economic reform, with the necessary powers. These are in particular the Ministry of Finance, the State Committee on Economics and the National State Bank. A High Economic Council has been formed comprising the leaders of these ministries and departments to achieve efficient decision-making and control in the implementation of reforms.

Because of the importance of a coherent monetary and credit policy, the National State Bank can be kept subordinate to the Supreme Council of the republic, or entrusted to the Cabinet of Ministers during the transition period.

It is particularly important to free ministries and departments from their present responsibilities for production, economic planning and the issuing of 'state orders'. Their role should concern market regulation, the growth of efficient production and high quality, investment policy and the implementation of scientific and technical policy.

To provide for such reforms there should be an inflow of high-class specialists to state administrative bodies. It is planned to adopt a Law on the Civil Service, and special institutions are being created to introduce reforms in the government of the republic.

As mentioned earlier, business concerns should be transformed into some 10–15 holding companies, the headquarters of diversified corporations on a multi-sectoral basis, in competition with each other. These would be administratively and managerially separate from the government.

LESSONS FROM KAZAKHSTAN'S PRACTICAL EXPERIENCE

Because of the economic and political situation in Kazakhstan, the main levers of reform must remain with the state. The task of government must be to achieve a consistent and systematic approach to the implementation of reforms. However, the results of economic reform in the reconstruction of industries and enterprises will depend upon both internal and external factors.

The most difficult ordeals for the economy lie ahead. It is crucially important to surmount the dogmas and stereotypes of the command economy, the psychology of levelling and social dependence, and to decrease the paternalistic role of the state towards business enterprises. There is no real option except a market economy. Formation of a social market economy is the way to achieving the highest values in a person's life, to his economic freedom and to an adequate standard of living.

5

POLAND – THE 'BIG BANG'

Pawel Bozyk

SOCIALIST BACKGROUND TO THE POLISH ECONOMY

Poland, with a population of 38 million, is strategically placed in northern Europe. It borders Lithuania, Belorus, Ukraine, the Czech and Slovakian republics and Germany (a direct link to the European Community). And it has a coastline on the Baltic Sea.

The country came under communist control in 1947. Market reforms were initiated in the late 1950s, but little came of them. This was because they stopped short of anything that might encroach on the essence of a socialist economy, especially its three cardinal dogmas: supremacy of the public sector, dominance of the state in the direction of economic activity, and egalitarianism in the distribution of income.

Interest focused on revitalization of market mechanisms in the public sector since private enterprise, though relatively well developed by comparison with other central and eastern European countries, formed only a small part of the economy – some 17 per cent of national income. It was confined mainly to agriculture (87 per cent of farm output), crafts, services and retailing. Almost the whole of industry remained state-controlled.[1]

However, revitalization of market mechanisms in the public sector faced difficulties. It was impossible to activate capital, foreign exchange or financial markets, or a labour market: in a socialist economy these markets simply did not exist. That being so, attention focused on revitalizing the goods and services markets, chiefly through decentralization of management.

However, the results were small and out of all proportion to the efforts of Polish reformers. In the mid-1970s, Poland began a slide into increasingly severe hardships, manifested in steadily worsening economic disequilibrium, dwindling economic efficiency and many other difficulties. Hopes that freer market mechanisms would remedy these anomalies came to nothing: they merely aggravated the disproportions and intensified the problems.

The reforms were superficial. They made no inroads into socialist dogma or into the monopolistic structures of production. Nor did they create institutions characteristic of market economies or introduce any appropriate mechanisms of enterprise management.[2]

THE INTRODUCTION OF FREE MARKETS

The Solidarity victory in the parliamentary election on 4 June 1989 opened the way to replace 'real socialism' with a free market system. In October a programme for the transformation of the Polish economy was published, and in December it was approved by the legislature. Its provisions were comprehensive and radical.[3]

They were comprehensive because they proposed a total overhaul of all areas of the Polish economy, including goods and services, capital, foreign exchange and financial markets; and radical because movement from a centrally planned to a free market was to be instantaneous, with 1 January 1990 set as the new system's launch date.

A *goods and services market* was created principally by decontrolling prices and leaving them to be determined solely by supply and demand. By the end of 1991 the prices of all agricultural products, 88 per cent of producer goods and 85 per cent of consumer goods had been freed. In the inputs markets, controls remained in force only for gas and electricity. In the consumer market they remained for 11 per cent of goods and services (essential medicines, central heating and hot water supplies to households, gas and electricity, spirits of domestic origin, rents and public transport).

Liberalization of prices was accompanied by abolition of the central allocation of inputs to public-sector enterprises. The state ceased to be an intermediary in this market. Rationing of foreign exchange was also discontinued.

The first step towards creating a *capital market* came with the opening of a stock exchange in Warsaw in April 1991 and the establishment of a Securities Commission. At mid-1992 the shares of 12 companies were being traded.

A *foreign exchange* market was created by unifying the value of the Polish zloty against other currencies and the introduction of internal convertibility. On 1 January 1990 the zloty was devalued to 9,500 per US dollar, a rate which remained in force until May 1992, when the zloty was again devalued (to 11,100 per dollar). In October 1992 the fixed exchange rate was replaced by a crawling peg mechanism linked to the interest rate and inflation.

The stability of the exchange rate was guaranteed by a Stabilization Fund of US $1 billion and the extension of a standby credit by the International Monetary Fund (IMF).

A *financial market* was created as a result of changes in monetary, credit budgetary, tax and banking policy. The principal measure was the introduction of a positive interest rate, encouraging saving and squeezing investment, consumption and inventories. All preferential interest rates (for exports, energy conservation, environmental protection and exports, etc.) were abolished.

One of the chief objectives of economic policy was a balanced budget. It was decided that the deficit could not exceed one per cent of GNP. To this end, there was a reform of the tax system which eliminated all privileges in both business and personal sectors.

The banking system was reformed, starting with state banks: the National Bank of Poland as the central bank, and nine of its branch offices, were hived off as separate commercial banks. New regulations opened the banking sector to private persons – including foreign nationals. In 1990–1 a total of 70 licences were granted for starting joint-stock banks. Despite that, private banks account for only 5 per cent of total bank business.[4]

THE POLICY OF 'SHOCK TRANSFORMATION'

The special feature of the Polish route to a free market economy was the policy of shock transformation, also known as the 'big bang'. It called for the transition from central planning to a free-market system to be made in a single leap, with direct government control of enterprises kept to a minimum. The economy was thrown open to foreign competition and market mechanisms were allowed to operate freely.

The inspiration for shock therapy was drawn from the programme prescribed by the IMF for insolvent debtors seeking credits. This made debt relief contingent on a restrictive monetary and budgetary policy (tight money, and government expenditures and revenues in balance), curtailment of domestic demand and growth of exports. The IMF also recommended devaluation of the domestic currency, reductions in real incomes and increases in interest on loans and deposits to the level of inflation.[5]

The government's responsibility was to be the supervision of such principles of transformation through periodic freezing of the exchange rate, wages and positive interest rates.

All of the IMF requirements were observed in full.[6] An additional element was rapid privatization of the economy, this being regarded as a *sine qua non* of the proper functioning of the free-market mechanism. The original assumption was that 75 per cent of the public sector would be privatized by 1995. In 1991 this target was reduced to 50 per cent.

GOVERNMENT INDUSTRIAL POLICIES

Poland embarked on the process of systematic transformation of its economy under the handicap of the unfavourable industrial structure bequeathed by the old system. This is illustrated in Table 5.1.

The mainstay of industry were sectors related to the primary sector (defined in Poland to include mining, fuel and energy, metallurgy, food

Table 5.1 Structure of industrial output in Poland 1986–91

	(%) 1986	1987	1988	1989	1990	1991
1 Extractive industry total	7.4	7.7	7.6	5.0	6.1	9.0
2 Manufacturing industry total	92.6	92.3	92.4	95.0	93.9	91.0
Of which:						
Fuel & energy	14.8	15.0	15.1	11.2	15.9	21.6
Metallurgy	9.6	9.9	10.0	10.1	12.7	10.1
Electro-eng.	25.4	25.8	25.9	25.3	24.2	19.8
Chemicals	8.7	9.0	9.3	9.1	9.5	9.2
Minerals	3.8	3.8	3.8	3.9	4.2	4.1
Wood & paper	4.4	4.5	4.4	5.0	4.9	5.0
Light industry	11.4	11.1	11.4	12.2	8.1	6.7
Food process	19.7	18.4	17.6	20.0	18.6	21.5
Other	2.2	2.5	2.5	3.2	1.9	2.0
Total	100	100	100	100	100	100

Source: Author's compilation on basis of Central Office of Statistics Yearbooks, Warsaw 1991.

processing). In 1989 they accounted for almost one-half (47 per cent) of total industrial output.

Unfortunately this situation did not improve in 1990–1. In fact, the share of primary production grew to no less than 62 per cent. This was due partly to raw material prices rising faster than manufactures. It was also the result of a plunge in output of the latter. The share of electro-engineering fell from 25 per cent in 1989 to 20 per cent in 1991, and in light industry from 12 to 7 per cent.

There were various reasons for this decline in manufacturing output. Firstly, there was a marked downturn in demand as a result of real incomes falling by almost one-third. For example, there was a much higher increase in the prices of agricultural inputs than of outputs, and this had an impact on farmers' real incomes. This drove down demand for farm machinery and equipment (by one-half) and tractors (threefold).

Secondly, opening up the Polish economy to imports resulted in consumer demand switching from higher-priced and lower-quality domestic products to superior and often cheaper foreign products. As a result output in many consumer goods industries fell by 50 per cent or more.

Thirdly, there was a decline in investment which led to reduced demand for construction machinery, cement, building materials, chemical products, furniture and other fittings. Again there was a substantial fall in output.

INDUSTRIAL STRUCTURES

The Polish economy inherited a considerable degree of monopolization. The greater part of industry had a monoculture structure with a high degree of concentration of many products in single enterprises. Large enterprises (over 1,000 employees) accounted for about 70 per cent of total industrial output. The share of small enterprises with less than 200 workers was less than 5 per cent.

In 1990–1 a process of radical restructuring and de-monopolization was introduced. An Anti-monopoly Office was established and rules laid down for preventing monopolistic practices. Some 290 large multi-establishment state and cooperative enterprises were split into 996 small and medium-sized units (the increases in the number of state-owned enterprises in Table 5.2 was for this reason). Nevertheless, at end-1991 large enterprises still accounted

Table 5.2 Changes in enterprise structure in Poland 1989–91

	*Number 1991**	*% change 1989–91*
1 **Industry**		
State-owned enterprises	8,969	20
Cooperatives	2,535	11
Private companies	9,182	64
Joint ventures	2,099	86
Sole traders ('000)	1,420	17
2 **Construction**		
State-owned enterprises	1,430	-8
Cooperatives	998	41
Private companies	8,387	62
Joint ventures	232	98
Sole traders ('000)	170	NA
3 **Transport**		
State-owned enterprises	531	70
Cooperatives	251	59
Private companies	645	82
Joint ventures	155	91
Sole traders ('000)	60	NA
4 **Trade**		
State-owned enterprises	609	26
Cooperatives	3,790	17
Private companies	14,784	87
Joint ventures	678	35
Sole traders ('000)	550	87

Source: Author's compilation on basis of Central Office of Statistics *Report on socio-economic situation* (Warsaw, 29 January 1991) and Government Economic Committee *Report on the Economy* (Warsaw, 3 December 1991, pp. 36–7).
Notes: * As of 30 September 1991, except Industry.
NA Not available.

for 62 per cent of the total work-force and 67 per cent of industrial output. The figures for small firms were 7 and 4 per cent respectively.

Changes in the structure of production have also been advanced by privatization. By July 1991 legislation was in place, and by the end of that year 1,260 enterprises were in the process of privatization (300 through transformation into companies and 960 through 'liquidation' – sale or leasing).

After two years of privatization the share of the private sector in total industrial sales was 24 per cent, while the share of public-sector sales declined by 20 per cent. Employment in the private sector grew to 38 per cent of the total work-force, mostly due to joint ventures with foreign capital (the number of which rose 2.5 times in 1991, from 853 to 2,099).

Structural change in industry has also come from the commercialization of public-sector enterprises – the number of Treasury-owned corporations increased from 41 to 177 in 1991.

A key element in industrial policy, from 1 January 1990, was the abolition of subsidies and tax reliefs, and the equal treatment of all enterprises. By 1992 only hard coal, pharmaceuticals, artificial fertilizers, school textbooks, rents, public rail and road transport, and a few less important goods and services were still subsidized.[7]

These measures had the effect of revealing efficiency (defined here as the ratio of profit to cost). In 1991 the figures (in percentages) were non-ferrous metals (26), transportation (–4), leather (–4), textiles (–5). Within these and other industries there were variations in profitability, with a range between profit and loss.

Government policy is firmly committed to eliminate unprofitable enterprises. The most effective method is to force prices to find their own level (which in practice means upwards). By end-1992, subsidies on energy, drugs, rents and transport will have been phased out.

There are plans also to reduce expenditure on education, research, health, culture and welfare. Commercialization will make all of these activities self-financing. Already tuition fees are charged in some types of schools and colleges, private facilities are appearing alongside those publicly provided. There has also been a growth in cooperative health care, which has a long tradition in Poland.

In 1992, however, the government of Prime Minister Jan Olszewski decided that (in contrast to the liberal policies of his two predecessors) extra interventionist instruments had to be introduced to help enterprises combat the recession. Farmers were offered credits at one-half the standard rate, and the same was done for medium-term housing construction loans. Minimum guaranteed prices were introduced for wheat, rye and milk and the Agricultural Market Agency was empowered to introduce price stabilization schemes elsewhere. Credit preferences and insurance guarantees, partial exemptions from dividend payments by state enterprises, and export and investment tax reliefs were also promised.

Under the old system, most foreign trade was subject to concessions and licences, raw material exports and imports were balanced and limited by quotas, and foreign exchange was centrally allocated. On 1 January 1990 new rules typical of an open-market economy were introduced.

Firstly, access to the foreign trade sector was liberalized (except for a few commodities which normally are controlled, such as military equipment, radioactive isotopes and inflammable materials).

Secondly, export quotas were abolished. In 1992 the only restrictions which remain are those resulting from international agreements on, for example, textiles and clothing, iron and steel, some food, and some construction industries. Also, exports of coal and liquid fuels are restricted for reasons of national energy security.

Thirdly, there was free access to foreign exchange and internal convertibility of the zloty in commercial transactions, and a unified exchange rate.

Fourthly, export stimulation through tax reliefs was scrapped, since the exchange rate was intended to determine export profitability, although in 1992 tax reliefs were reintroduced as a means of promoting exports.

Finally, tariffs were assigned as the fundamental instrument regulating the volume and structure of imports. For 18 months (January 1990–June 1991), Polish tariffs were among the lowest in the world. In mid-1991 they were adjusted upwards in line with EC standards but are still regarded as liberal. There are no non-tariff restrictions, which has greatly increased access to Poland's domestic market.

RESTRUCTURING WITHIN ENTERPRISES

During the period of 'real socialism', the functions of a state-owned enterprise were passive. A government department determined its production plan, allocated its physical requirements (raw materials, energy, work-force level) and its financial resources (in domestic and foreign currency). The enterprise was run by a management answerable to the appropriate industrial ministry, and was also subject (through the *nomenclatura*) to control by the Communist Party through its own channels. Unions and works councils played a marginal role.

In the 1980s a self-management system was introduced. Formally, state enterprises became self-financing, self-managing and self-sufficient (the 'triple-S' principle), although within the limits of restrictions centrally formulated by the finance ministry. Most of the industrial ministries were closed down.

The object of this system was to force enterprises to improve efficiency or, if unviable, to go into liquidation. In practice they simply pressured the Planning Commission (and the Central Planning Office, its successor) and the finance ministry into granting them subsidies, tax reliefs and other forms of support.

Administration within enterprises was now transferred to self-management bodies (employee councils) with powers of appointment and dismissal of managing directors. Management became completely subordinate to these councils. Formally, the central authorities could veto council decisions but in practice they almost always sided with the employees and, for example, upheld dismissals. This system also affected the distribution of enterprise funds, priority usually being awarded to pay increases while investment was considered to be of secondary importance.

In late 1991 there began a process of commercialization of state-owned enterprises. Control by employee councils could now be replaced by supervisory boards, representing the state as owner, managers and employees, with separate management boards. Under the new rules, employee councils are being either abolished or reduced to a purely advisory role.

Most Polish enterprises are finding it necessary to re-equip and to modernize their product range. They were developed during the period of 'real socialism' under autarkic conditions in which foreign competition was not a factor. From 1978 to 1991 there was no net increase in investment in Poland, and replacement of technologies and product development have suffered. On average 80 per cent of machinery and plant has reached the end of its asset life. Some enterprises are being closed and others are being modernized, partly with help from World Bank funds and with programmes drawn up by IMF experts.

An example is the holding company which controls Poland's two biggest steelworks – 'Sedzimir' on the outskirts of Cracow, and 'Katowice' in Silesia. Previously their product range was similar. Now, following a programme prepared by the Canadian consortium Hatch Associates Ltd (approved by EC experts and financed by the World Bank with Polish government guarantees), 'Sedzimir' will specialize in refining and processing and 'Katowice' in smelting, and there will be new technologies, changes in organization and a substantial reduction in employment.

THE SYSTEM OF INDUSTRIAL CONTROL

The market economy system introduced in Poland in January 1991 reduced to a minimum the role of institutions charged with monitoring anti-competitive practices and protecting the public against the pathologies of capitalism.

Apart from the establishment of an Anti-monopoly Office and the amendment of anti-monopoly legislation, no new regulations were introduced to counteract collusion in restraint of trade. The sole exception – a requirement to give notice of forthcoming price increases to fiscal authorities, which were empowered to defer them for three months – affects only 9 per cent of trade in intermediate products and 4 per cent of trade in consumer goods, and has done nothing to restrict the growth of economic rents.

Uniformly positive and high interest rates, a single exchange rate and high taxation discriminated against small firms competing with each other and made scarcely a dent in the position of monopolists. They reacted to increasingly difficult market conditions not by improving quality and lowering prices but simply by cutting output.

The only effective answer to such practices was to open up the economy, including liberalization of imports. However, this led to imports growing faster than exports and to deficits in the balance of trade.

The principal measures designed to protect employees against the drawbacks of capitalism were the introduction of a system of unemployment benefits and provisions of relief for the poorest households (rent allowances, free meals, etc.).

Policies in Poland are the most liberal in the whole of eastern-central Europe. They have, however, resulted in a very rapid and marked social differentiation and in extremes of wealth – the private owners of capital – and poverty – the millions of pensioners, large families, public-service employees (doctors, teachers, academics, civil servants), the overwhelming majority of the farming population, artisans and workers in state-owned enterprises.

CORPORATE GOVERNANCE

The privatization legislation introduced in 1990–1 provided for two methods of ownership change.

1 The transformation of state enterprises into Treasury-owned corporations, and
2 liquidation for the purpose of either leasing assets to the work-force or their sale in whole or in part.

The choice of route is decided by the Ministry of Ownership Changes (until 1991 this was the Ownership Changes Agency).

In transformation, the state-owned enterprise is transformed into a company governed by the commercial code. The whole of its capital undergoes this process, but relationships with third parties remain unchanged. A management and a supervisory board are selected. The powers of the general assembly of shareholders are exercised by a representative of the Treasury, who takes over the functions of the founding body.

Pending a share offer to third parties, the company is run on the same lines as before. Dividends are calculated in proportion to capital and profits after tax, and dividend payments (previously a tax, reduced in July 1992 to 10 per cent of capital employed) are retained by the company. Their distribution (remuneration, employee share scheme, economic development) is determined by the supervisory board.

With the approval of the Minister of Ownership Changes, shares in the company may be sold to small private investors, with up to 20 per cent offered to its employees at a discount.

The equity of a Treasury-owned company not sold within two years is assigned to a bank appointed to act as administrator.

The other route to ownership change is liquidation, with a view to either the lease or the sale of its assets. For leasing, the founding body, in association with the Minister of Ownership Changes, may liquidate an enterprise and lease its assets to a company or cooperative formed by its employees. Such an employee-controlled firm must meet the following requirements.

1 Its members must comprise a majority of its employees, and the decision to initiate the liquidation and the leasing process must be approved by a general meeting of the work-force.
2 The founders and members of the firm are all private persons.
3 The paid up capital may not be less than 20 per cent of the book value of its assets.

The purpose of these rules is to permit the establishment of employee-controlled firms in enterprises where there is strong worker participation but where they lack the financial resources to buy the assets outright.

Under the second liquidation variant, the assets of the liquidated enterprise may be sold to individual investors wholly or in part. The principles of such sales are decided by the Minister of Ownership Changes, the preferred method being by auction. Selling off state-owned assets piecemeal promotes small-scale privatization and the creation of new private businesses.

A growing role is being played by the Warsaw stock exchange. At its first session (16 April 1991) five companies were listed, with another four later in the year and three more in 1992.[8] There are now two sessions a week, and the volume of business is rising. So far the role of the stock exchange in Poland is marginal, and a gradual growth is forecast.

NEW INVESTMENT – DOMESTIC AND FOREIGN

Foreign capital investment in Poland is regulated by a law on companies with a foreign stake, enacted on 14 June 1991. Compared with previous legislation, it substantially liberalized the rules of foreign investment. It allows foreign investors to buy into Polish companies in the process of privatization and to transfer various forms of investment earnings.

The total influx of foreign capital in 1989–91 amounted to some US $700 million in joint ventures, US $88 million in privatizing enterprises and US $45 million in the banking and insurance sector.[9] The major foreign investors have been Fiat, General Motors, ABB, Hyatt Regency (hotels), Levi Strauss, Coca Cola, Reynolds Tobacco, Alcatel and Siemens, and Northern Telecom. Apart from Fiat, most companies have invested only small amounts.[10] By contrast, in the same period US $2.7 billion have been invested in Hungary and over US $2 billion in Czechoslovakia (most from Germany).

At end-1991 there were some 4,800 joint-venture companies in Poland, of which 2,100 were involved in industry. In 1991 the total number had trebled, those in industry being one-half of that. Most projects, however, were small businesses with the foreign capital contributed by investors of Polish extraction. The vast majority were involved in trade and many were of a speculative nature (capital invested for a year or so and then withdrawn).

Productive capital plays a useful role in the transfer of technology and patents to Poland, and so in improving the quality and sophistication of products. From this point too, it is good for Poland.

GOVERNMENT INSTITUTIONS FOR RADICAL RESTRUCTURING

The principal institutions supporting structural change in the Polish economy are the Ministry of Ownership Changes, the Industrial Development Agency, the Socio-Economic Initiative Bank, the Polish Development Bank, the Export Credit Insurance Corporation, the Employment Fund and a steadily growing number of consultancy firms.[11] In 1991, these institutions received for restructuring purposes grants totalling 3 trillion zlotys (US $316 million) plus various types of credit guarantees, leasing arrangements, etc.

Many of these institutions have obtained the right to implement ownership changes and industrial restructuring projects, with the help of credits provided by the Polish Development Bank and the Socio-Economic Initiative Bank, and targeted to both private- and public-sector enterprises. They are empowered to purchase shares and stocks in privatizing enterprises, banks and other institutions involved in the restructuring field, to provide credit guarantees and to activate leasing arrangements.

MANAGEMENT EDUCATION

The introduction of a market economy was accompanied by a rapidly growing demand for managers familiar with the rules of business, and capable of running firms on their own. The training of specialists of this kind is conducted by two methods: at regular higher education institutions, and at special management schools.

Undergraduate college courses in management, initiated on a broader scale in 1990–1, chiefly at schools of economics and technology, are replacing general economic subjects with courses in marketing, finance, civil law, organization, commercial negotiation, accountancy, etc. However, it will be about 1995 before the first graduates appear.

For this reason many schools of economics have started postgraduate courses in management. Their length varies, the shortest being several weeks, the longest one year or more. The aim is to provide people with different educational and professional backgrounds with an elementary grounding in business. These courses are fee-paying and attract much support.

In recent years several tens of private business and management schools have been started by various institutions, ranging from foundations to individuals.

In 1991 a Staff Coordination and Training Office was established to provide government support for management development. The principal aim is to coordinate assistance by foreign experts in such training, and the financial aid granted to Poland by various foreign foundations.

The education of businessmen is developing very dynamically in Poland. It is, however, in its infancy and still requires external financial and professional assistance.[12] Such assistance is being provided by the European Community and special funds to promote market transformation by the governments of the United States, the United Kingdom, France, Germany and other countries.

LESSONS FROM PRACTICAL EXPERIENCE

The evidence of the first three years of movement towards a market economy in Poland indicates that this will be a far more complicated process than was at first thought.

This applies above all to the problem of structural change in the economy. Over one-half of Poland's factories need to be reorientated to meet the requirements of an open-market economy. Some will have to be closed. This makes the costs of transformation that much greater, and drives down general living standards. Moreover, structural change cannot go forward without a substantial injection of foreign capital, and so far investors have been tentative in their approach to the Polish economy.

The shock transformation route (the 'big bang') has proved to be no alternative to evolutionary progress spread out over many years. Swift replacement of a centrally planned economy with a free market generates high social costs, and in its wake a backlash of popular resistance (as in eastern Germany).

The state must play an active role in the transformation process. This is not solely or exclusively a matter of the government's macroeconomic policy. Because public ownership is still present on a wider scale than in the West, the state must also exercise direct control of state-sector enterprises by means of microeconomic policy instruments. These may include preferential credits for selected enterprises, direct funding of government investment in selected industries or spheres of the economy and provision of credit guarantees to private banks for financing projects.

Poland's experience of the transformation process also argues in favour of certain changes in the methods of privatization. Although the share of the private sector in the Polish economy has to be appreciably expanded, this goal cannot be pursued at the cost of the complete destruction of the public sector.

No time should be wasted in setting up a Treasury Property Board, clearly separate from the central administration and responsible for all assets owned by the state. Its job would be to see that these assets are properly utilized and managed, and it should represent the interests of the owner – the state – on the supervisory boards of such state enterprises. The Ministry of Industry should be regarded as the body making governmental policy towards enterprises, state-owned and others (this issue is under discussion in the government).

The legal and financial rules governing the operation of the private sector and its obligations to the state are also in need of fundamental overhaul. A stable institutional base is necessary for the expansion of the private sector. New regulations therefore must be discussed in detail, and fine-tuned at the drafting stage, to prevent them having to be amended or replaced soon after their introduction. That would be a particular deterrent to private investors from abroad.

One of the first changes that has to be made is reform of the financial system. Failing that, pathological side-effects multiply. The first steps should be directed in particular towards reforming the banking system, which is the nerve-centre of a market economy. Banking regulations cannot leave loopholes in the system or scope for arbitary interpretation of the rules.

Summing up, it can be said that the direction of change chosen by Poland is right, but that many of the detailed measures could have been better designed.

6

THE CZECHOSLOVAK 'LARGE PRIVATIZATION'[1]

Michal Mejstrík and James L. Burger

OVERVIEW

Starting in the nineteenth century, the Czech lands had been the most industrially developed part of the Austrian-Hungarian Empire. The market system continued to develop in independent Czechoslovakia from the break-up of the empire in 1918 until 1948 (except under German occupation during the Second World War). The per capita GNP of the Czech lands during the 1930s was close to the Belgian GNP, and greater than the Austrian GNP by some estimates.

Gradually after 1945, and finally in 1948 under Russian influence, communists took over power in Czechoslovakia and started to build 'socialism'. On behalf of workers, and to achieve the redistribution of income, they dismantled the market system and implemented a command economy. The rapid redistribution of property rights through nationalization and collectivization followed as a basic prerequisite for the introduction of a centrally planned economy. Industrial (and all financial) enterprises with employment exceeding 500 persons were taken over by the government in 1945. Most industrial firms were actually nationalized before the communists came to power in 1948. Smaller enterprises with over 50 employees were expropriated by the new communist government in the same year. The process was completed in two final waves of nationalization in 1955 and 1959, when smaller enterprises such as private crafts and service establishments were either liquidated or nationalized and integrated into larger state-owned enterprises. By 1960, 93 per cent of produced NMP (the GDP arising from industry) was under state domination. As the mid-1980s approached Czechoslovakia found itself with 97 per cent of its NMP dominated by the state sector and only 0.7 per cent of NMP contributed by the non-farming private sector (see Table 6.1).

These systematic institutional changes were supported by a specific economic policy of so-called 'structural reconstruction' aiming at industrialization and concentration, based on the 'law of increasing returns' although without any conceptual limits or any definition of optimal size. Its goal was

Table 6.1 Size of the state sector in eight countries

Country	*% of output*	*% of employment*
Czechoslovakia (1986)	97.0	–
East Germany (1982)	96.5	94.2
Soviet Union (1985)	96.0	–
Poland (1985)	81.7	71.5
China (1984)	73.6	–
Hungary (1984)	65.2	69.9
Austria (1978–9)	14.5	13.0
West Germany (1982)	10.7	7.8

Source: Milanovic (1989).

to exploit available resources as well as the largest economies of scale possible for the country. This policy led to a steady increase of plant size. This in turn led the small and functionally closed Czechoslovak economy to the artificial formation of indivisible single plants with natural or technical monopolies (and sometimes oligopolies).

In addition, the hierarchical structure of the centrally planned economy generated institutional reasons for the formation of administrative monopolies. In an attempt to manage this central planning system more easily, and in turn to coordinate better industries and firms, economic authorities decreased the number of enterprises while increasing their size. For example, in Czechoslovakia between 1958 and 1980 the share of employment for state-owned industrial firms with less than 500 employees fell from 13 per cent to 1.4 per cent. In 1988 the average size of state-owned industrial firms (over 1,600 firms), that employed over 3 million employees (nearly half of the labour force) was 3,100–3,400 employees per firm.

The resulting coalition type of structure, often made possible by artificially created monopolies and oligopolies – many of which still exist – was characterized by a system of barter exchange. This was an informal distribution network of resources where formal monetary cost played a secondary role. The trump card in an exchange was the ability to deliver a deficit product, also known as 'natural revenues', such as industrial materials in short supply, the inside line on certain consumer goods, or a 'natural' bonus system of holidays. Basically, in a system where deliveries of certain intermediate goods were not always assured by central planning, possession of such goods or access to high-level personal contacts had a more valuable role than money. In fact, money often played a secondary role in purchases, being used only for accounting purposes. Unprofitable firms were universally subsidized and prices were set artificially by central authorities. The main goal of an enterprise was production in accordance with the plan – and not generation of profit.

Soon after the change in government in 1989 it became clear that certain important economic changes would be necessary. The introduction of a free market type of economy was seen as the only way to allow a greater degree of economic freedom in the nation, and at the same time as the best way to set the stage for Czechoslovakia's lagging economy to raise its standards to those of the West.

ISSUES IN THE FORMULATION OF PRIVATIZATION POLICY

The main controversy in Czechoslovakia between 'gradualists' and 'radicals' was over the speed, depth and tools of the transition process. Some external factors (disruption of oil supplies and oil price increases, and CMEA mutual foreign trade denominated in convertible currency) swung public opinion in the direction of the radical reform package. This was adopted by the federal government in May 1990. Although the radicals have been in control of policy since 1990, gradualists have continued to argue that the process is being implemented too quickly, creating unanticipated side-effects and leading to a level of social problem which the public cannot bear. For instance, they argue that price liberalization (enacted on 1 January 1991) should not have occurred until after monopolies were broken up and that therefore the inflation resulting from price liberalization was greater than it need have been.

The reappraisal of the long-standing tradition of the prevailing state sector, and the means of its transformation to private ownership, was a focus point for the wider controversy about economic policy. The gradualist reformers rooted in the 1960s wanted to postpone privatization to the future and saw it as a very gradual process (1968 reform process had not recognized its importance at all). Gradualist arguments against speedy privatization pointed to the possibility of large-scale lay-offs and unemployment, as well as the need to have more functional markets before businesses are forced to operate self-sufficiently. A further argument was that to minimize the problems associated with privatization and to receive maximal returns on the sale of these enterprises, it would be better to restructure firms' operations before privatization.

The radicals proposed speeding up the procedure and minimizing the privatization period for at least some state enterprises. Their main argument was that one cannot renew the functioning of a market economy without renewing private ownership. The main purpose of privatization is to create inviolable fields for sovereign rule by the owner (and the exclusion of interference by the government, except for generally recognized duties like taxes). Radicals also pointed to the fact that in the interim period preceding privatization, ambiguity about ownership and accountability has been generating economic and ecological irresponsibility as well as non-transparent financial relations.

Various means of privatization were considered. The desire for a rapid transformation meant that the use of standard methods alone (i.e. public sales, auctions) was not possible in Czechoslovakia, given that the level of public savings was not enough to buy all of the state property. This problem was especially acute because most citizens with a significant amount of savings were either ex-Party members or ex-black-marketeers, neither of them very popular. The inadequacy of relying on standard methods of privatization is one of the reasons why privatization seems to be stalling in Hungary and Poland.

Efforts to sell off to the first coming foreign company (i.e. 'FIFO', not auction) were seen as a politically unacceptable form of 'spontaneous' privatization. They might provide existing managers, often Communist Party functionaries (the *nomenclatura*), with 'golden parachutes' after selling out to foreigners at low prices. The experience of Hungary shows that the effort to reverse the prepared agreements with foreign investors could mean loss of government credibility abroad.

The blueprint which finally resulted involved a combination of standard methods with other processes and was designed to compensate for factors peculiar to Czechoslovakia. Basically, those proposing to privatize an enterprise may choose from a variety of means of privatization, with government organs responsible for deciding which proposed method is the most applicable. The original blueprint of the Federal Ministry of Finance, described below, envisaged a structure of the privatization process which has more or less held to date, although the role of certain actors in the process, and the timing of the process overall, have changed to some degree.

THE 'LARGE PRIVATIZATION'

Restitution

Part of the 'large privatization' process involved restitution, the return of property to the original owners or their heirs. The Large Restitution Law, passed in February 1990, covers assets expropriated through the nationalization effort which started 28 February 1948, and also covers forced gifts and out-of-law restitutions and rehabilitations. This law gives the full rights to return the property or to provide other forms of reimbursement to the original owners whose property was expropriated, or who were forced by tax and rental policy to provide their property to the state as a gift in the 1950s and 1960s.

Under this law, more than 20,000 demands for restitution have been met. Many involve financial reimbursement or ownership of shares rather than actual return of property. All privatization projects which are submitted (see below) must provide confirmation that restitution claims have been met, or must provide a means of meeting restitution claims. In order to compensate for restitution demands, 3 per cent of the value of every firm undergoing privatization will be set aside in a National Restitution Fund. The original property owners (physical persons, not former shareholders) are also given priority in buying back the parts of companies not subjected to restitution (i.e. parts which were newly erected after the firm was expropriated).

The design of the 'large privatization' process

In adopting their so-called 'large privatization' policy, the Czechoslovak government and Parliament decided, by an act passed in February 1991, to accelerate the large-scale privatization of state-owned enterprises. Overall, the large privatization will be divided into two *waves*. The government made a rough list of enterprises to be privatized in each wave, and final proposals for each wave are made by the branch ministries. Some enterprises – roughly 30 per cent – are not to be privatized at all. For each wave of privatization, each enterprise selected on the list must present its own *basic* privatization project before a set deadline. The structure of the privatization project is obligatory (see Figure 6.1). There have been no workers' councils since April

A privatization project must include the following information:

(a) The enterprise's name, and property for privatization;
(b) Information on how the state acquired the property to be privatized;
(c) Identification of the property unusable for business purposes (i.e. debts, unusable fixed assets and stocks);
(d) Valuation of the property to be privatized (usually book value, except in the case of foreign direct investment, in which case an official assessment of 'market price' is required);
(e) Manner of transferring the property to be privatized, including the settlement of claims of entitled persons;
(f) When establishing a commercial company, the definition of its legal form;
(g) When establishing a joint-stock company, the distribution of stock shares and their value or type, as well as information on whether and how investment coupons will be used;
(h) If local property is to be sold, the location and method of sales, pricing, and the conditions and terms of payment;
(i) In some cases, the proportion of the privatization process proceeds to be handed over to the National Property Funds of the republics;
(j) The manner of transfer of intellectual property rights, which must be discussed in advance with the Federal Bureau of Inventions;
(k) The privatization project implementation schedule.

In cases of direct sale, unpaid transfer or commercialization, the privatization project should also contain a business plan and recommendations concerning the object of business activities, information on potential buyers or investors, information on the existing and anticipated market position of the enterprise, and information on the number and qualification structure of the enterprise's work-force.

Figure 6.1 Privatization information requirements in Czechoslovakia
Source: Author's data.

1990 (which makes a great difference in comparison with Poland and Hungary), and thus company management has the main input on the formulation of a firm's basic privatization project.

Following the submission of basic projects, any other person or enterprise is allowed to submit a *competing* privatization project, again until a certain deadline. In order to promote the supply of new technology, better organization and management through Foreign Direct Investment, potential foreign buyers are permitted to collaborate with Czech firms in the elaboration of basic or competing privatization proposals, or to submit their own competitive proposals. Decisions about project approval are made by the relevant (Czech or Slovak) Ministry of Privatization, which also receives advice from the 'founding' ministries (i.e. the Czech or Slovak Ministries of Industry, Agriculture or Trade). If the project involves direct sale, the Economic Council of the appropriate republican government must approve it. In such cases, the government has two weeks to alter the decision of the Economic Council.

There are already many state-owned joint-stock companies that have been created in the past year through the 'commercialization' of state-owned enterprises. Other enterprises can propose commercialization as part of their privatization project. Through their proposed projects, enterprises can suggest what portion of their shares will be privatized through which means, including standard means such as direct sale, public auction or public tender, or more unusual methods such as the distribution of shares to the public through vouchers.

The original conception was that most projects would be basic projects, and would concentrate on the voucher method, and that the Ministry of Privatization would play a passive role in approving these proposals. Circumstances changed this conception, however. A larger number of competing proposals than had been expected led to the need for a greater degree of flexibility in employing various means of privatization, and it also concentrated a large degree of power in the Ministries of Privatization through the process of evaluation and approval of privatization projects.

The voucher method

A great strength of the Czechoslovak privatization process is its flexibility, allowing privatization through a wide variety of methods. At the same time, it is also enacted so as to guarantee that privatization will take place quickly. One of the main methods to ensure a speedy privatization is the application of the so-called voucher method, originally proposed by Vaclav Klaus in the Federal Ministry of Finance. Within the framework of voucher privatization, a significant volume of state property will be transferred into the ownership of private persons not for money but in exchange for investment vouchers. Each citizen over the age of 18 has the opportunity to buy investment vouchers – 1,000 points of investment 'money' with limited maturity – for a registration fee of 1,000 Kcs (equivalent to US $34 and about 25 per cent of the average monthly wage). These vouchers will entitle every citizen to bid for the ownership of shares of any company privatized by the voucher method, or to allocate their investment points to an investment fund which will make investment decisions for them and hold a diversified portfolio.

The voucher method solves several problems. Voucher privatization will above all guarantee that a large volume of state property will pass quickly into private ownership. Secondly, it will guarantee that a maximum number of domestic citizens can participate in the process despite the lack of capital among the population. Thirdly, it is perceived as a method that is fair to all participating individuals. In addition, each individual will be able to participate in decisions about capital with respect to his or her own preferences. Also, mutual funds (unit trusts) will be able to evolve in a natural manner, and not as state-administered entities. Finally, the widely dispersed private ownership will create new constituencies in favour of a market economy. This is very important in a country with a history of successful capitalism, but which, under socialism, had one of the highest proportions of state ownership in central-eastern Europe.

There are, however, clear drawbacks to this form of privatization. The wide dispersion of ownership could lead to a lack of corporate governance at a time when strong control is necessary in the restructuring of enterprises. Furthermore, this form of privatization does not provide enterprises with access to the financing which they will need in order to restructure successfully. Participating investors also lack the necessary knowledge and information. Such an operation is technically very difficult with no existing capital markets or financial intermediaries, and without relevant legislation. Also, at a time when there is a danger of budgetary shortfalls, this method provides no revenue for the government budget.

Other methods of privatization

Other methods of privatization also have their strengths and weaknesses. Public auction gains the highest possible returns for the government and guarantees fairness and transparency in determining the eventual owner. None the less, it is hampered by the fact that there is not enough money among the population and that the holders of the greatest concentrations of capital are still ex-communists and black-marketeers. Also, using the sole criterion of money that a buyer is willing to pay means that other factors may be neglected. The use of public competition, in which other criteria than money are used (e.g. willingness to maintain levels of employment, protect the environment, reinvest future profits), resolves some of these problems and is more sensitive to the character of the privatized property, but is vulnerable to subjective decision-making, favouritism and perhaps corruption.

Direct sale is a method that must be approached more cautiously. By its nature, it excludes competition and involves a subjective decision-making process. That is why in Czechoslovakia direct sales require further approval from the government's Economic Council. None the less, in cases where many different projects are submitted which all propose direct sale, the decision takes on the nature of a public competition anyway, and thus projects proposing direct sale are still encouraged.

Given the strengths and weaknesses of each type of privatization, Czechoslovakia has adopted a system which allows the proposal of various methods of privatization, with a case-by-case review of proposed projects in order to select the most fitting method of privatization for each business unit involved. This system provides flexibility, but at the same time concentrates much decision-making power in the hands of the project evaluators (generally the Privatization Ministries).

The 'rounds' of privatization

As mentioned above, there are two *waves* of privatization scheduled. The first wave is now under way – all privatization projects have been submitted, and the Ministries of Privatization have completed the approval process for all projects which will be included in the first wave of voucher privatization. In voucher privatization, one wave consists of several individual privatization *rounds*. During each round, a predetermined portion of enterprise shares will be 'sold' to the public in exchange for investment points.

There is also a 'zero round', in which voucher holders may delegate their points to Investment Privatization Funds (IPFs). These are investment funds which have been established by various institutions (see below for a more detailed description). The funds are allowed to collect voucher points from voucher holders only in round zero of the voucher privatization wave (i.e. funds cannot collect points once the sale of enterprises is actually under way). Subsequently, the IPFs invest their voucher points in the same manner as would individual investors.

Each round will last no longer than one month. It is expected that one privatization wave will consist of not more than five rounds. The voucher holder can spend all of his or her 1,000 investment points in one privatization round, or spend them gradually during several rounds.

Based on demand for shares available, new share prices will be publicized by the Federal Ministry of Finance at the end of each round. If demand for shares of certain firms exceeds supply by a significant amount (over 25 per cent), then share orders will not be fulfilled and the price of that firm's shares will be increased for the next round. This process should lead to the establishment of equilibrium between supply and demand by the end of several rounds. The wave will end when it appears that supply and demand are in equilibrium, i.e. few voucher points remain unused and few shares remain unsold. The process is not expected to last more than five rounds.

Although the process has basically been enacted according to plan, the

Supply	*Demand*
Vouchers sold and prepared (First wave: basic projects prepared first, by 31 October 1991, then competing projects, by 20 January 1992) (Second wave: all projects prepared at the same time, from April to 16 June 1992)	Vouchers sold and registered IPFs founded (October 1991–28 February 1992)
Review of projects by branch ministries (First wave: undefined, sometimes coinciding with review by the Privatization Ministries) (Second wave: branch ministries will have two months after projects are submitted)	
Review of projects by Privatization Ministries Primary review of projects involving vouchers (January–April 1992 in second wave, the Privatization Ministries will review projects only after branch ministries have completed their reviewing process)	'Zero round' – citizens allocate investment points to IPFs (1 March–26 April 1992)
Registration of firms by commercial courts (April–11 May 1992)	
Publication of list of enterprises in voucher privatization (18 May 1992)	
First round of voucher privatization (18 May–8 June 1992)	
Following rounds: end of voucher wave	
Further review of projects continues during the voucher process: remaining projects that involve vouchers will be included in the following wave.	

Figure 6.2 Timetable for one 'wave' of privatization in Czechoslovakia (including actual dates of the first 'wave')
Source: Author's data.

timetable of the large privatization originally envisaged was changed slightly (see Figure 6.2), and will be a little different in the second wave from the timetable in the first wave. The original goal was for all projects to be submitted by 31 October 1991, with the first round of voucher privatization getting under way soon after the new year. The Ministries of Privatization decided, however, to extend the deadline for submission of competitive projects for over two months. The start of the voucher process was further delayed because a larger number of competing proposals was submitted than had been expected, and thus the Ministries of Privatization required more time to evaluate and approve projects. Thus, instead of the originally planned January start, the first round of voucher privatization actually began on 18 May 1992.

Such a delay will not take place in the second wave. A list of all enterprises involved in the second wave was published on 16 April 1992, and all proposals – both basic and competing – must be submitted within two months of this date (i.e. by 16 June). This alleviates the perceived problem that writers of competitive proposals had somewhat of an advantage in the first round, since their projects were written later, and thus they were able to respond to changes in the rules and to use more complete information.

The supply side: submission of privatization projects

In the Czech Republic, by the final deadline for submission of first wave privatization projects (20 January), the number of submitted projects reached 10,949 (see Table 6.2 for a breakdown of submitted projects by proposed privatization method, and see Table 6.3 for statistics on the authors of privatization projects). This number (which actually increased to over 11,000 including projects which were accepted after the deadline) was much larger than had been expected. Part of the reason was that the original deadline for project submission (31 October 1991) was moved back by over two months to permit more submissions of competitive projects. The original Law on Large Privatization anticipated that privatization projects would *usually* be suggested by the enterprise that is the subject of privatization. Nevertheless, of the submitted projects, only 26.3 per cent were proposed by firms as basic projects, while nearly three-quarters of proposals came as competitive projects. In fact, competitive projects were strongly supported by the liberal approach of the Privatization Minister Tomas Jezek, who was the motivating force behind the decision to extend the deadline for submission of competing proposals. For some companies, there were as many as 20 or 30 different projects from various bidders.

As can be seen from Table 6.2, not all of these projects intended to utilize the voucher system, and in fact most competing projects suggested direct sale or other classical methods. From Table 6.3 it can be inferred that most basic proposals were written by management, while most competing proposals

Table 6.2 Czech Republic: privatization projects proposed by the final deadline

	*Proposed method of privatization**	*Number of projects*	%
1	Public auction	1,150	11
2	Public tender	872	8
3	Direct sale to predetermined buyer	4,905	45
4	Commercialization of state enterprise to joint-stock company: also a pre-condition for voucher privatization	2,452	22
5	Privatization of an already existing state-owned joint-stock company	432	4
6	Unpaid transfer to municipalities, pension funds, banks or savings banks	887	8
7	Voucher privatization (out of 4 and 5 above)	2,523	23
Total number of projects		10,949	100
Basic projects		2,884	26
Competing projects		8,065	74

Source: Karel Cermak, Czech Republic Ministry for the Administration of State Property and its Privatization.
Note: *Many projects proposed more than one method.

were written by parties interested in direct sale. The large influx of competing proposals actually changed the originally planned structure of privatization activity and made it more difficult to prepare the supply side sufficiently for voucher privatization. As mentioned above, the Federal Ministry of Finance originally preferred voucher privatization over other privatization methods, and saw the role of the Ministries of Privatization as one of ensuring that projects were properly processed, to ensure that restitution claims were addressed and to decide on the role of foreign investors. As a result of the unexpected storm of competing proposals, the Ministries of Privatization gained a great degree of decision-making power in an extremely short period.

The originally agreed amount of property to go to the voucher privatization was 260 billion Kcs (US $9 billion) worth of assets. Originally, this amount was supposed to include 140 billion Kcs from the Czech Republic, 70 billion Kcs from the Slovak Republic and 50 billion Kcs of federal property. The federal contribution amounted to only 12 billion Kcs (most former federal property has been transferred to the republics by now), so a new level of contribution of each republic had to be defined. The final

Table 6.3 Czech Republic: elaborators of privatization projects

Initiator	*Number of projects*	%
Enterprise management	2,804	25
Management of individual plants (subordinate management)	416	4
Interested buyer	4,379	39
Original owner	397	4
Ministry	22	(–)
Consulting firm	334	3
Local privatization council	760	7
Other	1,451	13
Local founding institution	431	4
Department organization	19	(–)
Not listed	153	1

Source: Karel Cermak, Czech Republic Ministry for the Administration of State Property and its Privatization.
Note: (–) = less than 0.5%.

calculated amount was 173 billion Kcs (US $6 billion) of book value of assets from the Czech Republic and 75 billion Kcs (US $2.8 billion) from Slovakia. This ratio between the two (2.29:1) corresponds to the ratio of voucher holders in the Czech Republic to those in the Slovak Republic.

The Ministries of Privatization reviewed projects involving voucher privatization first, in order to approve enough property for the voucher method to start by the target date of 18 May. By the deadline for approving projects for the voucher privatization, each republic had actually exceeded its required contribution (with a reserve in case some firms would not be registered in the commercial courts in time for privatization – firms that were approved for vouchers but not prepared in time for the first wave will be privatized in the second voucher wave later in 1992). The Czech Republic designated 201 billion Kcs (US $7 billion) worth of property for the first wave of voucher privatization, encompassing 943 joint-stock companies (actually, 216.7 billion Kcs worth was approved for vouchers, but some will have to await the second wave) and the Slovak side provided 85 billion Kcs (US $3 billion), including 487 joint-stock companies (Table 6.4). The total net value of property designated to the voucher privatization was thus about 300 billion

Kcs (US $11 billion), well above the originally planned 260 billion Kcs. In Slovakia, it was common for firms to allocate all of their property (except 3 per cent of each enterprise, which is put aside for paying restitution claims) to the voucher privatization, while in the Czech Republic this practice was less common. In fact, Slovak enterprises undergoing voucher privatization allotted on average 74 per cent of their equity to vouchers, while Czech enterprises allotted only 62 per cent.

To date (August 1992), the majority of property which has been approved for privatization is directed towards the voucher method. The reason for this is simply that the Ministry of Privatization decided to review projects involving vouchers before concentrating on other privatization projects, in order to allow the voucher system to get under way by the agreed date of 18 May. Now that this milestone has been reached, the shares of other forms of privatization (see Table 6.5) will increase.

For the first wave, nearly 3,000 basic projects were submitted in the Czech

Table 6.4 Voucher privatization in Czechoslovakia (CSFR)

	Czech Republic	*Slovak Republic*	*Federal*	*Total CSFR*
Total number of enterprises in voucher privatization	943	487	62	1,492
Total book value of property of these enterprises (bn Kcs)	362.2	133.6	72.8	568.6
Total equity of these enterprises (bn Kcs)	323.1	114.4	25.4	463.0
Total value of property to be re-distributed through vouchers (bn Kcs)	200.8	85.1	13.5	299.4
Workers employed by these firms (000)	864	344	50	1,258
Combined output of these firms (bn Kcs)	592.9	196.3	112.9	902.1
Combined profit of these firms (bn Kcs)	67.8	15.5	22.6	105.9

Source: Karel Cermak, Czech Republic Ministry for the Administration of State Property and its Privatization.

Republic (about 11,000 projects overall – see Table 6.2), which means that by the end of the wave, it is likely that between 3,000 and 4,000 projects will have to be approved (since some enterprises will be broken up). According to the latest figures (late June 1992), 6,748 projects have been assessed, out of which over 1,600 were approved. In sum, these statistics mean that the Ministries of Privatization still have quite a lot of work – over 4,000 projects – facing them, and that the structure of methods used to privatize will change greatly by the end of the wave. In Slovakia, 1,500 projects were submitted on 736 enterprises, of which 430 were approved for the voucher privatization (487 units after some enterprises were broken up).

Table 6.5 Approved privatization projects in the Czech Republic (30 June 1992)

Approved method of privatization	*Number of bus. units*	*(%)*	*Value (bn Kcs) of property*	*(%)*
1 Public auction	218	(8)	2.7	(1)
2 Public tender	147	(5)	6.0	(1)
3 Direct sale	524	(19)	14.1	(3)
4 Commercialization into joint stock	943	(34)	263.3	(61)
5 Privatization of existing state joint-stock companies	177	(6)	126.7	(29)
6 Unpaid transfer to municipalities, pension funds, banks, savings banks	786	(28)	7.4	(2)
7 Voucher privatization (out of 4 and 5)	943	(34)	229.4	(53)
Property to be returned to original owners			0.6	(–)
Property partly written off as unusable			8.5	(2)
Remaining value of assets partly written off			1.5	(–)
Property to small privatization			1.1	(–)
Expected earnings on auction of stocks			0.4	(–)
Total (Total number of projects = 1,344)	2,795		432.3	

Source: Adapted from Karel Cermak, Czech Republic Ministry for the Administration of State Property and its Privatization.
Note: (–) = less than 0.5%.

The structure of methods used for privatization is already changing as a result of how early it was in the approval process. In early March, voucher privatization accounted for almost three-quarters of all property approved for privatization, but by August it accounted for only a little more than half. Privatization by direct sale covered 19 per cent of all business units approved for privatization, whereas in the beginning of March it accounted for only 9 per cent. These proportions are certain to change even further. Direct sale was the proposed means of at least partial privatization in almost 45 per cent of all projects submitted (see Table 6.2), and thus the share of enterprises privatized in this manner will increase significantly in the coming months. The share of enterprises transferred to the private sector through public tender or auction is also likely to increase, since many enterprises for which there are several competing proposals will be privatized in this manner.

The demand side of voucher privatization: public voucher registration and Investment Privatization Funds

The demand side also encountered some unexpected twists. Originally, people had postponed buying booklets until the last months, perhaps because they were not attracted by the official campaign. By 10 January, only 2 million voucher booklets had been purchased in both republics, and it appeared that the expected number of participants, 4–5 million, would not be attained. But then privately established Investment Privatization Funds (IPFs) opened their advertising campaigns unexpectedly early, promising options to buy back their shares if the voucher holders would invest into their funds. This option was interconnected with a promise to pay back not the actual market value of portfolio, but at least *ten times* the registration fee of the coupon book. Expected book value per voucher holder at that time was close to 70,000 Kcs, with 3–4 million expected participants.

These aggressive advertising campaigns and the impending end of the registration period attracted large crowds to the registration places and increased the number of participants to a level much greater than had been foreseen. The final number of registered voucher holders was 8.56 million citizens. This massive scale of participation – *nearly three-quarters of all eligible citizens* – was quite unexpected.

Intermediaries in voucher privatization – Investment Privatization Funds (IPFs)

An important role in the demand side of voucher privatization will be played by the recently established IPFs. These are closed-end funds, organized as joint-stock companies, which are allowed to collect voucher points from the public and invest them during the voucher privatization. Some of the IPFs were purely private, some were established by existing state-owned banks or joint-stock companies. By the end of the registration period, there were over 430 IPFs registered by commercial courts and the Ministry of Finance.

The significance of the role which the IPFs will play is tremendous. In the so-called 'zero wave', during which voucher holders were able to entrust their points to the various Investment Privatization Funds, 5.8 million people (about two-thirds of those involved in the voucher privatization) chose to designate all of their 1,000 investment points to IPFs, and a further 420,000 allotted part of their points to IPFs. In total, IPFs received 72 per cent of all vouchers in circulation, about 6.13 billion investment points (see Table 6.6).

Table 6.6 Structure of funds in the 'first wave', by size of fund

Size of funds (investment points)	*Number of funds*	*Share of total points (%)*
Over 100 million	13	(Top 10 funds = 40%)
10–100 million	65	
5–10 million	43	
Under 10 million	313	(All funds = 72%)

Source: Hospodarske Noviny, May 1992.

Altogether, the 10 largest IPFs control about 40 per cent of all investment points and about 56 per cent of all points that were allocated to IPFs. The largest IPF, Ceska Sporitelna, controls over 800 million points. The other largest IPFs are the Funds of Komercni Banka, Investicni Banka (Czech and Slovak branches), Ceska and Slovenska Pojistovna, Slovenska Sporitelna, Vseobecna Uverova Banka, Creditanstalt, Zivnostenska Banka and Harvard Capital and Consulting (the only non-banking institution among the largest funds). Only 78 IPFs gained more than 10 million points. In general, future shareholders appear to have put most of their faith in traditional monetary institutions, which have a wide network of affiliates and large advertising capacity. These institutions also have the largest number of financially trained experts, although it remains to be seen whether or not they actually have enough know-how to oversee the acquisition of property worth 'billions'.

After the end of the 'zero wave', and before the end of the first wave, IPFs were required to obtain computer diskettes containing information on the voucher holders from whom they received investment points. Six IPFs, representing 649 citizens and over 412,000 investment points, failed to pick up their disks and thus have been eliminated from the first wave. Citizens who had entrusted their points to these Funds may now either invest their points as individual investors, or attempt to lodge a complaint against the unsuccessful IPFs in court.

Unfortunately, until the recent (28 April 1992) passage of a law regulating

IPFs, they have been subject to very limited regulation, covering only the rules regulating their establishment or by *ad hoc* governmental decrees. These rules provided only very weak regulation, and this problem was widely criticized (see Mejstrík *et al.* 1990b). The principles included in the Law on Regulation of IPFs – a disclosure rule, diversification requirements, prevention of conflicts of interest, rules regulating operation, etc. – were not applied in time. Usually a full prospectus of an IPF, with full disclosure of its capital stock, personal history of members of the board of directors and description of operational charges, is not widely available. In fact, it was disclosed that many IPFs had appointed to their boards of directors governmental officials who sometimes play important roles in the voucher privatization procedure. Finally, the 28 April Law on Investment Funds and Corporations addressed this issue.

Problems of the 'large privatization'

There are many problems which have been associated with the large privatization process. On the supply side, they are often related to the quantity and quality of submitted privatization projects and the difficulty involved in writing them. On the demand side, they are mostly related to the lack of regulation on IPFs and the inadequacy of currently existing institutional structures. In general, the whole process suffers from a lack of foresight in regulation and a willingness on the part of the authorities to summarily change the rules. For the second wave, however, a more secure system should be in place. The following is a list of the most important problems encountered.

1 The privatization process requires the evaluation of firms' market value, which is not easily established given past pricing systems, inadequate benchmarks of value and poor accounting systems. The market value of the firm in the initial fixed price offer might, of course, be equal to zero for a poor asset (with low expected cash flows, etc.) or might be many times greater than the book value for a good asset (especially for internationally competitive firms). To assess the market value of the firm from expected cash flows on the base of distorted product and input prices (based on domestic individual costs and mark up combined with non-transparent subsidies) is somewhat naive. Hence modifications of common evaluation procedures are required case by case to indicate potential (international) competitiveness or bankruptcy of the firm. Nevertheless, under existing conditions of trade expressed in a book value, the citizens are often wary of foreign buy-outs as there are accusations that the national heritage is being sold too cheaply. Even with the help of the voucher process, with its unique method for establishing a 'market price' for stocks, a real price equilibrium will probably not be attained for some time.

2 Many competing projects propose the break-up of existing large enter-

prises. For the most part, this is a positive development, because of the over-concentration of Czechoslovak state-owned enterprises. It would allow the creation of a currently missing sector of small and medium-sized firms. Unfortunately, in many cases competing projects are trying to divide something which is technologically indivisible.

3 Often, management of enterprises refused to deliver (or delivered very slowly) information necessary for other parties interested in developing competing projects. This conduct was made legally punishable by the amendment to the Law on Large Privatization, which was passed in February 1992.

4 A loophole in privatization legislation allowed existing management to sign long-term rental agreements, which *de facto* predetermined the fate of the property before privatization. This loophole was also addressed by the amendment to the law on privatization.

5 Many projects present weak or poorly elaborated business plans.

6 Constant changes in legislation during the transition period (e.g. a new commercial code) are not reflected in these projects, which therefore need time for adjustment.

7 The 'mother' supervising branch ministries also review the projects and their conclusions are sometimes at odds with those of the Privatization Ministries, and often support existing management. In fact, the inherited hierarchy and coalitions are still largely in place.

8 Selection procedures and rules were not prepared in time and there cannot be a consistent, transparent means of evaluating projects. Some rules do exist. For example, in cases where there are two or more competing projects, competitive forms of privatization (e.g. public auction, public tender) are preferred over direct sales to predetermined buyers. Decision-makers are under permanent time pressure as well as lobbying pressure from various groups with vested interests.

9 Many firms entering voucher privatization have inherited heavy debts from the past (e.g. due to distorted price structures), creating a bad precondition for privatization and an obstacle to the formation of feasible business plans.

10 Foreign capital participation is seen as an important contribution to the development of Czechoslovakia's industry. None the less, foreigners are often discouraged by the tangled web of negotiations which must be undertaken in order to participate in privatization. Given the standard process, it is quite likely that foreigners would have to negotiate with enterprise management, then with branch ministries, then with the Privatization Ministry and its advisers, and perhaps then with the government's Economic Council. In such a case, it is easier to wait until the enterprise has been privatized and

then try to buy in. However, potential limits to be imposed on share trading in the near future may create further difficulties for foreigners interested in investing in Czechoslovakia.

11 The newly created Funds of National Property of the Czech and Slovak Republics serve as temporary owners of privatized property. These Funds implement decisions made at the Ministries, including decisions on enterprise contracts and the composition of enterprise boards of directors. It is extremely demanding to expect that these Funds will start to operate smoothly in such a short time period, although so far their activities have been promising.

12 Laws concerning the establishment and regulation of stock markets in Prague and Bratislava have just been passed. Whether these markets will be able to function effectively by the fourth quarter of 1992, when they are expected to commence operation, is still questionable.

13 The law regulating the behaviour of IPFs was not passed until 28 April 1992, after IPFs had completed gathering investment points from citizens (some problems with the IPFs were elaborated above). This law does provide needed guidelines on diversification of risk and on general disclosure, but it was passed very late and the continual changing of the rules can only have a negative effect upon their performance. The law also requires that by the end of 1993, IPFs must adjust their operations to become real investment funds, which may reduce their ability to function efficiently in the short run.

14 Given the (possibly excessive) option offers that were made by the IPFs, it is possible that many will face bankruptcy when these options mature. This is especially true because the average book value of assets per coupon book was almost 70,000 Kcs (US $2,300) when the IPFs began making their offers, but because more than twice as many coupon books were registered before the registration deadline, this figure has fallen to around 35,000 Kcs (US $1,100) per coupon book. Large-scale bankruptcies in the IPF sector could have a shock wave effect upon the whole economy. The new law on investment funds may alleviate this problem by recognizing open and closed funds, the latter of which are not obliged to fulfil their promises. The government is further considering a high capital gains tax which would discourage citizens from cashing in their options, unless used for reinvestment.

15 It is still unclear when dividend payments and share trading will begin. The often proposed regulated delay of dividend payments would seriously harm the entrepreneurial interests of new shareholders. Also unreasonable could be similar administrative regulations for new shareholders to allow trading with marketable shares only with some delay. It could postpone the secondary market with shares far into the future and block the endeavour for corporate governance on the base of shareholder ownership. It is mostly believed that the market mechanism will force citizens to generate additional

pension and social security funds, and that they will behave as responsible investors and will not convert their capital (shares or derived options) into liquid money for consumption, even if they do sell off their shares.

PROGRESS TO DATE

By late June 1992, the Czech Republic Ministry of Privatization had evaluated just under 7,000 of the roughly 11,000 submitted projects, of which over 1,600 have been approved (see Table 6.7). This still leaves over 4,000 first-wave privatization projects before the Ministry, with second-wave projects due by 16 June. The Slovak Republic had received about 1,500 projects on 736 firms in the first wave, of which 430 were approved for voucher privatization and over 70 others will be privatized through direct sale, with the remainder still to be judged. First-wave projects which involve voucher privatization, but were approved too late for the first wave of vouchers, will be included in the second wave of voucher privatization.

Table 6.7 Czech Republic privatization status, late June 1992

	Total projects	*Total firms*	*Property (bn Kcs)*
Projects submitted	11,163	2,883	766.9
Projects reviewed	6,748	1,642	474.9
Projects remaining	4,415	1,241	292.0

Source: Karel Cermak, Czech Republic Ministry of Privatization.

So far, most projects that have been approved have involved vouchers, simply because both republics hurried to evaluate voucher projects earlier than other projects in order to fulfil their quotas for voucher privatization (see Table 6.4). In the future, the shares of other means of privatization, especially direct sale, should increase (see above).

As for foreign participation, in the first wave of privatization, negotiations are under way with 220 potential foreign investors in the Czech Republic. The total book value of assets involved in these negotiations is almost 50 billion Kcs (US $1.7 billion). By mid-April, 50 deals had been closed with 15 billion Kcs (US $500 million) of investment. Considering that book value of these properties was only 8 billion Kcs, the potential for inflow of foreign capital in the remaining 170 properties – which employ 100,000 workers and encompass about 40 billion Kcs (US $1.4 billion) in book value – is quite likely to exceed the estimated book value. A special group of American advisers, supported by USAID, has been assisting the Czech government in negotiations with potential foreign investors. Foreign participation is significantly smaller in the Slovak Republic.

In voucher privatization, the first round of the first wave started on 18 May 1992. Because the value of property going into the first wave of voucher privatization was approximately 35,000 Kcs/coupon book, the price of all shares was initially set at 3 shares per 100 voucher points (100 points is the minimum investment in any given firm, the value of each share is 1,000 Kcs – US $35). This value was chosen because stock splits are not allowed, and thus a rate of 3.5 shares would not be possible, and because to undervalue the vouchers (rather than to overvalue them using a rate of 4) will allow greater flexibility.

The first round of voucher privatization, after a slow start, was marked by a very high rate of participation – over 90 per cent of all available voucher points in this round were 'invested'. As a result many firms were oversubscribed and over 60 per cent of share orders were returned. None the less, over 35 per cent of all voucher points were successfully invested and 30 per cent of all shares, worth almost 90 billion Kcs (US $3.2 billion), were successfully sold. The price structure of shares will be very different for the second round, with some firms much cheaper and others (such as popular breweries, hotels and financial institutions) going for significantly higher prices. Given that 30 per cent of shares have already been sold, it seems almost certain that the process will not require more than the five rounds which were originally anticipated.

POTENTIAL FUTURE DEVELOPMENTS

There are two major problems which may arise in the aftermath of privatization. Firstly, enterprises are currently saddled with a huge amount of (mainly inter-enterprise) debt, which is hampering their ability to function properly and limiting possibilities for investment. If firms begin to use bankruptcy laws to enforce payment of these debts, however, a string of bankruptcies could result in a general collapse. The state has initiated several programmes intended to clear enterprises and banks of their bad debts in ways that will not result in continued subsidization of poorly performing enterprises.

The first step which was taken was to ease the burden of so-called 'working capital loans' which enterprises had been forced to take out under the former regime. It was considered fair to mitigate this debt burden, since it was a product of the former system and not related to choices made by enterprises on the basis of efficiency. As a result, 110 billion Kcs (US $4 billion) worth of loans were transferred to a special 'Consolidation Bank', and the loans were changed to eight-year loans with a relatively mild 13 per cent interest rate. Although this policy step helped with the debt burden for many enterprises, it did not address the growing problem of insolvency caused by inter-enterprise debt.

Table 6.8 Inter-enterprise debt in Czechoslovakia: involvement of the banks

Debt clearance for selected banks	*Debt clearance (bn Kcs)*	*Recapitalization (bn Kcs)*
Komercni Banka	16.7	0.6
Investicni Banka	3.3	2.3
CS Obchodni Banka	2.2	1.1
Ceska St Sporitelna	–	3.8
Total	22.2	7.8

The first step in addressing the inter-enterprise debt problem was to use a 50 billion Kcs (US $1.7 billion) bond issue by the Funds of National Property (38 billion Kcs in the Czech Republic, 12 billion Kcs in the Slovak Republic) to help banks entering voucher privatization clear their portfolios of bad debts. The management of these funds was actually transferred to the commercial banks themselves (see Table 6.8). It is likely that further funds received by the Funds of National Property from privatization will be used in further bond issues to help relieve enterprise debt.

Another programme to relieve enterprise debt is an attempt to trace chains of mutual indebtedness among enterprises, i.e. groups among which enterprise debt can be cancelled out. The first wave of this programme managed to cancel 50 million Kcs worth of debt, a small amount, but there are hopes that later it can relieve enterprises of up to 50 billion Kcs worth of so-called 'secondary' debt (i.e. debt which the enterprise is unable to pay only because of the illiquidity of its accounts receivable).

Policy-makers hope that these programmes will be able to relieve the danger of insolvency spreading throughout the economy, but will not amount to a new programme of subsidization of these firms. Of course, programmes of debt relief must be handled very cautiously in order to ensure that they do not simply create a new degree of dependence on government subsidization.

The second potential problem is that of the IPFs. Having promised large pay-offs to their shareholders within a year, many of these institutions may be driven into bankruptcy due to the illiquidity of their assets, again possibly having a knock-on effect throughout the economy. On the other hand, if the funds have access to enough financial resources, it is possible that they will be drawing on the savings of those with a lower propensity to consume and converting it into 'hot money' for those with a higher propensity to consume, thus generating inflation in the short run. The best way that these problems can be avoided in the IPF sector is through careful IPF regulation (especially with regard to risk diversification), and through a continued restrictive monetary policy. Furthermore, a healthy economy and successful enterprise restructuring will naturally support the activities of the IPFs, although these are conditions which cannot be guaranteed.

CONCLUSIONS ON PRIVATIZATION

The most important observation to make about the privatization process in Czechoslovakia is that it is well under way. Privatization is seen as an extremely important part of the reform package and is supported both by the public and by Parliament. This is a key consideration in assuring that the process maintains its momentum. One of the most important goals to keep in mind is to make sure that the whole process does not get mired in details or in controversies about its problems.

It is clear that there have been many problems. But no process of such large-scale economic change can be problem-free. Several problems and loopholes were addressed by the amendment to the Law on Large Privatization. The most important policy pursued within the large privatization was the promotion of competitive privatization bids, allowing various offers including the voucher system and also direct sales, public auctions and tenders, and other means of property transfer. This policy, however, altered the process from its originally conceived form, and caused many unforeseen problems which required immediate attention.

Perhaps the greatest problem of the large privatization has been the lack of a firm legal framework, and the government's resulting willingness to make changes in important policies in the middle of the process of privatization. The effects of such changes have been to make the rules of the game unclear for potential investors and others submitting projects, and for the organizers of the IPFs. In spite of this problem, however, the first wave is under way and should be completed by the end of 1992. The second wave will be able to learn from the lessons of the first, and thus have a much sounder foundation for operation from its beginning, not suffering as much from the government's frequent changes in policy.

Czechoslovakian privatization, even with all of its controversies and criticisms, is happening, and is still supported by the public. What will be more important in the near future is to concentrate on the restructuring and reorganization of newly privatized enterprises in order to create a properly functioning market economy.

7

EAST GERMANY: SCALING DOWN

Robert Bischof, Gottfried von Bismarck and Wendy Carlin

INTRODUCTION

The face of industry in the former German Democratic Republic (East Germany) has changed dramatically since economic reunification with the Federal Republic (West Germany) in July 1990. A significant proportion of the industrial capital stock has been scrapped and employment, especially in industry, has collapsed. Although several hundred thousand small private businesses have been founded, as elsewhere in eastern Europe, the singularity of the east German experience of transition has been the role played by the government agency the Treuhandanstalt (THA) in privatizing a substantial proportion of the former state-owned enterprise sector.[1]

A simple indicator of the active role played by the THA in splitting up firms is provided by the fact that the number of enterprises which are or were owned by the agency has risen from 8,000 in mid-1990 to 12,000 by mid-1992. Of this total, 4,600 have been privatized, 1,600 closed and 900 returned to their previous owners. The THA still has over 4,000 enterprises on its books. There were originally about 4 million employees in the THA's enterprises; now about 800,000 remain. Although jobs have been guaranteed for nearly 1.25 million employees by the new owners of the enterprises sold by the THA, the shrinkage of employment as a consequence of restructuring is clear.

In the first part of this chapter, we present a brief summary of the way in which this agency has undertaken its threefold task of privatizing, restructuring and closing enterprises. This is followed by two detailed case studies illustrating the process of transformation of large state-owned enterprises into private-sector companies. In each case the transformation is virtually complete. The remaining parts of both large conglomerate enterprises as they existed in the German Democratic Republic – the so-called Kombinats – are in the process of liquidation. (Kombinats were designed to create vertically and horizontally integrated units which undertook intermediate and final production, capital investment, R & D and domestic and foreign marketing for entire industries. By the end of the 1980s, in East Germany there were

126 national Kombinats in industry, each employing on average more than 20,000 workers.)

Both cases lie at the highly problematic end of the spectrum of enterprises to be restructured and privatized in east Germany. The first case study is of the heavy machinery Kombinat called *baukema*. Baukema was engaged in two main industries: construction equipment and foundries. It was a medium-sized Kombinat which employed 16,000 workers and was highly dependent on the former Soviet Union for its sales.

The second case is the microelectronics Kombinat *Mikroelektronik Erfurt*. This was a huge enterprise with more than 55,000 employees and was the main supplier of microchips and microelectronic components to East Germany. Its share of the East German market for microelectronic components was 80 per cent. The Kombinat was also engaged in numerous other activities, from being sole supplier of colour television tubes to East Germany to producing watches, watch straps, photocopying machines and radar.

The moderate size of baukema means that the story of the restructuring and privatization of the entire Kombinat can be told. The microelectronics case study serves a rather different purpose. It highlights the way the THA has dealt with the specific problem of the fate of a high technology and possibly strategic industry. The focus in the second case study is therefore on the microelectronic core of the Kombinat.

THE CENTRALIZED PRIVATIZATION AGENCY – THE TREUHANDANSTALT

When drawing comparisons with other formerly planned economies, it is striking that the East German former communist government under Hans Modrow had decided to change the legal status of firms from so-called Volkseigene Betriebe (owned by the people) to AGs (Aktiengesellschaften – German public companies) and to GmbHs (German limited liability companies) owned by an independent state agency, the Treuhandanstalt. This process was viewed as a route to commercializing the activities of enterprises and was in full swing when economic unification with West Germany took place.

With German economic and monetary union (GEMU) in mid-1990, the Federal German authorities took over the THA and established a supervisory/administrative board (Verwaltungsrat) to oversee its activities. Represented on the THA's supervisory board are the major interest groups in the German economy: the Federal Government, the Bundesbank, the governments of the new east German Federal States, German (and a couple of foreign) businesses and the trade unions.

Some 30,000 very small businesses, mainly in the retail sector, were privatized rapidly soon after GEMU. The process of restructuring and privatizing the 8,000 medium-sized and larger state-owned enterprises was decentralized in two ways. Firstly, all enterprises with less than 1,500 employees were transferred to the 12 regional subsidiaries of the THA. The remaining larger firms remained the responsibility of the Treuhand-Zentral in Berlin.

The second method of decentralization involved the private sector and the German institution of two-tier boards of companies. All German companies with more than 500 employees must have a supervisory board in addition to the management board. On the supervisory board are representatives of the owner(s) and, for most enterprises, of the employees as well. The supervisory board's job is to monitor the performance of the management. An early task of the THA was to ensure that all large enterprises had a supervisory board.

Most supervisory boards are chaired by a west German – about one-fifth of chairpersons come from west German banks and the remainder from west German companies. In the process of transition, an important role of the supervisory board has been to provide the east German management board with information and contacts essential for recasting the business in a form compatible with survival in the market economy.

In addition to setting up a governance structure for east German firms within the German legal framework, the Treuhand's early preoccupation was with preventing the bankruptcy of their portfolio of firms after GEMU. The threat of bankruptcy arose from pressures on both cost and demand. Firstly, the one-for-one conversion rate from Ostmarks into Deutschmarks used for wages meant that real wages were higher than average productivity. After reunification, wages in east Germany rose rapidly without a parallel rise in productivity, exacerbating the problem of cost (see Akerlof *et al.* 1991).

Secondly, the order books of east German firms, orders from within east Germany and from the Soviet Union, collapsed. East German firms were no longer competitive in the domestic market (once faced with open competition from the rest of Germany and the European Community) and the Soviet market was beginning to disintegrate. To stave off widespread bankruptcy, the THA had to provide liquidity. This was done through issuing 100 per cent THA guarantees on loans from commercial banks.

To decide the long-term future of enterprises, the THA undertook to evaluate the likely viability of each firm and the extent of restructuring required. Although many economists argue that the Treuhandanstalt should simply have put its firms up for auction to the highest bidder, there are a number of reasons why this method was not adopted.[2] There was the slow and uneven emergence of a market for real estate in east Germany, the complex organizational structure of the large Kombinats and the problems of the existence of old debts of enterprises to the former GDR state banking system. Most important, since the German government was concerned with the employment effects of privatization, a simple auctioning of enterprises to the highest bidder was not a feasible procedure. Had this been done, there would have been great interest in enterprises with property in the Berlin area or in other desirable locations, but little interest in industrial activities.

The process of evaluating each enterprise was coordinated by a special team set up within the Treuhand. The team (called the Leitungsausschuß) was made up of 80 top managers from west Germany. Its aim was to decide whether there were any *core business activities* in the enterprise which could be made profitable. Evaluations were done by the Leitungsausschuß in conjunction with both the THA case officer responsible for the enterprise (usually a west German, often seconded from industry) and the local management. The overall outcome of their work was that in about 70 per cent of Treuhand enterprises there was judged to be at least one potentially viable core business. Making the enterprises viable would generally entail large reductions in employment and finding an outside investor with expertise and a market position in the industry.

In order to sell its portfolio of firms, the THA has had to break up the large concerns to produce saleable units. Restructuring of this kind has not been dictated by concern with the abuse of monopoly power by the former Kombinats: in the east German situation, there are few sectors in which east German producers are protected from vigorous competition from west German and international suppliers. Nevertheless, German and EC anti-monopoly law applies and all sales above a certain size are referred to the Kartellamt for approval.

Anti-competitive practices by *west German* companies, however, have caused concern in the THA. One of the disadvantages of using the supervisory board system to devolve the process of transferring ownership and control from the state is that a west German chairman of an east German enterprise's supervisory board can abuse his position to enhance the competitive position of the west German company.[3]

Enterprises or parts of enterprises which are not deemed potentially viable are closed down. There is a 'winding up' division of the THA which deals with these cases. Most enterprises are closed through a procedure of negotiated liquidation which involves attempting to maintain as many jobs as possible for former employees on the site. On average between one-fifth and one-third of jobs are saved.

RESTRUCTURING AND PRIVATIZING A HEAVY MACHINERY KOMBINAT – BAUKEMA OF LEIPZIG

The baukema Kombinat[4] consisted of more than a dozen enterprises scattered across East Germany, operating in four main business areas: road construction and earth-moving equipment, residential and commercial construction machinery, plant engineering and foundry equipment, and foundries. In mid-1990, this giant enterprise employed 16,000 people; just over two years later, 19 companies have been sold to private owners, with total employment guarantees of 2,500, and the rest are in liquidation.

Before tracing the process of restructuring and privatization, there is one source of employment loss unrelated to questions of business viability. Baukema, like all Kombinats, included a substantial amount of employment in non-business-related activities. There were 19 blocks of flats, polyclinics, kindergartens, a polytechnic and numerous other services provided by the enterprise for its work-force. Most of these activities and the associated employment were taken out of baukema AG in 1990, leaving some 12,000 employees in business-related activities.

An important feature of the method of enterprise restructuring used in east Germany is the delegation of monitoring and strategic decision-making from the Treuhand to the supervisory boards of the enterprises. The baukema case illustrates both the costs and benefits of such an approach. In one of baukema's four business areas (the Gisag foundries), the supervisory board provided a source of realistic information for the management board about the route to survival in the market economy. The chairman of the supervisory board was instrumental in devising the strategy for breaking up the enterprise in a manner that would secure the survival of its core business, albeit in a much reduced form. In the main part of baukema, however, the supervisory board shielded the managers from having to confront pressing decisions about the break-up of the firm. We begin with the story of Gisag.

Restructuring and selling Gisag AG

It was clear to all at an early stage that the foundry business was unrelated to the rest of baukema and should be dealt with separately. Gisag AG was therefore sold by baukema AG to the THA for the nominal sum of DM 1. As an AG, Gisag already had its own supervisory board. This board was chaired by the head of the west German foundry industry association, who provided an early assessment of the restructuring required in the east German foundry industry in general, and at Gisag in particular, if it was to survive in a sector shrinking right across western Europe.

Gisag's markets in east Germany had virtually disappeared with the dramatic cut in production of the enterprises it supplied – for example, the shut-down of the Trabant car plant cost one foundry the bulk of its orders. The extreme case was a foundry which only produced chains for Soviet tanks. Production of tanks ceased in 1991 and the foundry closed.

The strategy developed by the management of Gisag in conjunction with the supervisory board was to hire an international foundry industry expert to help locate possible buyers who would bring their market with them to Gisag. An extensive Europe-wide search was partially successful. Possible buyers were found for all four foundries. Sales have resulted for two of them (see Table 7.2 below).

Business strategies for baukema AG

With Gisag hived off, baukema AG was basically a construction equipment and plant engineering concern. For 1991, based on the results for the second half of 1990, the management board projected a *profit* of DM 6 million on a turnover of DM 820 million (of which sales to the Soviet Union would account for 65 per cent) with employment falling by 1,000 to 4,700 over the course of the year. The out-turn was dramatically different: a *loss* of DM 105 million on a turnover of DM 150 million, and a fall of employment to 2,800 by the end of 1991. In the course of 1991, baukema received liquidity credits guaranteed by the THA of DM 70 million. This provides the background against which the conflicts over restructuring strategies took place.

Until the spring of 1991, baukema AG, like many Kombinats, lived a life away from the Treuhand, supervised, protected and guided by its supervisory board. Its first supervisory board originated from the period before GEMU and, unlike the Gisag case, it did not play a constructive role in shaping the future of the enterprise. Under German law, the owner of an AG has access to the managers only through the supervisory board. Only as the need for liquidity arose was the management persuaded that cooperation with the owner – the THA – was necessary. At the same time, the THA moved to dismiss the original supervisory board. The new board was headed by a retired chief executive of a major west German road construction equipment manufacturer.

The 'business concept' of the baukema management played an important and negative part in the process of restructuring baukema. The idea of baukema management – i.e. the management board of the baukema AG which was a holding company with 12 subsidiaries – was to keep the concern together and find a buyer for the entire unit (see Table 7.1). Their view was based on baukema's traditional role as a supplier to the Soviet Union. A typical 'state order' for baukema from the Soviet Union combined the output of several of baukema's subsidiaries and was of the following kind: from 'teltomat', asphalt mixing towers (DM 80 million), 'Gatersleben' asphalt laying machines (DM 75 million), 'NOBAS' excavators (DM 30 million) and 'Welzow' concrete mixing towers (DM 5 million) – a total of DM 190 million. In 1991, baukema had in hand signed contracts for DM 244 million worth of orders of this kind from the Soviet Union. In the Soviet market, baukema's strength was in being able to supply the full package of products required for major construction projects. The management also emphasized baukema's reputation and contacts in the Soviet Union.

Management's view was that there were important synergies between the constituent enterprises. This had two important consequences. Firstly, management tried to find a consortium of banks which would buy baukema. Although negotiations were begun such attempts came to nothing. Secondly, they were aware that if just one of the key companies was to break out and

Table 7.1 East Germany: three business strategies for the baukema Kombinat

Originator	*Proposed Strategy*
Management board of baukema AG	**Maintain the concern intact** Sell to a consortium of banks. This strategy was based on the expectation of a lasting high share of sales in the former Soviet Union.
New supervisory board of baukema	**Rebundle assets** to form integrated businesses at a small number of locations.
Treuhandanstalt	**Break up the concern** and, if necessary, also its individual enterprises. Sell off the core businesses.

find a buyer, it would be the end for the concern, as the synergy effects vital for the Soviet market would be lost. They therefore ensured that all potential investors interested in individual enterprises were discouraged – in clear contradiction to THA policy.

A second strategy for baukema (Table 7.1) combined recognition of the existence of synergies in supplying the Soviet Union with an ambitious plan to restructure the company along divisional lines so as to take advantage of economies of scale. The idea was developed by the new supervisory board chairman. Key parts of the baukema enterprises would be shifted to two chosen locations. The other locations would be sold off as business parks. The logic of this second strategy rested on a confidence in the long-term future of markets in the Soviet Union.

In the summer of 1991, the THA's company evaluation team (the Leitungsausschuβ) turned their attention to baukema. The Leitungsausschuβ, in conjunction with the THA's baukema case officers, took the view that the concern was unviable as a unit and that the only option was for the speedy disposal of individual subsidiaries (Table 7.1). Baukema's heavy losses and the worsening prospects for the existing Soviet orders being honoured, and of stable markets in the former Soviet Union emerging, were reflected in the judgement made by the Treuhand's company evaluation team.

Using a classification running from '1' (for an enterprise operating profitably) to '6' (closure), with '3' for enterprises with a business concept which appears to be viable, most of the baukema subsidiaries were classified as category 3.1.2, with 4.1 for 'EBAWE' and 5 for 'Ludwigslust'. The sub-category '3.1.2' refers to so-called 'cash gobblers'. Such firms must be privatized by a certain date or be liquidated. By contrast, firms in category 4 are deemed potentially viable but where the company strategy needs revision. More time is also available to those in category 5. A deadline for privatization of the bulk of baukema was set by the THA committee for the end of 1991, but at the request of the Treuhand case officers working on baukema this was extended to April 1992.

Management obstruction to the restructuring of baukema finally ceased in November 1991 when they agreed that splitting up the concern was inevitable. The tenacity with which the management had stuck to their belief that baukema should remain together can be understood partly by the personal costs to them of its dissolution. In the early days of the THA, supervisory boards were able to write quite unrealistic contracts for the management board. Baukema managers sat on five-year contracts entitling them to Mercedes cars and private pension rights set at 40 per cent of final salary. (The Treuhand only sanctions contracts that entail six months' notice and no pension rights above the standard maximum of DM 5,000 in redundancy pay available to all employees of THA enterprises.)

Selling the subsidiaries of baukema AG

The east German managers of the subsidiary companies of baukema who had been discouraged by the main management board from pursuing potential investors were now the major source of contacts with the eventual buyers. (The Treuhand officials also contacted all international competitors of the baukema enterprises. For the bulk of baukema subsidiaries, there were less than a dozen competitors in the world.) The managers of individual baukema firms had been in touch with many of their competitors, attended trade fairs and travelled extensively in Germany and abroad. Many had attended management and English-language training courses. As a result, they had begun to pull in new work (e.g. 'Ludwigslust'), had signed licence agreements (e.g. 'Gatersleben'), diversified their products (e.g. 'NOBAS') and opened up new markets (e.g. 'EBAWE' in Iran and Israel).

Table 7.2 shows the sales of the baukema subsidiary companies. It is clear from the table that the most frequent type of buyer is a west German firm. However, foreign companies have also bought parts of the concern. The small business services companies set up by baukema have been sold as management buy-outs (MBOs) to east German members of the management board. East German equity participation through MBOs has also occurred in two other cases. Whilst most enterprises have been sold as going concerns (share deals), there have been a number of asset deals. In the latter, specific assets have been bundled together for prospective buyers so that, for example at 'Gatersleben', three new enterprises took the place of a single baukema firm. In the majority of cases, the Treuhand's policy of trying to save core business activities has been achieved. As elsewhere in east Germany, it has only been possible to find buyers for enterprises with much reduced work-forces. In the Gisag case, for example, accelerated structural change is being observed. Rationalization and structural change from the use of steel to light materials

Table 7.2 East Germany: restructuring and privatizing the baukema Kombinat

Name of enterprise in baukema	*Sold to a company from (country) (or as MBO)*	*Type of deal*	*Core business retained?*	*Employment* at end-1990	*Employment* guaranteed by buyer	*Investment guaranteed (DM million)*
Gisag AG	1 WG	Asset	Yes	3,300	600	40.0
(foundries)	2 Sweden/WG	Asset	Yes	(total)	125	10.0
	3 and 4	Liquidation				
from Gisag AG	MBOs (EG)	Asset	No		250	1.0
Langensalza	WG	Share	Yes	200	120	4.5
Ludwigslust	WG + 10% MBO (EG)	Share	Yes + new products	500	230	3.1
Welzow	Switzerland	Share	Yes + new products	480	250	16.5
teltomat	WG/Indian	Share	Yes + development	525	350	15.0
Gatersleben	1 WG	Asset	Yes	1,000	185	3.5
	2 WG	Asset	Yes	(total)	45	2.0
	3 WG	Asset	No		70	1.5
Bernsdorf		Liquidation		235		
Gisag Maschinenbau	MBO/MBI EG/WG	Asset	Yes + new products	400	80	2.0
Gisag Anlagenbau	Netherlands	Share	Yes	500	100	3.0
EBAWE	WG/Indian	Share	Yes + new products	640	205	15.0
Baustoff Bautzen	MBO/MBI EG/Swiss	Share	Yes	100	40	1.0
NOBAS	WG	Asset	No	1,470	100	5.0
Grundstucks und Verwaltungs Gmbh	MBO EGs from management board of baukema	Share	Yes		10	
baukema Bau und Miepartner Gmbh	(as above)	Share	Yes		20	2.0
baukema Engineering Gmbh	(as above)	Share	Yes		20	
baukema Handel	(as above)	Share	Yes		10	
Total				9,000 (approx)	2,500 (approx)	100.0

Note: In September 1992, an order for DM 250 million was confirmed from the former Soviet Union. This includes orders for 'NOBAS' and has forestalled the threatened liquidation of this large subsidiary. A part of the business has been bought by a west German firm (shown above in the table); the remainder of 'NOBAS' will be managed by that firm while ownership remains with the THA. The west German firm may eventually buy all of it.

has been proceeding in west Germany since the 1950s, while the equivalent transformation of the foundry industry has been forced on east Germany in 18 months.

The final column in Table 7.2 shows the investment committed by the new owners. In several cases, the new owner will demolish the existing factory and start with new capital equipment.

Problems in negotiating sales

The difficulties of concluding a deal with a potential buyer are enormous. First is the problem of restructuring the target company to the size the buyer wants to acquire. This relates to the number of employees, the amount of real estate and the specific fixed assets and stocks that should remain in the company.

Secondly, there are problems related to the balance sheet. As the balance sheets were 'created' (in DM) in June 1990, the accounts of all companies are inaccurate and riddled with distortions. For example, the profit and loss accounts are rendered meaningless by the inclusion of subsidized short-time workers and workers employed in temporary employment programmes. Stocks are generally overvalued because of the inclusion of unsaleable output that had been intended for the Soviet market. Large question marks exist over the valuation of land, the building stock, plant and machinery.

The third set of problems relate to restitution claims, those claims on property from previous owners whose assets were nationalized. For two baukema subsidiary companies restitution claims were lodged for the whole company, but claims for parts of companies (for example, land and buildings) were made for all others. Under a new law, compensation rather than restitution will take place if a new investor is prepared to invest more in the company than the former owner. Hence although sales contracts can be signed, they have legal force only after all restitution claims have been dealt with. This lengthy legal process means that the new owners are unwilling to spend money in a company until the situation is clear.

Fourthly, there are administrative and physical infrastructure problems. The courts are full and there are delays of months and even years in the company and land registers. Telecommunications and roads are still inadequate in some areas. At a key meeting at 'Gatersleben', two people were on time, three were up to two hours late and a merchant banker gave up completely and made it known that he would only fund companies in accessible locations.

The fifth problem relates to pollution. Lengthy surveys are frequently necessary to establish the extent of the damage. This is followed by a further lengthy process of determining the allocation of financial responsibility for dealing with the pollution. A purchaser of a THA firm must first put in a claim to the various levels of government for compensation. Depending on the outcome of this, the financial burden is divided between the purchaser and the THA. The THA insists that the buyer pay a substantial entrance fee so as to prevent unnecessary or 'luxury' cleaning-up from occurring. Above the entrance fee and up to a certain maximum limit, the THA typically bears the burden of the clean-up costs. Beyond this limit, the buyer bears the risk. The aim of this formula is to ensure that only essential cleaning-up occurs and to allow the THA to calculate its total costs.

Finally there are problems associated with the THA itself. Because of the accusations about poor deals and manipulation by speculators, a complex controlling system was introduced which makes the process of selling firms bureaucratic and cumbersome.

The terms of the sales

All of the sales of baukema enterprises have involved a substantial subsidy. In the share deals where the purchaser buys a going concern with all its assets and liabilities, the subsidy from the THA to the buyer can be expressed in terms of the reduction in net worth of the enterprise which the THA allows per job guaranteed by the purchaser. In baukema's case this subsidy varied from DM 10,000 per employee in the case of 'teltomat', with good real estate near Berlin, to DM 80,000 per employee for 'Welzow', which is located in a completely depressed coal-mining area.

In the case of asset deals such as occurred at the Gisag foundries, sales negotiations are confined to the specific assets the buyer wants. The same rules of thumb are used to calculate the 'justifiable' subsidy to purchasers in such deals. In the Gisag case, for example, the subsidy was some DM 30,000 per job guaranteed. The arguments used by the THA's case officers to justify this to the Board of the Treuhand included the importance for the regional engineering industry of retaining a foundry industry in the Leipzig area. The THA took into account industrial, social and regional aspects of unemployment.

RESTRUCTURING AND PRIVATIZING THE MICROELECTRONICS KOMBINAT MIKROELEKTRONIK ERFURT

The Kombinat *Mikroelektronik Erfurt* has presented the Treuhand with one of its most difficult cases. It has revealed deep-seated problems with the division of responsibilities between the THA, the Federal Government and the governments of the new east German *Länder* when privatization is bound inextricably to industrial/structural policy. Microelectronics was one of the prestige industries in the GDR, dominating research, development and manufacturing in this sector for the entire Eastern bloc. It was an industry which received priority in the allocation of resources for investment right up to reunification. This set it aside from the many sectors which had languished with low levels of investment in the 1980s.

In following the case of the Mikroelektronik Kombinat Erfurt we are following the fate of the microelectronics industry in East Germany. The key microelectronics enterprise in the GDR was the principal member of this Kombinat. It had the GDR's most modern factory for the production of integrated circuits. The extraordinary levels of investment in this enterprise are demonstrated by the fact that in 1988 when sales were 970 million Ostmarks, investment was 920 million. (Over one-half of investment in the entire Kombinat took place in this enterprise.) Of this investment, 175 million Ostmarks was in research and development. Although the microelectronics industry in East Germany was behind developments in the West, it was not totally backward. Despite the isolation of the R & D workers, considerable progress had been made. The prestige and privileged status of Mikroelektronik Erfurt in the GDR as well as its high level of employment (some 36,000 in microelectronics-related business) have strongly influenced the process of restructuring the enterprise.

The THA's first sweep at restructuring

Around the time of reunification, 17 enterprises in microelectronics were stripped out of the Kombinat and gathered into a new holding company PTC-electronic-AG (PTC), owned by the THA. The collapse in demand for east German microelectronics output was sudden: only one month after GEMU, less than 30 per cent of the 36,000 employees were working full-time, a further one-third were working half-time and the remainder were not working at all.

At this time, the management of PTC (all east Germans from the original Kombinat) formulated its 'business concept' as required by the THA. The management foresaw the continued existence of the PTC with most of its subsidiaries (but only half the number of employees), and sought relief from the old debts incurred to the GDR state banking system, the supply of liquidity to cover losses and for investment for a two- to three-year period of restructuring.

The THA's internal evaluation team (Leitungsausschuß) judged this concept to be unworkable. The PTC holding was viewed as a collection of enterprises without economic logic. The cost of restructuring along the lines proposed by the management was viewed as too high (DM 750 million for investment and DM 1.1 billion for liquidity to the end of 1991). There was always a strong strand of opinion in the THA that the whole project of saving the microelectronics industry in east Germany was mistaken. Some of the key players had connections with Siemens and experience of the persistent difficulties of the *west* German microelectronics sector.

But advocacy for the retention of the industry was strengthened with the appointment of the supervisory board for PTC. It was headed by Professor Lorenz, the former chief executive of a major west German electronics company. He was fully aware of the state subsidies provided to industries considered vital for Germany's technological leadership – the so-called key industries (Schlüsselindustrien). He emphasized the prospect of the deindustrialization of east Germany consequent on the shut-down of microelectronics. His case for saving the microchip business was based on the achievements of the east Germans, the concentration of highly skilled workers and on the importance for the *German* economy of success in the development of specialized microchips. These customer-specific integrated circuits (ASICs) are playing an increasingly important role in the automobile industry. The Japanese are already using them in cars; the German car manufacturers have not yet begun to use them but are becoming interested.

The division of responsibility between the THA and the government

It is clear from the earlier description of the THA's procedures, and their application in the baukema case, that the Treuhand takes account of the employment, industrial and regional consequences in its decision-making. However, it has refused to conduct 'structural policy'. Although it has never been made clear how structural policy is defined, in practice, the THA does not take on the job of deciding on the fate of an *entire* industry. This is viewed as a political decision to be made by the Federal and *Länder* governments.

Once the THA's Leitungsausschuβ had judged that PTC was neither worthy nor capable of being restructured successfully, the Federal government was confronted with the problem of the future of the microelectronics industry.

The second phase of restructuring: separating out the core business

In a new report commissioned by the Federal government it was recommended that the *core business* of *microchip* production should be separated from the rest of the PTC's subsidiaries. What resulted by mid-1991 was the stripping out of PTC the non-core subsidiaries; these were sold to the THA for DM 1 each and became independent companies to be privatized – or liquidated. A new limited liability company was set up as a subsidiary of PTC AG. It was Mikroelektronik & Technologie GmbH (MTGmbH) and was formed by the merger of the three core microchip businesses of PTC with a fourth microchip enterprise from the Carl Zeiss Jena Kombinat. Since the location of the four enterprises of MTGmbH plays a major role in the restructuring strategies, it is easiest to simply refer to them by the name of the town in which they are located: Erfurt (in the state of Thuringia), Neuhaus (Thuringia), Frankfurt an der Oder (Brandenburg) and Dresden (Saxony).

The merged company MTGmbH had 8,400 employees when formed, and this had dropped to 4,500 by January 1992. By the beginning of 1992, MTGmbH had received DM 500 million in liquidity credits.

Selling the core microchips business

Strategy 1

Early in 1990, before the currency union, a US company, LSI Logic Inc., had established contact with the management of the East German microchip producers. The merger to form MTGmbH in mid-1991 was partially driven by the concept of LSI – although only a vague 'letter of intent' had been signed by the US company. The THA/LSI strategy was that LSI would 'buy' 19.8 per cent of MTGmbH, and they would be given the enterprise in a debt-free state. LSI would produce specialized chips known as ASICs at Erfurt, use Dresden as an R & D facility (large-scale production had never taken place at this enterprise) and use Frankfurt/Oder for mass chip production. The remaining 80.2 per cent of equity would be 'sold' to the federal states in which the enterprises were located. According to US law, companies owning less than 20 per cent of a foreign company do not have to disclose this on their US balance sheet. Management was to be supplied by LSI. The THA would pay DM 250 million to LSI to cover its start-up losses to the end of 1993.

Strategy 2

This strategy involved splitting up the new MTGmbH and was driven by the appearance of a competing purchaser. By the autumn of 1991, it became clear that the life of the newly formed microchip enterprise MTGmbH was to be very short. A US competitor of LSI Logic, called VLSI, became aware of the possible subsidies available from the German government to save the microchip industry. It sought a deal with the MTGmbH enterprise at Dresden. The management at Dresden were strongly opposed to Strategy 1 (LSI) since they wished to expand into production from being a pure R & D facility. The VSLI proposal was to produce at Dresden virtually the same product (ASICs) as LSI had been planning to produce at Erfurt. The prospect of a separate deal for Dresden helped to shatter Strategy 1.

In the light of this development, the THA gave serious consideration to two other strategies. The THA's preferred strategy was to close the Dresden enterprise and push through the LSI deal for Erfurt and Frankfurt/Oder. Political opposition from Saxony, in the context of an apparent offer from VSLI, led to the adoption of the alternative – Strategy 2 – as the most feasible option. In Strategy 2, Dresden is taken out of the MTGmbH and separate deals are done for Dresden (with VLSI) on the one hand and Erfurt and Frankfurt/Oder (with LSI Logic) on the other. In each case, a 19.8 per cent deal with the respective US buyer was envisaged with the remainder of the equity being taken up by the state (*Länder*) governments.

Strategy 2 was expected to result in 1,900 jobs at a cost to the THA of between DM 184,000 and 254,000 per job. This is almost an order of magnitude greater than the cost per job in the baukema case. The economic justification lay in the potential strategic importance of the industry.

Strategy 3

This strategy involved yet further fragmentation and was driven by conflicts between the federal states. The Treuhand was not intended to be an institution taking long-term financial responsibility for enterprises, let alone for an industry. Its goal was to shift from itself the ownership of the microchip industry, and given the limited stakes the US buyers were willing to take, a central part of the strategy was to persuade the *Länder* governments or other institutions to acquire the majority of the equity.

Once this task had begun in earnest, cracks appeared in Strategy 2. The problem was that the *Länder* governments were not prepared *jointly* to take over an enterprise with a subsidiary in another Land. Thus the LSI deal, which included Erfurt and Frankfurt/Oder, would have required ownership of the merged enterprise jointly by the states of Thuringia and Brandenburg. The Premier of Brandenburg refused to take on ownership of any part of MTGmbH. The THA had not foreseen that a coordinated approach to the preservation of the microelectronics industry was only possible *inside* and by the THA itself. Once reponsibilities had to be shifted to *Länder* governments, the coordination fell apart. It became clear that the restructuring of enterprises carried out by the THA to create synergies and economies of scale would not survive the transfer from Treuhand to regional government responsibility.

The third strategy then emerged: MTGmbH would be split into its constituent enterprises, each of which would be privatized separately. The THA would split DM 280 million (roughly the amount involved in Strategy 2) three ways: 125 million to go to Erfurt (LSI); 125 million to Dresden (VLSI); and 30 million to Frankfurt/Oder. The *Länder* governments agreed to this and there was even a change of heart in Brandenburg about participating in a 'US-19.8 per cent' deal with a small Californian company called Synergy.

The Federal Finance Ministry

The THA is an autonomous trust but is obliged to submit decisions over major expenditure to the German Federal Finance Ministry for approval. After the contracts with LSI had been approved by all the THA governing bodies, the Finance Ministry refused to sign the deal. Their argument was that the sale of 19.8 per cent to LSI and 80.2 per cent to the Land Thuringia accompanied by a cash subsidy from the THA of DM 125 million was a case of 'structural policy'. The Finance Ministry stated that the *Länder* are responsible for structural policy and hence should make a contribution of part of the cash subsidy. In late summer 1992, both Thuringia and Saxony agreed to pay DM 40 million of the DM 125 million.

Winding up the remainder of the microelectronics industry

The deal with LSI has been signed. On 1 September 1992, the remainder of PTC, and with it the MTGmbH, went into liquidation. The liquidator who organized the restructuring of AEG in the early 1980s is managing the disposal of the remaining assets. It is still unclear whether the deals for Dresden and Frankfurt/Oder will proceed. Figure 7.1 provides a summary of the stages in the restructuring of the core business of the Mikroelektronik Erfurt Kombinat.

During the process of negotiation over the privatization of the core business, there was considerable activity in privatizing non-core activities (sales of non-core businesses are shown in dashed boxes in Figure 7.1). For example, a machine-tool building plant in Erfurt was sold to Vaillant (60 jobs); a clean room in Erfurt was sold to a chip producer (50 jobs); an electrical measuring apparatus production facility was sold (60 jobs) and parts of Neuhaus were sold as MBOs.

CONCLUSION

When assessing the east German experience of restructuring and privatization, it is essential to bear in mind the macroeconomic context, namely, the economic and monetary union with west Germany. A full EMU with mobile labour, common trade unions, industry-level wage setting and a starting point in which east German productivity was less than one-third that of west Germany's was bound to result in a swathe of east German industry being made unprofitable. Added to this was the loss of east German sales to the former Soviet Union. Given the decision for immediate reunification, the only method of retaining jobs in the open sector of the economy would have been through an employment subsidy. This policy option has been widely debated (see for example, Akerlof *et al.* 1991).

In this chapter, we have taken the macroeconomic setting as given, focusing instead on the transfer of ownership and control of enterprises from state to private ownership. However, as the case studies have illustrated, government subsidies based on employment levels are being used in conjunction with the sale of firms. The baukema case shows how the supervisory board system has enabled the Treuhand to delegate and decentralize the restructuring task. However, the abuse of supervisory board power (in preventing the Treuhand from having adequate access to monitor the activities of AGs) suggests that greater care should have been exercised in the appointment of supervisory board chairpersons.

An important theme running through both case studies is that the number

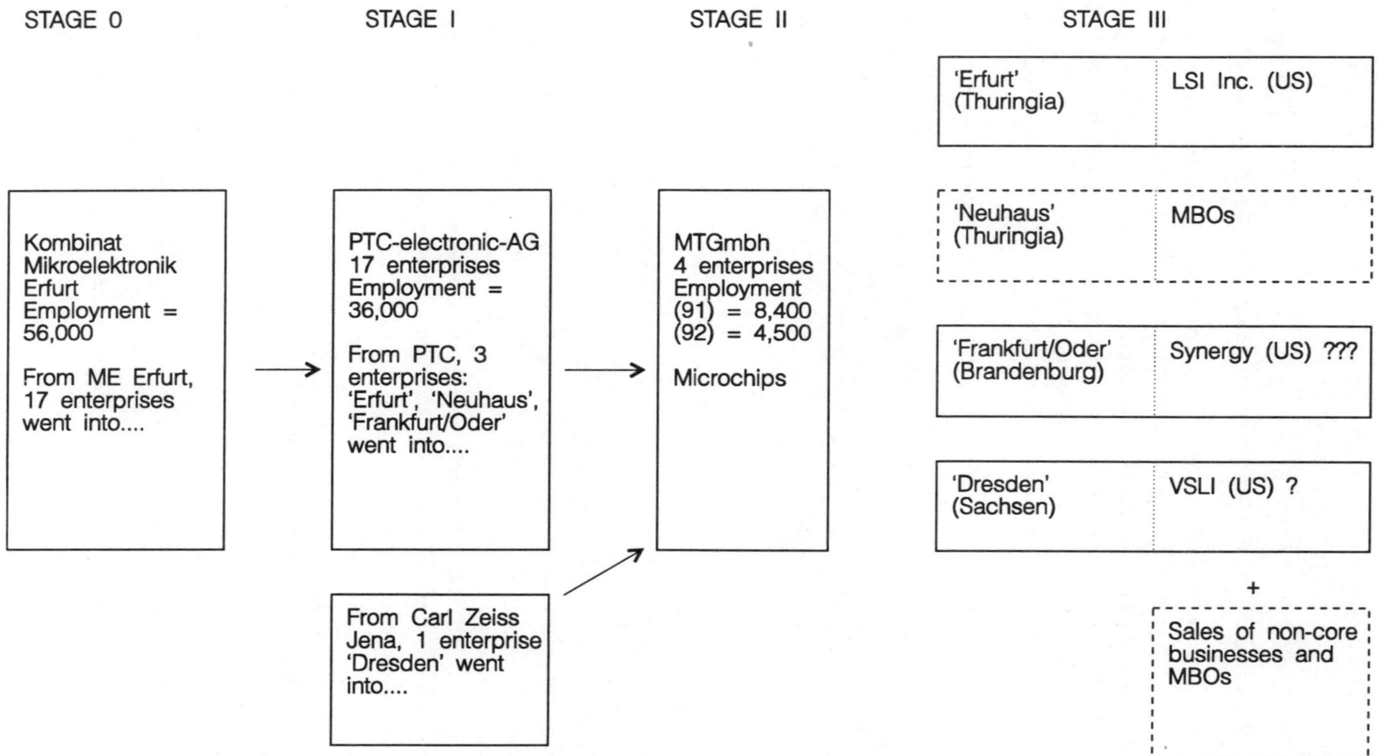

Figure 7.1 Stages in the restructuring and privatization of microelectronics in east Germany
Source: Author's data.

of potential buyers for these enterprises in international terms is very small. Taking the microelectronics case, none of the big west German electronics firms is engaged in microchip production. There was no interest at all from Japanese producers and only one fleeting show of interest from the Korean firm Samsung. While it is quite evident that the THA's negotiating position was very weak when only one or possibly two players were involved (LSI/VLSI), there was simply no interest from other companies at all. It is worth underlining the fact that even in a case where it was well known that government at the highest levels was committed to saving the industry (and therefore that the possibilities for rent-seeking were considerable) that only two companies in the world showed a serious interest in taking over this business.

As both case studies have illustrated, the Treuhand has not been offering for sale what an economist would think of as a firm. Rather, it has been offering combinations of physical assets, human capital and cash in exchange for management/organizational capabilities, technology and markets or market access to investors viewed as likely to transform the east German enterprise into an internationally competitive firm. In selling the Gisag foundries, for example, one tactic was to search for foundry operators in Europe which, for environmental reasons, were being forced to leave inner-city sites. In addition to management, they would bring their market with them to east Germany. In some cases, a very high risk has been taken. Given the paucity of interest in the microchip industry, LSI were able to secure a rather loose contract from the THA. They could take the DM 125 million subsidy and walk away in a few years.

It will be many years before the Treuhand's record can be properly evaluated. Will employment and investment guarantees be honoured? Will the weight placed by the THA on industrial and regional externalities be borne out by the evolution of industry in east Germany? For the Treuhand strategy to be deemed a success, it must create a critical mass of viable firms able to compete in the international markets.

8

REFORMING 'SELF-MANAGED' ENTERPRISES IN SLOVENIA

R. Jayashankar

BACKGROUND

History

Slovenia is one of the smaller nations in Europe. Formerly part of Yugoslavia, it is squeezed between the upper reaches of the Adriatic Sea, the Alps and the Pannonian plains. Its population of 1.9 million live in a fertile territory of 20,251 sq km – the size of Wales or the state of New Jersey.

Historical ties of Slovenes with Austria to the north and Hungary to the east were established in the sixteenth century when most Slovene regions were under the control of Habsburgs. With the downfall of the Austro-Hungarian empire at the end of the First World War, a united kingdom of Yugoslavia – Serbs, Croats and Slovenes – was proclaimed in 1918, with Belgrade its capital. Political subordination and economic hardships within the Yugoslav federation then prompted Slovenia to begin building its own statehood. Attempted subjugation by its powerful neighbours during the Second World War further strengthened national feelings of the Slovenes. Yugoslavia became communist in 1945 but broke with Moscow in 1948, developing its own version of socialism.

The last two decades have seen Yugoslavia gradually slipping into political and economic crisis. Slovenes pressed for a looser confederation of states. This proposal was initially thwarted by the federal government. However, Slovenia's first free parliamentary elections in April 1990 pointed clearly towards the formation of a sovereign nation. The declaration by Slovenia of its independence on 25 June 1991 provoked military attack by the Serbian-led Yugoslav army. With the prompt diplomatic intervention of the European Community, the attack was subdued quickly and troops withdrawn. Eventually, on 15 January 1992, after centuries of Habsburg rule and decades of a communist regime, Slovenia was recognized as an independent nation by the international community.

Slovenia shares some common problems with eastern Europe in the transformation to a market economy and political pluralism, although its self-management system combined with (after 1948) an indicative form of central planning makes the adjustment relatively easy.

The communist system has given way to a more liberal democratic system, following which a comprehensive restructuring and stabilization programme is being implemented at both macro- and micro-levels. The shift towards a market-orientated economy implies tougher competitive situations, an impending fall in market share to imports and low profit margins for industrial enterprises. Thus a central element of the reform process is the restructuring of industrial enterprises.

The industrial base of Slovenia

The country's total annual GDP is approximately US $10 billion and its per capita GDP of US $6,200 is nearly double that of Yugoslavia as a whole.

The republic's average annual foreign trade turnover is US $12 billion and accounted for 29 per cent of Yugoslavia's exports in 1990 (with 15 per cent of its population) and 18 per cent of GDP. Nearly 75 per cent of it is with developed industrial countries (60 per cent with EC partners). However, trade with other republics in the former Yugoslavia has fallen away sharply, except to Croatia. Trade relations with Italy, Germany, Austria and Hungary are strong. Approximately 250 Austrian investments in Slovenia are envisaged, the primary interest being in banking, insurance and construction. However, Slovenia still needs markets, especially following the drop in sales to other republics of the former Yugoslavia.

The Slovene economy consists of roughly 12,000 enterprises, 90 per cent of which are small and medium scale (large-scale corporations have never dominated Slovenian economy as in other communist countries). Small enterprises (maximum 10 employees) employ 9 per cent of the 607,000 working population (a rising share), and there has been a rapid growth of self-employed persons, employees in the private sector and small private enterprises. However, large companies still employ 62 per cent of the total.

Manufacturing industry is the strongest economic sector of the Slovene economy, contributing 50 per cent of GNP. The main industries are electrical apparatus and machinery, metal processing, electronics, machine building, automobile production, textiles and garments, leather, wood processing and furniture, and pharmaceuticals. The raw material base of Slovenia is not very extensive. Half of the total land area is covered by forests. Other natural resources are coal, mineral and thermal springs and good agricultural land. For the country's energy requirements there is an adequate supply of power, particularly hydroelectric (with further potential). There is one nuclear power plant and a few thermoelectric power stations. Crude oil is imported mainly from the Commonwealth of Independent States.

The steel industry, machine building, manufacture of transport vehicles, textile and leather industries and base chemicals have experienced the greatest recession. Liquidity has deteriorated because of payment defaults, and there is no legal or personal security in business links with other parts of former Yugoslavia. Thus civil war, politics and economic conditions in Yugoslavia have changed the growth trends of industry and services.

Nevertheless, the Slovenian economy is further advanced than in many nearby eastern European countries. Its strong ties with the West have meant that it has been exposed to market economies – an advantage over other transforming economies. Its sophisticated labour force also distinguishes Slovenia from eastern and central European countries. The work ethic is strong.

THE WORKERS' 'SELF-MANAGEMENT' SYSTEM

The system of workers' self-management was unique to Yugoslavia in the socialist world. Its legal principles were codified between 1950 and 1953 and remained the basis of the system until 1974. Until that time enterprise self-management operated approximately as follows.

An enterprise comprised two legal entities – the *collective* (all permanent workers over 18 years of age, who produced, managed and distributed the income), and the *assets*, which were socially owned by 'all the people' (not by the state or the government).

The collective elected a *workers' council*, to which formal control for economic decision-making was passed if the enterprise membership exceeded 30. The collective had influence through electing the council, making personal proposals or choices in general meetings, or voting in the referenda that were called on most central issues. Large enterprises and multi-plant firms had more complex structures.

The workers' council determined overall policy and general direction. Its primary function was legislative, with the executive role played by a sub-committee it appointed – the board of management – and the director. The council therefore set general aims and ensured that they were carried out by the executive, using a machinery of reports, rules (called 'statutes'), plans and accounts. It could have between 15 and 120 members elected for a two-year term, of whom 75 per cent had to be production workers (initially, the elections were organized by the trade union but the role was later assumed by the outgoing council). A rotation principle was introduced to ensure that there was a fast turnover, with members not sitting for longer than two terms consecutively on any self-management committee.

The board of management, the executive branch of the workers' council, had responsibility for the development and supervision of detailed plans to achieve the general policy goals framed by collective meetings, referenda and by the council. It included the director as *ex-officio* member and had 3–11 members, of whom 75 per cent had to be manual workers. It could appoint specialist committees. Membership of any self-management organs entailed no work exemption, nor higher earnings (except for expenses) but did guarantee freedom from dismissal, transfer or ordinary disciplinary procedures during the term of office.[1]

The enterprise director, appointed by the workers' council, was the principal executive agent. He could only be dismissed during his years of office if he broke the law or if the enterprise was liquidated. The director's legal responsibility for business practices left the collective and the members of the various self-management committees free from legal liability. The director appointed a conventional enterprise hierarchy of managers who were responsible to him in the execution of policy, at the head of which was a 'collegium' of departmental heads.

Thus the system aimed at retaining decision-making at the enterprise level, with employees actively running the enterprises in which they work. They chose, worked closely with and supervised a management team. Workers possessed some of the property rights of ownership in that they had custody and *usufruct* of the assets they managed (the right to use and profit from certain property without damage to it). They could even, in special circumstances, alienate assets through sale. However, workers did not have unlimited rights with regard to the dissolution or change of form of the enterprise. The workers were not the owners in the strict, Western legal sense of the term. Three of the most important tasks for the self-management organs were the schedule of wage distribution, the distribution of net revenue and the adoption of internal statutes.

In principle the Yugoslav system of self-management was, and remains to this day, established by a fundamental distinction between decision-making, to be undertaken by the self-management committees, and execution, which is empowered to the managerial hierarchy. The imperfections of this distinction in practice, and in particular the fact that managerial staff appeared to dominate much of actual decision-making, has been a major theme in Yugoslav literature. It was a principal factor behind the 1974 reforms. These further devolved decision-making authority to the economic units later known as 'Basic Organizations of Associated Labour' (BOALs).[2]

The constitutional system of 1974 sanctioned certain already accepted principles, with the goal of further promoting self-managements, and legally and materially guaranteed the organizations of associated labour. The constitution of 1974 further stipulated that workers are entitled to receive the income of their BOAL, and a personal income for the satisfaction of personal, common and general social needs. The workers themselves establish the principles for the distribution of personal incomes and, in cooperation with other organizations of associated labour, jointly establish criteria for the distribution of income.

Slovenia has therefore never relied on the state as the most prominent form of economic ownership, as in conventional socialism. Self-managed enterprises were free to decide their market strategies and had great freedom in fixing prices and wages and in trading with foreign markets. Slovene enterprises were therefore much more used to markets and marketing, and were much better equipped, than their eastern European counterparts. The central planning system was more 'indicative' than controlling. Large multi-plant enterprises could be developed in most sectors of the economy, and market competition existed. The technical capabilities of many Slovenian enterprises were up to Western standards.

Some problems with the worker self-management system

One of the prime considerations in its development was the efficient management of enterprises. A series of economic instruments was introduced for the purpose of placing enterprises in a position to make rational use of all the factors of production. These included a national system of inter-firm comparisons, using a variety of productivity ratios.

While the system provided good results in the beginning, it later became a barrier to development as it discouraged investment in new and more expensive technology.[3] Workers' councils tended to take a short-term view, and employees took most of the proceeds. The basic way of financing investment therefore became credit approved by the banks on the basis of economic and technological proposals. Because of the great demand for investment resources, interest rates were high and loan periods short so that the annuities were also very high. The banks put a great burden on enterprises. This led to links between the administrative groups in the work organizations and the centre of financial power beyond them, and the influence and social position of the direct producers became weaker. There also appeared a tendency for individual managers to become rich, not on the basis of work but from their status, or because they disposed of social resources free of any control.

PRIVATIZATION

Present institutions and policy

Two government institutions were established in Slovenia in December 1990 (one year before its independence) with the purpose of supervising, structuring and assisting privatization transactions in the Republic. These were:

1 *Agency of the Republic of Slovenia for Privatization* (which has a monitoring and control function), and
2 *Development Fund of the Republic of Slovenia* (which acts as the seller and recipient of the proceeds when shares of socially owned companies are sold, as well as the investor of privatization proceeds).

Both institutions are accountable to the Council of Ministers of the Republic of Slovenia. However, they enjoy a great degree of independence in their operations. The general principles followed by the Agency and the Fund in the implementation of privatization transactions are:

1 competitive and transparent procedures,
2 business and asset valuation on a standard and professional basis, and
3 assuring proportional voting and profit-sharing rights for socially owned companies in the case of joint-venture private (including foreign) investors.

In preparing for privatization, the company and (if appropriate) the foreign partner must follow certain procedures, required by the still-valid Federal Law on Social Capital, and the Company Law, supervised by the Agency for Privatization. These consist primarily of the mandatory business and asset valuation of the company and the rules for tender offers, auctions and public sale of shares through which the Agency tries to ensure the competitiveness and transparency of the privatization process. There are exceptions to the rule of competitiveness in the event that the potential investor has been a long-term contractual joint-venture partner with a domestic company. In that case the Agency adheres to the value assigned by a 'licensed business appraiser' and foreign investors should not expect to get major concessions on this value if there is no competition.

The licensed business appraisal system was set up by the Agency for Privatization. A core group of highly qualified accountants in Slovenia, recognized generally as being experts in the field of valuation and business appraisal, was appointed to form a Valuation Commission. They were granted licences on the basis of their valuation reports by international professional organizations. Their tasks were:

1 to prepare standards and principles for business valuation practice;
2 to prepare training courses and examinations for candidates applying for licences; and
3 to supervise the work of the business appraisers by reviewing their valuation reports.

If a candidate for a licence is not satisfied with the examination results he may appeal to the Agency for Privatization. The Agency will then forward the case to the Board of Examiners of the American Society of Appraisers for review and comment. At present there are 45 licensed business appraisers in Slovenia who have been trained and certified by the Agency.

The government cannot force a company into privatization because neither the government nor the state is owner. The initiative must come from the enterprise. But the Agency has to approve transactions and the creation of joint ventures where a socially owned enterprise contributes assets to the new company. In transactions involving the sale of shares of existing capital stock, the Development Fund (acting on behalf of the state) has the authority to sign the contract with the buyer.[4]

The way to successful acquisitions and joint ventures in Slovenia therefore lies in achieving a consensus among various interests, ranging from the two government agencies, the firm's employees (workers' councils) and management, and sometimes even local communities. When this consensus is achieved, then practically any type of transaction is possible. So far, 20 privatization transactions involving trade sales and management buy-outs have been executed by the Agency. The Privatization Agency and Development Fund would then ensure proper financial restructuring of these enterprises.

The workers' councils of some socially owned enterprises in Slovenia are to be transformed into social boards. They will comprise representatives of the state, creditors (typically the banks) and employees. Such boards will be vested with the power to hire and fire managers and to take other decisions typically made at the level of board of directors in a capitalist firm.

The dilemma of whether to privatize first and restructure later, or vice versa, has been proven in practice to be no dilemma at all. The state is not able to restructure the economy on such a large scale. It is the future owners who will have to undertake the comprehensive restructuring, while the state will have to limit its actions to short-term financial reconstruction. If the state were able to restructure these companies and run them efficiently, it would have done this a long time ago and there would be little need for privatization.[5]

A case study on the work of the Agency and the Fund

The Tobacco Company of Ljubljana (TCL) was established 120 years ago as a state concern. This largest industrial facility in Slovenia has been run for the past four decades within the system of workers' self-management. Accordingly the managing directors and heads of various organizational units were elected by the workers' council, which was chosen by the employees. The council did not interfere with management decisions and in most cases agreed to the proposed policies.

In addition to cigarette production, TCL was also a cigarette wholesaler and had retail outlets in Slovenia, Croatia and Serbia. TCL distributed 80 per cent of all cigarettes consumed in Slovenia. Its profits showed a progressive decline during the late 1980s and early 1990s. Both the national and international market share declined primarily due, it was thought, to the lack of attractive new brands to meet consumers' demands.

TCL's management felt that the company could be put on a sound footing only through a strategic alliance with a big international cigarette manufacturer. Other privatization techniques, such as management and employee buy-outs, sale of the company to financial institutions or individual investors, were not the desired options. Their aims were to produce a new brand of cigarettes, to have access to international markets and to introduce new technology and managerial skills.

The management of TCL identified two potential investors: Reemtsma/Seita from Germany and a large multinational company from the United States. Advice from both the Privatization Agency and the Development Fund was sought relating to the privatization plan, analysis of the offers and negotiating the deal with the winning bidder. The Privatization Agency was legally to approve the transaction, and the Development Fund had to sign the contract with the foreign partner.

Both bidders employed international accounting and auditing companies to appraise the value of the company. On the TCL's side the valuation report of the appraiser, licensed by the Agency for Privatization, was prepared according to Slovenian valuation standards and principles. After the completion of the analytical work, both prospective investors were invited to submit their offers, explaining the financial and commercial arrangements. A detailed plan of action was also sought about developing new products, modernizing technology, marketing strategies, changes in internal organization and developing human resources. During the first presentations it was felt that both proposals were satisfactory from the point of view of further development of the company. However, the offered purchase prices were too low in comparison with the appraised value. After two rounds of negotiations there was a significant improvement in the prices offered.

The selection committee decided in favour of Reemtsma/Seita, proposing a partnership that would preserve the tradition of one of the oldest Slovenian companies. A final draft of a sale contract was prepared and approved by the board of directors of Reemtsma/Seita, by the workers' council of TCL and the boards of the Agency and the Fund.

The structure of the deal consisted of purchase of a 76.5 per cent share of TCL from the Development Fund by Reemtsma/Seita. Firstly, the socially owned company was transformed into a limited liability company with the Development Fund as the only shareholder. During the bidding stage, both bidders were required to make an asset transaction. This involved the purchase of TCL assets by their newly established Slovenia subsidiaries. Following the awarding of the contract, these assets would be cashed in, the old company would be liquidated, and the residual money would go to the Fund. In order to allow the employees of TCL to take advantage of certain benefits expected to be guaranteed in the privatization law once passed, the remaining 23.5 per cent of the shares was reserved by the Fund for the future discount sale or even for free distribution to employees. Foreign purchasers were willing to accept employee-share participation only on the condition that employee shares stayed indivisible. The contract therefore established a new joint-stock company in which individual employees would be shareholders and for which the sole purpose would be to hold and manage the shares of TCL.[6]

To ensure that there would be no redundancies, a modernization plan for TCL was prepared. A minimum of 20 per cent rise in real wages was promised and all fringe benefits were retained. This positioned TCL on the upper-wage-level range of companies. An extensive training programme was proposed to enhance productivity and to introduce new standards of quality for employees. A new seven-member board of directors was nominated. The chairman of the board was the chief executive of the buyer company. Three members of the board were nominated by the foreign shareholders; two of the other three were representatives of employees and one was a representative of the Fund. Specific provisions for corporate governance and minority shareholders' rights were contained in the shareholders' agreement.

TCL took new orders after the acquisition and a new international brand of cigarettes was introduced in Slovenia. However, considerable discontent arose among employees as the work-load was substantially increased, though at present a strong sense of discipline prevails. The managing director retained his job and some new executives were nominated. The board of directors approved the business plans and introduced new incentive schemes. Due stress was also laid on training of managers and production foremen.

The absence of a privatization law

Everyone in Slovenia agrees on the need to privatize socially owned enterprises, but the mode of doing so has evoked much controversy. Thus, although the Agency and the Development Fund have been in operation for two years, a law on privatization has not yet been passed by the Slovene assembly. There may be many reasons for this omission.

Firstly, the timing is wrong. In the extreme turbulence and terror of the civil war next door, and the severe adverse effect on Slovenia – dislocation and recession – a major privatization programme might be very risky. The government will want to keep a handle on the situation at this time since intervention in industry for over-riding national interest reasons may be necessary.

Secondly, there is no settlement yet of the restitution of property to former owners, and that must be cleared up first. Clauses to protect the interests of former owners have been accepted in principle. They entail separating parts of an enterprise, or a portion of the enterprise's capital, and putting them under government supervision pending resolution of the denationalization claim. This also protects future owners of privatized enterprises from later claims by former owners.[7]

Thirdly, there are blocking actions by some former communist officials.

However, it is sensible policy to position all of the legal structure and institutions of a private-sector market before the main privatization takes place, so delay has a benefit. Also the Agency and the Fund are going through a learning process in preparation for the main thrust. The lessons can be fed back into the main policy initiative. It is a cautious approach so that Slovenia, when it decides on the main scheme, will get it right.

It is expected that the forthcoming comprehensive privatization law will mandate the initiation of the privatization process for each company and a definite time schedule will be implemented. It is envisaged that a certain portion of the equity of socially owned enterprises (perhaps up to 20 per cent) will be given to employees free of charge or with substantial discounts. Along with this, the employees may have a first option for an additional 40 per cent of the equity that will otherwise be sold to domestic and foreign investors using traditional privatization techniques. The residual 40 per cent of the equity may be transferred to the Development Fund and a number of other financial institutions (investment companies, pension fund, compensation fund). These institutions would be free to keep or dispose of these shares. New boards of directors representing owners would replace the workers' councils in governing the companies. The full implications of such a law, which is expected to be passed in early 1993, on foreign direct investment are still somewhat unclear. However, there is little doubt that the current legal uncertainty in Slovenia will be greatly reduced when a law is passed.

Two specific privatization options

Two detailed options are being considered by the government.

Firstly, there is a proposal by Dr Joze Mencinger, a prominent Slovene economist, that at least one-third of employees in a self-managed enterprise can purchase from the Development Fund a fixed 10 per cent of the company value in the form of preference shares, at a 50 per cent discount. The state would receive a 2 per cent fixed dividend, paid by the company, with no rights of management. The company itself also would have the right to purchase preference shares within the following 10 years, as would other institutions. At the end of the period any remaining preference shares would be converted to ordinary shares and given to the company.

Furthermore, employees would be able to buy up to a further 10 per cent of the preference shares, the purchase money being left in the company for its development.

If the workers' council of an enterprise decided not to accept either of these two tranches then the enterprise would have to be privatized by a direct method or public auction of all or part of its property, supervised by the Agency for Privatization. If none of these methods succeed, the state would itself attempt the sale.

The Slovene government has argued that the book value of companies will be lower than their actual worth. Leading Slovene economists argue that the 10 per cent 'threshold' for employee participation is too high and that if this proposal were to be adopted few companies would be privatized and would become a burden on the state.

The other proposal under serious consideration, called the 'Umek model', has been made by Dr Jeffrey Sachs, adviser to the Slovenian government. Share vouchers would be distributed free to all citizens rather than being sold to employees at a discount. Citizens would exchange them for shares in mutual funds (unit trusts), which would in turn hold shares in companies. The risk to citizens in holding individual company shares would therefore be reduced.

Four types of mutual funds are projected: an indemnity fund would receive 15 per cent of the value of enterprises being privatized, pension funds 20 per cent, various investment associations 35 per cent – and the remaining 30 per cent would be left in a national fund which would have to sell them within a few years or transfer them to other financial institutions.

Mutual funds would therefore take over all large enterprises and thus gain control over the present management. (Small organizations would be privatized according to Mencinger's model with some minor differences.) The Sachs approach is shock therapy, compared with the gradual approach of Mencinger. It prescribes a centralized blueprint to cover all enterprises, based on size. Its selling point is that it sorts out the tangled legal situation bequeathed by the social ownership system, under which property rights are frequently unclear.

THE BANKING SYSTEM

Slovenian banking has inherited a peculiar feature of the Yugoslav federal system under which enterprises could establish their own banks. Enterprise managers could be represented on the board of their banks. A local bank manager could issue credit to the owned enterprise. There was, however, practically no accountability as the banking system was devoid of checks and balances.

The federal government initiated a process of restructuring the banking system in 1989.[8] However, there were conflicting and vested interests at stake which prevented any effective reform. Enterprises accustomed to soft loans advanced by the banks and inter-enterprise banks were not in a position to survive without credits.

Successful banking reorganization was a necessary condition for a firm basis of the national currency. With independence in Slovenia and the establishment of the Bank of Slovenia as its Central Bank, measures have been initiated for effective credit and monetary policies for optimal liquidity management amongst the banks. The 'Agency for the Rehabilitation and Reorganization of Banks' was created in January 1992, comprising experts from the Bank of Slovenia. This agency has a large task ahead documenting the actual balance of accounts of the country's banks. Its first task is to ascertain the real value of the banks concerned.

The composition of the banking market in Slovenia is fairly unusual. Many have judged it to be monopolistic or oligarchical as the result of the privileged position enjoyed by the Ljubljanska Banka and its affiliated banks. According to a survey conducted by the Bank Association of Slovenia, the Ljubljanska Banka is the parent bank and the entire bank structure of the Ljubljanska Banka accounted for 60 per cent and 90 per cent respectively of the total balance sheet of all Slovenian banks. The total number of commercial banks, including the ones set up after independence, is 30, and they have also begun diversifying the scope of their services. The restructuring of the Slovene economy and the enterprises to a great extent depends on the restructuring policies for the Slovene banks.

Banking problems

The problems facing the Slovenian banks are as follows:

1 *High provision for doubtful loans*. Ljubljanska Banka, which has a 90 per cent share of the Slovenian market, last year posted a provision charge of US $186 million against non-performing, bad loans and off-balance sheet exposure, which resulted in a net loss after tax of US $65 million.
2 *High unit costs of establishing and maintaining independent systems*. The number of employees in most banks is too high and this is linked to business costs.
3 *Temporarily unresolved relations with the National Bank of Yugoslavia*. In addition to the burden of non-performing loans of Slovene banks, the other problem is the claim against the National Bank of Yugoslavia (NBY), based in Belgrade. In the past, any foreign-exchange deposits made by Slovenes to the banks in Slovenia were transferred to NBY. Since independence the National Bank of Yugoslavia has not released these deposits to Slovenia (some economists in Slovenia believe that they have been spent). However, the rejection of the Slovene banks' plea concerning their acute foreign-exchange shortage may be due to the intransigence of the NBY in impounding Slovenia's reserves. The problem is not simple and cannot be laid entirely at the door of the Yugoslav federal government. It also arises from Slovenia's flagging, uncompetitive exporting sector which brings in successively lower foreign-exchange inflows, while the level of domestic government spending remains unaltered.
4 *High investment in the retail network, new office space and information systems*. The Slovenian banks need an inter-banking information system with stored data on their customers, accessible to all banks, which is the accepted banking practice.

Thus the greatest difficulty for the Slovenian banks is that their owners are to a large extent self-management enterprises which themselves have no owners (except the 'whole people') and are often debtors to their banks. The consequence is a large number of bad debts. It is unhealthy for the Ljubljanska

Banka's lending to be controlled by its own client shareholders since this prevents healthy companies with no capital stake in it from obtaining investment funds, which much less deserving cases can access.

Banking reforms

The Law of Central Bank was passed in June 1990 (a Law of Savings Banks is due to be passed early in 1993). The banking reforms were directed at minimizing the adverse effects just mentioned. They should also reduce the expenses of monetary trade, enable more favourable loans and a greater choice of services. Foreign banks do not contribute to this at present. They do not invest in the Slovene economy but only 'export' the foreign currency deposits of Slovenian customers. Only with the help of foreign capital will the Slovenian banks be able to extend their services and to modernize their technology.

The rehabilitation and privatization of banks will also offer the possibility that reformed banks could give loans to companies with a positive credit rating and to those who wish to become the banks' shareholders, thereby changing the bank's loan into their share investment in the bank.

There is a debate on the level of statutory reserves deposited with the Central Bank. The banks' claim is that the interest paid by the Bank of Slovenia does not keep pace with inflation, which under the conditions of restrictive monetary policy negatively reflects on their liquidity.

When Slovene banks and the Bank of Slovenia were cut off from Yugoslavia's foreign-exchange reserves, amounting to some US $2.6 billion, savers were left without their own cash. However, the sale of socially owned apartments to their existing tenants increased Slovenia's external liquidity and foreign-exchange reserves because many savers had their deposits put in safe places abroad, and when the sale, at favourable prices, of 230,000 apartments began, a large amount of these deposits was drawn back to domestic banks. In allowing the privatization of state-owned apartments the government combined its privatization and monetary goals into one.

Monetary sovereignty was established with the introduction of new Slovene currency, the 'tolar' (shortened to 'SIT') on 8 October 1991. The tolar (a Slavic version for the old German 'thaler') was initially fixed at one to one against the (Yugoslav) dinar, but within a few days a dinar was worth only 0.75 SIT.

DEVELOPMENT OF A CAPITAL MARKET AND STOCK EXCHANGE

The absence of the capital market over the past 50 years, and the common ignorance of, and mistrust in, long-term forms of the mobilization of capital, have given way to a range of laws designed to provide for the financial and economic restructuring of the economy. A turning point in the introduction of a capital market into Slovenia came on 12 December 1989, when 33 banks and financial institutions founded the Ljubljana Stock Exchange. At present 25 securities, with a total capitalization of nearly DM 500 million in value, are traded on the Exchange.

The funding statutes of the Exchange restrict its ownership to banks – only they are permitted to buy its shares although other institutions may become members. Discussions are under way to allow other financial intermediaries, such as insurance companies and pension funds, to become shareholders.

Membership of the stock market is open to both public- and private-sector companies, provided they are from Slovenia. There are still limitations on the participation of foreign brokers in stock-market trade. A foreign broker can only become a member of the domestic stock market through the foundation of his own firm in Slovenia. Similarly, securities issued by foreigners are not admitted to the market except those issued by joint-venture firms. However, these limitations may be changed with the anticipated privatization legislation.

Most of the trading (88 per cent) is accounted for by bonds, primarily the bonds of the Republic of Slovenia. In certain periods it was possible to buy the bonds of the republic at a price ensuring a 14 per cent or higher return on maturity. Shares account for an insignificant part of stock-market trade for the time being.

Securities traded on the market can be bought by domestic and foreign investors alike. Investments by foreign persons are not subject to special legal limitations, barring investments in the purchase of immovables. Reinvestment of profits from direct investments are not liable to tax. The repatriation of profits, interest and invested capital is guaranteed by law. Minor limitations do exist still in the repatriation of foreign and domestic securities, where a special permit is required from the Bank of Slovenia. Domestic and foreign investors are both exempt from payment of capital gains tax until the end of 1993.

The present situation on the capital market still leaves much to be desired. The consequences of deficient legislation, and the lack of firms capable of providing good quality services to those interested in participating in the capital market, are sharply felt.

FOREIGN INVESTMENT

The most popular and widely used format of foreign investment in Slovenia is an equity joint venture with a socially owned enterprise. This type of deal is closed directly with the company. However, for the inscription of the new legal entity into the court register, approval by the Agency for Privatization is necessary. Where shares representing social capital are sold, close cooperation with the Agency and the Fund (acting as the seller) is even more important.

Foreign investors are required to contact the Agency or the Fund in the early stages of the process to avoid potential problems in the final stages of negotiation, particularly when the proposed transaction includes complexities such as organizational and financial restructuring prior to the transaction, restitution issues and deferred payment schemes.

The Slovenian attitude is positive and realistic towards foreign investments which are designed to integrate the republic into international economic process and qualitative restructuring of the economy in general. According to the current foreign investment law, foreign capital can be engaged in business in Slovenia in various legal forms:

1 wholly or partially foreign-owned company;
2 contractual joint venture;
3 concession; and
4 a build-operate-transfer agreement.

A company owned by a foreigner may take the form of a joint-stock company, limited liability company or partnership. A special form of partially foreign-owned company can be created under the current Company Law by partial sale of a socially owned enterprise or by raising additional equity capital. In this event, foreign private equity coexists with social capital stock that has no clearly defined owner.

Foreigners can invest in any company on a contractual basis. The foreign investment itself does not change the legal status or ownership structure of the enterprise in which it has been made. Investment capital on a contractual basis in a domestic enterprise does not entitle the foreign partner to ownership rights in the enterprise. He acquires the right to participate in its management and to share in the profits in proportion to his invested capital.

Concessions may also be granted to a foreign investor operating from abroad or through a wholly owned Slovenian enterprise. Although private ownership of natural resources is not allowed, the investment rules permit the granting of a concession to a foreign investor for the exploitation of a given renewable or non-renewable natural resource or public good.

A foreign person may also be allowed to build, manage and exploit for a fixed period of time a certain facility, installation or plant under conditions specified in the permit. Once the contract expires, the facility becomes a public property and is constituted as a public-sector enterprise. The foreign investment law specifies the form which domestic and foreign capital contribution may take. These include cash, tangibles and rights. The law does not specify a minimum or maximum percentage for foreign investment and hence no ratio of domestic to foreign investment is prescribed and all combinations are possible.

Thus the Foreign Investment Law has been strategically drafted to define the different ways in which foreign capital can be invested in Slovenia and the attitude towards these investments. This was not clearly spelt out in the former Yugoslavia and hence investments were haphazard. Establishing a clear policy in relation to a foreign investment is the essence of the strategy. When the Slovenian market economy is entirely open and the risk is transferred to individual companies, such a legislation will be redundant.

So far, most investments are from Italy, Austria, Germany and France. Slovenia is a country where some risk exists and the new legislation will help to safeguard the interests of foreign investors. The priority tasks that Slovenia wishes to carry out with the aid of foreign investments are projects concerning the rehabilitation of Slovene waterways, air and waste management.

SLOVENIAN TAXES

The first reform in the economic field, implemented by the new Slovenian government after the first multi-party elections, was tax reform. In December 1990 Slovenia changed the previous system of 48 direct taxes and social contributions to a system of personal income tax, corporate income tax and three social contributions towards the pension fund, social security and unemployment. The most important Slovenian indirect tax – the sales tax – remained as it was until a new sales tax was adopted in January 1992, in preparation for the introduction of a value added tax.

The tax reform from December 1990 has, through the introduction of the above mentioned taxes, also introduced other changes. Prior to the personal income tax, a complete decentralization of tax policy existed in Slovenia. Within the state only certain taxes and contributions were fixed and the communes had a large degree of autonomy in fixing rates, tax exemptions and many income-tax reliefs. The same was true also for all social contributions (except for the contribution to the pension fund). Such decentralization of the tax policy caused much confusion in Slovenia, especially in Ljubljana, which consisted of five city communes, divided by particular streets.

The second important consequence of the reform was the introduction of an integral budget at the level of state and communes. Prior to this many independent budgets existed in the state and in the communes, with the help of independent taxes. Thus public consumption was indeterminable and the savings measures were inefficient. Public money dispersed through particular accounts was not enough for the special tasks of the state.

The third important consequence of the tax reform is the tax equality of citizens. Prior to the reforms, the citizens of Slovenia were divided according to their profession in special tax groups, with the tax on income ranging between zero and 35 per cent. With the tax reforms introduced in December 1990, Slovenia now has a law on financing public consumption which represents the main law of all public finances.

MANAGEMENT EDUCATION

Development of managerial skill is an integral part of enterprise restructuring. The interaction of central planning, 'self-management' and the market, previously provided an overall conceptual system. Changes in the weighing of different parts of the system will lead to a new balance of forces.[9]

The market dimension will be greatly enhanced. 'Macroeconomic management by government' will replace central planning, and more independent trade unions might be a substitute for 'self-management'. Managers will have to interact with both government and trade unions. Hence management training, to be effective, should be focused on managers performing their role in the new circumstances.

At present in Slovenia long-duration management programmes at the postgraduate level are offered by the University of Ljubljana and the University of Maribor. The International Center for Public Enterprises launched an international MBA programme in 1989 by collaborating with the University of Ljubljana. There are also other training centres offering short-term executive development programmes.

Because of the large number of managers in need of development, there should be short-term executive development programmes in basic areas such as accounting, finance and marketing for middle management and supervisory staff. Strategically orientated programmes should be the focus for top-level management. It is also essential to have relevant cases prepared over a period of time to introduce trainees to situations prevailing in the transition economies. The most effective way to transfer knowledge is through training of capable local management teachers. Most of the existing training institutions rely primarily on foreign faculty. Thus there is a need to train Slovene trainers, as in the end only local faculty will be relevant and most effective.

As the perceived need to address uncertainty in the strategic planning process is assuming importance, a few firms have begun to use 'scenarios' as tools of management. Enterprises should devise contingency plans as part of the strategic planning process, to test strategies against major sources of uncertainty. In the restructuring process of the Slovene enterprises, 'scenarios' can be a powerful device for taking account of uncertainty in making strategic choices. Also, decision support systems, which deal with unstructured decisions through the facility to provide answers to 'what if' and 'goal seek' questions, can be extremely useful in such situations. In the transformation process of Slovene enterprises, such approaches can be of special relevance.[10]

CONCLUDING REMARKS

Slovenia, unlike its neighbouring republics from the former Yugoslavia, has not allowed nationalism to prevail over pragmatism. Efforts are being directed towards establishing an export-orientated industry structure, to be achieved through privatization, liberalization, economic transformation and restructuring. Where the practice of self-management has been abandoned it has resulted in a better work ethic and improvements in productivity.

Restructuring and privatization of socially owned enterprises, coupled with the growth of private business units, will accelerate the growth of the economy. Speedy restructuring and internalization of Slovene enterprises will be faster once the privatization law is passed. Private property is gaining recognition and the existing social enterprises are being transformed into companies with share capital. The process of privatization has commenced. The introduction of a securities market has facilitated the transition from loans to venture capital investments.

The Slovene economy has already gained a considerable foothold in the European economic arena. The relations with western Europe are very important for Slovenia's further development. In the longer term, Slovenia hopes to become a member of the European Community. The aim of becoming closer to Europe in the monetary field has been achieved through introduction of the Slovene national currency and liberalization of the exchange rate. The range of economic measures, such as the liberalization of imports, the restrictive monetary policy and the changed role of the Bank of Slovenia, will support the development of a competitive and export-orientated market economy. The work carried out by institutions, enterprises and the Central Bank serves to reassure the international community and foreign investors that Slovenia is stable. Given the desired accessibility to exports, finance and markets, confidence and stability can be a permanent feature in this part of Europe.

9

RESTRUCTURING DURING THE CIVIL WAR IN MOZAMBIQUE

Salomão Munguambe

BRIEF OVERVIEW OF MOZAMBIQUE

Mozambique is situated in the southern part of Africa. It shares common borders with South Africa, Tanzania, Zambia, Zimbabwe, Malawi and Swaziland. It has an area of 786,000 sq km, the size of Turkey. The population is about 14 million, the majority of whom are peasants living in the countryside (the 1980 census showed that 85 per cent of the active population were engaged in agriculture, 6 per cent in industry and 2 per cent in commerce), with many strongly diverse ethnic groups.

Mozambique, a Portuguese colony since 1490, achieved its independence in June 1975, through the military efforts of the liberation movement Frelimo under its then leader Samora Machel. Immediately before independence there were nine months of transition government composed of Mozambicans and Portuguese. Then, until 1986, it was a Marxist socialist country with a centrally planned economy and widespread state ownership.

However, during this period since 1975, and especially after 1981, a guerrilla group called Renamo has been trying to oust the Frelimo government. This civil war, which has devastated the country and has created vast numbers of refugees, now seems at an end. In August 1992, after two years of negotiation, President Joaquim Chissano, leader of the Frelimo government, reached agreement with Alfonso Dhlakama, leader of the Renamo rebels, and a cease-fire took effect on 16 October 1992.

One result of the civil war is that Mozambique's GDP per capita is less than US $200, which makes it one of the world's poorest countries. The life expectancy at birth is 46.6 years, and the rate of illiteracy is 70 per cent. International aid is vital, and accounts for 25 per cent of Mozambique's food consumption. More is now needed because of the renewed drought. The country has large deficits both in trade and in its external current balance.

During the first five years of independence there was a mass exodus of about 80,000 Portuguese, many of whom were skilled workers, managers and owners of enterprises. Virtually the entire educated population left, including those in the vital middle and upper levels of the bureaucracy who had run the country. For example, of 487 technical staff in the Ministry of Finance, only 13 remained after independence. All 28 regional offices were left unattended. Abandoned farms, commercial and manufacturing enterprises were commonplace. The Portuguese went back to Portugal for many reasons, one of which was the fear of vengeance from the blacks.

During the 1975–80 period there was much emphasis on education (literacy rose from 7 per cent to 30 per cent during this period), and on health care, in which there was less dramatic progress. Real improvements, however, were being made, with the help of large amounts of foreign aid, in spite of the extremely unfavourable legacy of the past. Political cohesiveness was being achieved.

Then, between 1981 and 1986, the civil war intensified, and natural calamitics – floods, drought and storms – resulted in a most serious setback to the economy. Progress was reversed. Over 1980–6 the GDP declined 40 per cent. Around 1.6 million people were displaced by the war, and by 1991 it is estimated that about 900,000 people had died. There was huge physical damage and 10 million people (70 per cent of the population) were living in absolute poverty.

This period also introduced much help from abroad. The IMF and World Bank programmes began in 1984, which marked the beginnings of recovery.

The year 1987, following the assumption of Joaquim Chissano as President in 1986, saw the introduction of some degree of economic liberalization and of some cautious political reform. A free press was introduced, and an independent judiciary. The Economic Recovery Programme 1987–90 showed considerable success (as will be described later), and with the cease-fire the future prospects now look good.

THE SITUATION FOR ENTERPRISES DURING THESE PERIODS

Pre-1975

During the colonial period enterprises were privately owned and the countryside was dominated by big concerns employing forced labour. Even after the abolition of the system of forced labour, which happened after the beginning of the armed struggle against colonialism, peasants were still exploited by the fixing of very low prices for raw materials and commodities produced by them and sold to big companies.

Private enterprise was the fundamental form of organization for both production and distribution. There were a few public enterprises, in transport for example. Public bodies were supposed to control abuses in fixing prices, but most were simply economic coordination boards. And there was some attempt at regulation to adjust supply and demand.

1975–80

From 1975, since there were no experienced Mozambican owners or managers, the state was forced initially to 'intervene' in, and subsequently to take over and to manage, almost every economic unit, from small shops to big companies with branches abroad. Intervention was the only way to secure the normal functioning of enterprises at a time when there were deliberate attempts at economic paralysis. Most people had seen private enterprise as an instrument of oppression (to enrich the Portuguese settlers). Private enterprises were in consequence much despised.

There was during this period much foreign aid, from Sweden (large grants), the Soviet Union (military aid and commercial loans), East Germany (commercial loans and experts) and Cuba (experts). The amount, however, was too much, far greater than the country could absorb with its limited capabilities at that time. But the influences were strong.

In 1977 the government formally decided to adopt state socialism. State enterprises came into being, and cooperatives were formed. Frelimo's attitudes and policies towards economic organization, as identified through their statements and texts during the armed struggle for independence, were:

1 Colonial companies are a system of economic organization which depend upon force. Private enterprises are associated with exploitation.
2 In the zones liberated from colonial oppression, people should organize themselves into cooperatives.
3 New forms of economic organization through state ownership will produce better results for the people.
4 It will be necessary to establish a central organ for management control.
5 All workers are called to participate actively in discussions and solutions of all kinds of problems in each enterprise. Workers at all administrative levels will have a decisive influence in all matters from production to distribution.

The administrative commissions to implement these policies faced extremely difficult problems – a very bad financial situation, the exodus of technicians and those with most education, generalized disorganization and the incapacity of the state to organize and to define tasks for every enterprise. To recover from colonialism and the armed conflict, to reorganize and to manage enterprises in the manner recommended by Frelimo, was extremely hard.

In Decree 17/77 of 28 April 1977 the government issued some important rules for the organization and functioning of state-owned enterprises. They were to be one of the principal elements in the establishment of a socialist society and of planned economic development, to meet the basic needs of the people. They would be directed by the state through the National Commission Plan, by provincial planning commissions and through National Directorates within ministries, in a hierarchy of levels. Each level had consultative councils whose job was to coordinate the implementation of party and state policies. Objectives and targets would be defined in general terms by the ruling party, Frelimo, and detailed annually in the Central Plan.

Until 1991, the constitution of Mozambique assigned to the Frelimo party the task of 'guiding and supervising the activities of state agencies in order to ensure that the state policy is in conformity with the people's interests'. So party cells were installed in all state institutions, and their members participated in the discussion and implementation of the national plans at all institutional levels. Their influence was very strong.

Central planning therefore had its effect on the functioning of every enterprise through a hierarchy of commands, as in the army. The instructions covered both broad targets and the detailed means by which the different targets should be achieved. In most situations, however, the central authorities extended their functions beyond the possibilities of feasibility. The mechanisms of price control never worked properly, and the objectives of efficiency and control to meet people's needs were not as effective as had been desired.

The social obligations of enterprises were very significant and costly. The main target of enterprises was seen as benefiting the workers, by transforming and using their capabilities. Reorganization through laying off workers was not possible. Enterprises had to provide restaurants, creches and sports facilities, as well as offices for the party cells.

Boards of directors were set up for the larger enterprises, and the general director of each enterprise was nominated by the minister of the government department responsible, although the workers could influence both the nomination and the appointment through their opinions on the behaviour of the candidates. But general directors were in a difficult position because they received strict vertical commands directly from the ministries, and also proposals and pressure from the workers below, well organized in party cells.

In addition to some 300 state-owned enterprises, mostly in light industry and the rest in heavy industry such as metal, paper and petroleum refining, during the period 1975–85 there were also 'people's shops' (*lojas do povo*), supposed to belong to all people, and cooperatives. Because of the mass exodus of the former white owners of local shops (*cantineiros*) new shops had to be set up to distribute basic goods, especially food.

1980–3

After five years of progress since the end of colonialism, in 1980 the President launched an organizational and political offensive, a kind of cultural revolution. Its aims were:

1 to decrease the subsidized prices established by the state;
2 liberalization of prices;

3 progressive denationalization;
4 hard work;
5 to encourage the growth of small and medium-sized firms in non-strategic sectors;
6 to open discussions with IMF and the World Bank; and
7 to stop political movements against socialism.

A series of Decrees followed. In the Decree 2/81, 30 September 1981, sole responsibility for decision-making was given to general directors of enterprises. Boards of directors were in future to be only for consultative purposes. State enterprises achieved economic and operative independence. Managers and workers were to have a material interest in the success of their enterprises. Enterprise profits were to become the principal source of revenue of the state. Worker assemblies were deprived of power, though a general director could consult them if he wished.

The unrest in the early 1980s, however, forced the government into drastic measures of austerity, and led to more centralization. The role of commercial departments in enterprises responsible for buying and selling was considerably diminished. Further structures for controlling enterprises were introduced in the National Commission Plan and in the Central Bank. An *ad hoc* body of representatives of the economic ministries controlled the execution of monthly targets for the strategic sectors (imports/exports, mining, textiles, sugar, food oil, soap, beverages, fishing, cement, petroleum), and allocated resources in accordance with the needs of different sectors and enterprises. Most profits were channelled to the state budget and the rest were used for reinvestment. It was a wartime-type measure in which the state gave not only the targets for production but also allocated the raw materials, received the output and then decided the distribution in accordance with its own criteria.

Targets were, however, difficult to achieve. Because of state ownership, workers were not interested in the results of their enterprises. Their monthly salaries were assured, despite annual losses. Also the central plan and the Direction Units in ministries retained their power in controlling state-owned enterprises (accounts had to be presented weekly), while worker assemblies, despite having lost their powers of decision, kept their influence through dependency upon the hierarchy of Frelimo party appointees.

The civil war was a tragedy. It severely disrupted but did not prevent the establishment of a central planning system, or the formation of state-owned enterprises and cooperatives. What it has prevented is effective results from such changes being of benefit to most of the people of Mozambique, because of the territory controlled by Renamo and because of the destruction of some railways and roads. Many of the gains of the first five years since independence, in education and health care, were lost.

The state had taken control of all large enterprises, and by 1983 the public sector accounted for 70 per cent of industrial production.

1983–6: the first stages of restructuring

In 1983, through economic and social directives, the government began to encourage the inflow of foreign capital for import substitution and for exports. This policy was consolidated in the Law 4/84 of 18 August 1984. Under it the state guarantees the protection of foreign property. Nationalization would only take place exceptionally, on the basis of national interest, and with 'just and equitable compensation transferable in free convertible currency'.

As incentive, the state guarantees the transfer of exportable profits and of re-exportable capital, and exempts from customs duties imports for investment purposes, and raw materials for export goods not available locally. There are also tax holidays for up to ten years, and income-tax deductions for expenses incurred in training Mozambique cadres.

From 1983 the state also encouraged the development of privately owned small and medium-sized enterprises, to complement the state sector. There were special incentives through credit for investment and for raw materials and spare parts. The purpose was to promote local industrial units that could easily transform raw materials to help solve the basic needs of the rural population at low prices and distribution costs, and to achieve a better balance between the countryside and the cities.

1986–91: the Economic Recovery Programme, liberalization and restructuring

In 1986, after 10 years of failure to reach the initial goals set by the ruling party Frelimo, the breakdown of the social services which had been built up earlier, the overgrown bureaucracy in government and the rise in state subsidies – all due to the civil war and to natural disasters but also to the unduly rigid central planning system – the new government of President Chissano began thinking of a better strategy for state enterprises.

The result was the three-year Economic Recovery Programme 1987–90 (the ERP was signed in 1986) and the World Bank's rehabilitation programme (soft loans) for infrastructure, institutional development and aid to small and medium-sized enterprises. Some programmes still continue. The ERP, which was based on the IMF's measures for stabilization, had the following aims:

1 to halt the steady fall in economic activity;
2 by 1990 to initiate a progressive recuperation of the vital sectors of the economy;
3 to reduce the deficits of the state budget; and

4 to reduce the debts of the banking system.

After the steep decline of previous years, GDP grew some 4 per cent in 1987–8, but subsidies to state-owned enterprises had begun to represent a significant burden to the budget, some 6 per cent of current expenditure. However, under the ERP it was decided that 1993 will mark the gradual elimination of these subsidies (except that, because of social pressure, subsidies on sugar, infant milk, maize and flour will continue for some while). This reduction should force state-owned enterprises to become more competitive with the private sector, which does not receive any subsidies.

However, the ERP has also led to new fiscal and price policies to stimulate private enterprises to reinvest their profits, especially in small and medium-sized firms that can easily generate new employment. Grants are given to enterprises that use local raw materials and inward investment was encouraged with guarantees concerning the repatriation of profits and incentives for reinvestment.

The ERP required the independence of state-owned enterprises from the state budget, and as a result they have become more autonomous financially and managerially. State enterprises were also allowed to issue bonds for external financing, as in the private sector, and they were also permitted to engage in mergers and other forms of participation with any enterprise. 'The market', the use of money, prices and profit have become the criteria of management. Although ownership of state enterprises remained with the state, the directors and workers were allowed to share in their profits. Managers no longer seek solutions from the ministries for their problems.

One problem apparently still unresolved (in 1992) is the role of the party organization within state-owned enterprises. These enterprises are supposed to concentrate their attention on mobilizing all managers and workers to increase efficiency and to play a leading role in seeking solutions. Party cells are primarily meant to use political means of persuasion, although they interfere in all management decisions.

But for party members to understand matters of production, quality of goods, productivity, finance and profitability they should have at least minimal qualifications. They do not have a clear picture of the economy as a whole, generally do not understand their own enterprises, and many are unclear of their role. So the question has been raised: what kind of education should a cell secretary have? Since President Chissano has rejected Marxism, do they have a role at all? The answer now emerging is that they have no role.

Further developments in 1991

State-owned enterprises not working in strategic sectors are being reorganized with a view to conversion to wholly or partially owned private enterprises, through public bidding. Foreign concerns have been invited either to take over or to participate in such enterprises. Already the largest sugar plant in Mozambique (Sena Sugar Estates) has been retaken by its former owners and is being managed by them. The remaining 'intervened' enterprises not taken into state ownership earlier were also to be disposed of, through a bidding system.

A CASE STUDY IN ELECTRICAL GOODS

The enterprise used as a case study has some 300 employees engaged in electrical installations and in the sale of electrical goods. It is based in Maputo, the capital, with branches in Beira, the second city, and Nampula, the third largest city. It was formed out of 13 mergers before independence.

When the Portuguese departed it was abandoned in extreme disorganization, and crucial accounting documents were missing. It became an 'intervened' organization, prior to being taken over by the state. It was expected that this enterprise would supply all of the construction sector, especially at the state level, and it was planned that output would increase by 30 per cent per annum.

In 1977 a general director was appointed by the ministry, with a board of directors. After 1981 the board became purely advisory. The enterprise has three departments: (1) projects, works, electrical installations and selling; (2) finance and administration; and (3) control of the two branches in Beira and Nampula.

Until 1989 the enterprise was closely controlled by the state, through regular reporting to the National Directorate within the Ministry of Construction and Waters. After that time these controls had no effect on the enterprise other than to make sure that the general policy for the sector was being fulfilled. This general policy for electrical energy and fuel was defined by the Economic and Social Directives of the ruling party Frelimo as being strategic for the whole country.

The principal client was the state, through individual ministries. The main problem was getting customers to pay. By 1989 the enterprise had some 700 debtors, of which other state enterprises and the ministries were the most important. There was no obligation on state clients to pay their bills.

Moreover, the enterprise lacked skilled workers. Only the general director and the head of finance had university degrees. The engineering department had no skilled workers. There was no marketing undertaken. Heavy losses were incurred, and the enterprise made no contribution to the state budgets. The planned 30 per cent per annum increase in output was not achieved. Because this was a state-owned enterprise, and the largest in this sector of activity, there was little incentive to work hard and a lack of aggressiveness to improve the situation.

The enterprise is now in the process of being privatized.

EFFECTS OF THE ECONOMIC RECOVERY PROGRAMME

Any positive effects from the restructuring described above have not been fed through to the people of Mozambique. The already rich have benefited most. To achieve real peace is crucial if the benefits are to become widespread. Unless there is an effective cessation of the fighting and banditry, restructuring cannot be effective, and Mozambique will not have the capacity to use the measures introduced by IMF and the World Bank for the interests of the people. But the prospects now look better than at any time since liberation.

Mozambique remains extremely poor and illiterate (in 1987 only 47 per cent of state employees, including those in state-owned enterprises, were literate). The majority of the population are in the countryside, yet regional organizations are not well developed (under the Portuguese there were no 'district officers' as in some other colonial territories), coordination to achieve effective action has been absent, and communication with the centre remains inadequate except through the Frelimo party apparatus. However, the United Nations Development Programme has a major three-year project to assist in the improvement of local organizations, working with the National Directorate for Local Administration in the Mozambique government, which is part of the Ministry of State Administration.

There is still a lack of flexibility in state enterprises, and much economic mismanagement. Decisions take a long time. Practical results from the liberalization of trade, prices, credit and foreign investment cannot be expected for four to five years. The inheritance of the colonialist period – obsolete machinery and production processes, inadequate infrastructure – has not been overcome. The quality of goods remains poor, prices too high and international competitiveness weak.

To overcome these problems one has to rethink all management structures from top to bottom, to avoid the dispersion of economic power between managers, party workers and trade unions, to resolve the contradictions between the demands of the ERP and the real capabilities of the enterprises, and between the present social obligations of enterprises and the need to become more business-minded and efficient. However:

1. The cease-fire has yet to be proven. Gangs of bandits still roam the country. Once true peace is achieved it will take time to rebuild the economic infrastructures.
2. Some of the largest exporting industries are in the countryside where the war still has its effects.
3. The change from a one-party state to a multi-party democracy, as promised by President Chissano, with no previous experience in the country as guide, will create uncertainties for foreign investors.
4. Most enterprises have large debts, either to the banks or to private creditors.
5. There is no money for start-ups of new enterprises.

6 State-owned enterprises are still seen by their managers and workers as like any other public office. They never commence work on time. They have neither interest in nor enthusiasm for improved results.
7 There is still a great shortage of skilled workers and technicians.

Restructuring of enterprises continues and has a high priority. Some enterprises are being sold through bidding. Many new small enterprises have been formed, especially in exporting and importing. The market system still requires a much broader participation. New initiatives were launched in April 1992 at a seminar organized by the Ministry of Industry and Energy designed to introduce new technology in industry, to improve organization and management and to re-capitalize enterprises, with the state being concerned only with strategic development of the economy.

CONCLUSIONS

The main lesson from the experience of Mozambique is that although much can be done in terms of revitalizing the economy after centuries of colonial rule, to be effective a country needs peace.

Pragmatic responses were needed to respond to the worsening economic situation, with party dogma taking second place. From 1986 President Chissano has provided this kind of leadership.

There is a need for self-discipline among state organizations. If the state is a customer, albeit of a state-owned supplier, the state should pay its bills on time like any other customer – and should set an example in so doing.

Motivation is crucial. In enterprises this comes down to good management, and to clarity about who is in charge. Mozambique cannot afford to have a parallel hierarchy, with party functionaries doubling up. If it is now agreed that they no longer have a role this should be recognized in organizational change. Everyone must work effectively, to earn his or her keep, and for the sake of the future of Mozambique.

Part III

THE SOCIALIST GROUP OF STATES

10

THE PEOPLE'S REPUBLIC OF CHINA: SOCIALISM WITH A DIFFERENCE

Gu Yang

INTRODUCTION

History

China's 5,000 years of culture and history have left a legacy in its people which has powerful influences today. The most relevant period, however, starts in 1949 with the overthrow of Chiang Kai-shek and the rise to power of the Communist Party under the leadership of Mao Tse-tung. Before the split with the USSR in 1960, the Soviet planning system had become firmly entrenched in China, and a complete system of state ownership and control had been introduced.

The country experienced great forces of hope, fervour, destruction and chaos during these years. The losses were devastating. After Mao Tse-tung's death in January 1976, the leadership alternated between periods of immense power and sudden eclipse. Deng Xiaoping was dismissed as Secretary-General of the Communist Party in 1960, reinstated in 1973, and was eclipsed again by the Gang of Four in April 1976 following Mao's death.

With his reinstatement in 1977 he then assumed the position of China's effective leader (Hua Guofeng was the titular head and Mao Tse-tung's successor). In December 1978, at the Third Plenum of the Eleventh Central Committee, he launched the great reform movement – the 'four modernizations' – which built upon ideas put forward by premier Chou En-lai in his last government report in 1975. These reforms were not undertaken for ideological reasons (Deng Xiaoping is not a liberal) but for pragmatic ones, because he perceived the need for fundamental change. His earlier support for incentives, following the disaster of the Great Leap Forward, had proved to be successful.

In his speech of January 1992 he called for more rapid and bolder reforms, including the liberation of ideas and freedom from the ideological strait-jacket of the past. This speech has brought forth a surge of new concepts and debates in the media, in the literature and among academics, and has released new energy and drive in the reform movement.

The development of reforms

Since 1979 the Chinese economy has gone through major structural and institutional reforms. These changes can be summarized as:

1 expansion of the market mechanism in resource allocation;
2 the shift from an extensive, broadly based development strategy to an intensive, more targeted, strategy; and
3 the 'open door' policy for foreign investment.

On the use of the market mechanism, during the 30 years before 1978 the Chinese economy had operated under a centralized command system. The state acted as the market and allocated investment resources, the means of production, the supply of raw materials and the employment of human resources. It also took full responsibility to distribute the finished products. Despite rapid industrialization and economic growth, this centralized allocation system resulted in a misallocation of resources and low economic efficiency.

Since 1978 a market system has gradually been developing. The control and management systems have changed from central planning alone to a dual system under which both market and planning mechanisms are applied.

To shift from a mandatory system to market orientation, and from administrative control to competition, the authorities have taken the initiative over the last 13 years to reduce the extent of planned prices and allocations. Markets now control two-thirds of prices and allocations.[1]

Secondly, there has been a shift from an extensive development strategy to an intensive one. A characteristic of the command economy is its emphasis on quantity rather than quality, and on the rate of growth rather than the achievement of a balanced growth according to market requirements. Investment programmes favoured heavy industry at the expense of light industry and agriculture.

However, since 1978 the authorities have emphasized that the main source of growth should come from science and technology. A series of medium- to long-term development plans for those sectors have since developed.[2]

The 'open door' policy is designed to integrate the Chinese economy into the world economy and to encourage the foreign direct investment which will bring capital and technology for China's drive for modernization. Over the past 13 years, US $80 billion has been utilized in infrastructure and technology transfer.[3]

These structural changes have necessitated widespread institutional changes in agriculture, in enterprises, in commerce and distribution networks, in financial systems, the price system, the planning system and the system of foreign trade management. According to the director of the Economic Reform Commission, Mr Gao, these reforms can be divided into the following stages:[4]

1978–84 There was both rural area reform and the expansion of enterprise decision-making power in the cities. The policy measures include increasing the purchasing price of agriculture produce and contracting out land. In industry, enterprises were given more autonomy in decision-making and could keep part of the profit.

1984–8 Reform was concentrated on the enterprise sector. During this period, the 'contract' system (under which managers endeavoured to fulfil a contract reached with the government, including tax rates) was practised by 90 per cent of state-owned enterprises. The share ownership system was also tested experimentally on a selected basis.

1988–92 The reforms were deepened during this period. They concentrated on the following areas:

a) to separate government administration from enterprise management;
b) to correct the sectoral imbalance between primary and secondary industries, and between industry and service sectors; and
c) to reform the government function, for example from mandatory planning to guidelines, from micro to macro, from administration to policy control.

During the period 1988–92 the focal point for reforms was the state enterprise sector. By the end of 1989 there were more than 10,000 such enterprises, some 1.2 per cent of the total number. However, they had contributed 55 per cent of the total industrial value and 70 per cent of corporate taxation.[5] A collapse of this sector would mean the collapse of the whole economy. It would threaten the political and economic survival of the country.

In contrast to the eastern European reforms, the Chinese government policy towards the big and medium-sized enterprises is to strengthen and revive, not through privatization, but through reforming the role of the enterprises under the public ownership. The central issue is to free enterprises from government intervention at the micro level, to give enterprises full autonomy in production, investment decisions, finance, production, sales, etc., so that they will become independent entities operating in the market situation.

The structure of enterprises in China

At present there are four types of ownership in China:

1 *State*: state ownership, within the central planning and allocation systems;

2 *Collective*: including those under 'township' control in the rural areas and cooperatives in the cities, all of which are outside of the state planning and allocation systems, and which range from completely publicly owned to 'almost private';
3 *Private*: including 'one-man', 'household' family businesses and partnerships; and
4 *Foreign ownership*: 100 per cent foreign and joint ventures.

Table 10.1 Structure of Chinese enterprises: end-1989

State-owned	*Collective*	*Township and individual*	*Foreign*	*Total*
100,000	1,740,000	6,124,000	7,000	7,971,000

Source: *People's Daily*, 27 November 1990.

The above categorization is not quite what it appears to be. With the further liberalization following the Deng Xiaoping speech of January 1992, it transpires that some unknown number of enterprises in the 'collective' sector were only categorized as such for ideological reasons. In fact they are privately owned, although with some control from local authorities.

Between 1978 and 1990, the total share of industrial value (output at 'factory gate' prices, not value added) by the state sector had decreased by 23 per cent to 55 per cent of the total. There have been correspondingly large increases in other sectors.[6]

Industrial value in the collective sector has increased 11.5 times during this period to nearly 40 per cent of the total. The 'township' sector in particular has grown rapidly, especially and most dramatically in Guang Dong and Fujian provinces, the former associated with the proximity of Hong Kong and the latter with Taiwan, and both driven significantly by ethnic Chinese from abroad.

Private 'household' businesses have also grown dramatically, and many have diversified into high-technology activities, including computer software, for example. But their share remains small (with some 21 million persons, 0.2 per cent of the population).

These developments have been associated with the opportunities provided by inefficiencies and failures of state-owned enterprises and of central planning, and with the great encouragement and support given personally by Deng Xiaoping to areas and to enterprises outside of the state planning system.

THE PROBLEMS OF STATE-OWNED ENTERPRISES

Throughout the 1980s, economic efficiency in the big and medium-sized state-owned enterprise sector continuously declined. Between January and May 1992, 34.9 per cent of state enterprises were reported as making losses. They have grown to Yuan 14.2 billion (US $2.8 billion) annually, an increase of 8.5 per cent compared with the same period in 1991. Among all loss-making enterprises, 52.2 per cent are central-government-controlled state enterprises, and 46.2 per cent are local-government-controlled.[7] The losses have been a great burden on the state budget.

The causes of those losses are complicated. There are two main categories. The first is due to the distorted price and material allocation system, referred as the 'policy losses'. These include the social costs imposed on state enterprises which in the West are part of separate state or private budgets (health, education, welfare). The second cause is poor management and inefficiency, which is referred as the 'management loss'. The two are not, however, independent of each other.

Since 1980, the central issue of enterprise reform has been to free enterprises from government interference – one of the 'policy losses'. Despite laws and regulations to the contrary, government interference at various levels has continued. They range from large-scale political matters to small economic controls, like the money spent on entertaining customers.

According to a survey in ChunChing municipality (one of the biggest in the south-west), interference has taken a new form, although typical of what went before. On top of numerous inspections, assessment sessions and political studies, enterprises now have to attend endless conferences and join various societies and associations. More importantly they must pay conference registration fees, membership fees and donations of all kinds.

When enterprises are allowed to keep part of the profit earned, government units want to claim a share. Over the past two years, expenditures of the five bureaux of the ChunChing municipal government have each exceeded their incomes by Yuan 200,000–600,000. These deficits have been financed by forcing enterprises to pay 'fees' and donations. Last year, five enterprises had to attend 163 conferences and paid Yuan 129,000. A government unit could make a net profit of hundreds of thousands Yuan in a single conference! Since the 1980s, numerous societies and associations have been set up; many of them have become the vehicle for government units to rob enterprises. The funds were spent on fringe benefits, bonuses and extravagant banquets. This has damaged the enterprises and has bred corruption.[8]

Instead of being the supporters and promoters of the reform, government departments – for pursuing their own interests – have often become obstacles. The Beijing Sheet Cutting plant is an example. Construction began in 1977 with Yuan 105 million investment and 900 work-force. It was designed to be the only plant to supply the whole country with cut iron sheet (at that time, cut sheet was an item of state allocation). In 1986, when the plant was near completion, iron sheet was no longer subject to state allocations. End-users throughout the country were allowed to import the sheet. Some local governments set up their own cutting plants. As the result, the Beijing plant has managed to obtain contracts of only 90,000 rolls a year. The plant makes serious losses.

In 1989 the Beijing Motor Manufacturing Group approached the cutting plant for a merger. This would have provided an opportunity for its survival. However, their proposal was rejected by the government department in charge. Most of the equipment and machinery in Beijing Sheet Cutting is now idle; some has gone rusty. This modern plant now relies on making cold drinks, storing grain and raising fish (by using the cooling pond) for survival.[9]

Why do government departments feel reluctant to let go the enterprises under their control? Why do they still have such power over them? Firstly, because government departments see the number of enterprises under them as their power base. A merger would mean the loss of a big enterprise to another government department.

Secondly, under public ownership in China, nobody is responsible for the efficient use of state assets. It does not make much difference to government departments whether an enterprise makes a loss or a profit.

Thirdly, government departments still retain the power over investment decisions and finance. Until July 1992 mergers and take-overs were also subject to their approval. However, it is extremely difficult at present to separate the government from the enterprise until ownership rights are clearly defined. So long as the government decides investment and controls finance, enterprises cannot be fully responsible.

To address this problem, the July 1992 budgetary reforms and new regulations on separating the government from its enterprises have removed these two powers from government departments, although whether it will succeed remains to be seen. A clause in the July regulation clarifies the share of financial responsibilities among the decision-makers. An 'investor's responsibility system' is being implemented.[10]

Reforms in the state-owned industry sector in the 1990s

The government's policies to revive the state enterprise sector are based on matters external to enterprises and on internal management within the enterprises. External measures are mentioned later and include separating government administration from enterprise management, establishing a comprehensive market structure, reducing the financial burden and financial claims on enterprises and correcting sectoral imbalances.

Internally, the government has called on enterprises to turn to the markets for profit, to improve quality and efficiency and to bring out their full potential and initiative (including those suppressed by the planning system).

Enterprises should work hard, it is now said, on product design and changing product mix to respond to demand. As the reform deepens, changes are beginning to take place in the following three main areas, although progress is slow.

1 In the past, enterprises were competing for the allocation of government investment funds, for key inputs and subsidies. Their only worry was to fulfil the production quota; marketing and sales were irrelevant. Now they have to obtain everything from the market. This does not come easy because they now have to compete with other producers on product design, mix, quality and variety. They also have to market and sell their products themselves.

Mr Bao, the plant manager of the Shanghai Analysis Instruments, said that in the past most of his time had been spent in and out of the government departments. Now he has to work hard to study the market. In order to catch the market, he has reorganized his plant by reducing administration staff and expanding the R & D and sales departments. In the past, distribution of the products was carried out by a girl in a half day. Now a sales force of 80 have to spend more than 200 days a year on the road in every part of China.

Another joint-venture manager said that in the past, at least one-third of his time was spent on meetings, assessment and study sessions run by the bureaux and receiving inspection teams from them. Now most of his time is spent with customers. The boss has changed. All managers have agreed that the efforts to change enterprise behaviour are also dependent on the government reducing its interference.[11]

The market has put pressure on enterprises but also has brought opportunities and vitality to enterprises. The An Yang Iron and Steel plant was set up in 1958. For 21 years it barely broke even. By 1979 its accumulated loss reached Yuan 1.5 billion (1,500 million). The five-year contract has pushed it to the market. After a serious study on the production process, the enterprise has invested in updating technology in key processes. It has also changed the product mix, improved quantity and initiated a sales promotion campaign by offering fixed selling prices and free delivery. After 21 years of bottle-feeding by the state, the enterprise has finally stood on its own feet. In 1990, the production reached 900,000 tons and it paid tax of Yuan 200 million.[12]

2 The internal reforms on work, wage systems and personnel management are most sensitive and difficult tasks. The conservatives see them as 'the return of capitalism'. A veteran worker described it as 'after 40 years of socialism, capitalism came back overnight'. Some feared that workers would be thrown out in the street suffering from hunger and cold as was the case pre-1949. Others worried that this would change the nature of equality among the employee and employers. Because of political sensitivity and practical difficulties, the authorities emphasize that a cautious and slow approach is necessary. The experiment started on selected bases.

The Shanghai No. 3 Iron and Steel Complex was among the first to carry out the experiment. The old wage system was based upon egalitarian principles. A job was guaranteed for life no matter whether one worked or not. There was little wage differential among different jobs. There was no link between economic performance and financial reward. The system failed to reflect the effort, skill and the degree of difficulty of the job. Also in terms of personnel management, the practice was 'promotion only'. There was no demotion or resignation required from managers even if the performance was very poor or the person was not suitable for the job. These phenomena are referred to as the 'three irons' – the 'iron rice bowl' (job for life), 'iron wages' (guaranteed equal wages) and 'iron position' (no demotion or dismissal).

To demolish the 'three irons' the Iron and Steel Complex organized a special team to carry out work study, job analysis and job specification from which a new formula was worked out to calculate wages and salaries. The formula was designed to break the degree of over-equality and to implement the principle of 'more work, more pay'. Based on these studies, the team worked out three proposed reform programmes. These were discussed by all the work-force and voted by the workers' representative congress with the aim of achieving total consensus. Every worker had to be reassessed against the job requirement and their performance. The final decision was made on the strength of the combined assessment of self, fellow workers and management. Enterprises then signed contracts with each worker on a short-term and long-term basis. Some workers were not to be employed again. In the Shanghai No. 3 Iron and Steel Complex, 10 per cent of the 32,000 work-force were in this category. The following measures were taken to deal with the situation:

1 To recommend people to other employers.
2 To relocate through the internal labour market within the company.
3 To set up service companies.
4 To set up development companies where the workers are trained for new skills.

In Shanghai No. 3 Iron and Steel Complex's case, a service and development company was formed which employed 900 workers.[13] This is considered to be a near-ideal set of arrangements. It will, however, take a long time before such an example becomes commonplace in China.

Another case has had a most significant impact on the country. A firm in ZuHai (SEZ) recently rewarded a scientist (who had made a most significant contribution) with a house, a car and Yuan 100,000. This new practice and concept shocked the whole country. But it has finally brought effort in line with reward. The new incentive and reward system is a cultural shock to the socialist work-force. It has, however, brought high productivity, has significantly changed the behaviour of the lazy workers and had educational value.

3 The third area is concerned with plant managers' responsibility and the democratic process of decision-making. Under the central planning system, a plant manager worked as a civil servant who was responsible for the fulfilment of production quotas and material consumption targets. His appointment and the terms of office were determined by the relevant government department. The appointment was often based on political loyalty rather than production performance. There was little involvement of workers in decision-making (as they were made from above the enterprises). Under the old system, trade unions looked after welfare and the Communist Party organizations concentrated on political and ideological education.

The plant manager system is designed to make plant managers responsible for the economic and productive performance of enterprises. It has given plant managers power and autonomy in decision-making. A plant manager is elected by the workers' representative congress. He has to sign the contract. When he fails in his duties, he will be disciplined, demoted or dismissed. All decisions must be discussed, consulted with and approved by workers, although the final decisions are made by managers. The workers' representative congress is involved in all decision-making and handles disputes between management and workers. The workers are encouraged to make suggestions and criticisms to the plant manager.

Again, such procedures will take time to be widely implemented, but the model of desired management behaviour has been clarified.

State enterprises and the community

Traditionally, Marxism favoured 'productive' manufacturing activity over that of 'non-productive' service activities, and earned income over unearned income. Proceeds from properties, trade and financial services were considered less favourably and were sometimes dismissed as 'speculative'. In an economy of shortages there was little need for service in terms of information and advertising. The vertical controls and decision-making processes did not leave room for a service and distribution system. As a result, the service and distribution sector declined rapidly after 1949. In the 1970s, there were very few services such as restaurants, hairdressers, launderettes, hotels, etc.

It has become normal that Chinese enterprises run everything from schools, hospitals, hostels, groceries and detention centres for workers and their families. On top of their production activities, they have to run a community which has become a big financial and administrative burden, as well as a large social responsibility.

For example, the Nanjing Chemical Complex has 390,000 employees. For their 19,000 youngsters, the company runs kindergartens, infant schools, primary and high schools, a technical college and an open university. These cost the enterprise Yuan 7 million annually. The company also pays for medical care (Yuan 6 million), pensions (Yuan 13 million) (the state pension scheme is operated by employers), labour insurance (Yuan 3 million), housing, transport, etc.[14]

Another plant in Hongzhow runs 12 social services employing 6,000 persons, 20 per cent of their total labour force. There is a modern hospital with 56 beds and 72 doctors and nurses. The average utilization of the hospital beds is no more than five to six patients. It has a transport fleet of 86 vehicles, of which 10 are coaches. On average the 10 coaches are in service for two to three hours a day. To free enterprises from so much social obligation, the reforms have concentrated on:

1 contracting out the non-production functions to existing employees, or setting up independent service companies; and
2 establishing social security and social benefit systems operated by the state.

For example, the No. 1 Plastic Plant in Shi Jia Zuang has contracted out its kindergarten. The canteen has been contracted out to a catering firm. The hostel has been rented by the former employees. In the mid-1980s, the company not only recovered its investment but also made several hundred thousand Yuan in the form of profits and rent. These micro-level activities have promoted and helped the government macro-policy of rapidly expanding the service and distribution sector.[15]

Secondly, the process of setting up a social security system has been accelerated. One difficulty in implementing a bankruptcy law in China is that there is no safety net provided by society. At present anyone who is not in state employment has no claims on social benefits (the state benefit system is operated through enterprises). Those who quit a job to join the private sector would automatically lose their pension, fringe benefits, subsidies on food, fuel and free medical care. In the 'Regulation on Transformation of Functions in the State Enterprises', published 23 July 1992, the state is to establish a state pension system, an unemployment benefit system and medical and labour insurance systems.

THE COLLECTIVE SECTOR ('TOWNSHIP' AND COOPERATIVE ENTERPRISES)

Over the past 13 years there has been a rapid expansion in the township sector to become extremely important in China. For example, between 1980 and 1985 the total industrial value (output at 'factory gate' prices) of the township sector increased 187 per cent, an annual average of 23 per cent. In 1991 GDP reached Yuan 850 billion (US $170 billion), contributing one-third of total industrial value.[16]

How it began

In 1980, after listening to the morning's report by two governors from Guang Dong province, Deng Xiaoping said to them 'The report is good. You could designate an area in Guang Dong as a special zone. The central government has no money. You have to rely on yourself to break a path' (Chen Bingan, Hu Ge, Liang Zhaosong 1991).

This event marked a significant event in China's history. It started not only the system of 'special economic zones' but the whole reform movement itself.

Although the central government provided only Yuan 30 million (US $6 million) in loans, it appointed a strong management team of the two best provincial governors and the three best county directors in the province (a very significant sign of high-level commitment), but also 108 of the best qualified engineers and architects were brought together from all over China. Two army construction battalions, headed by a well-educated general, were sent to build the infrastructure and other basic facilities. The management team was given full autonomy. No policy constraints were attached.

To finance the first phase, the management team decided to lease the land to the Hong Kong business community. This was unthinkable in China in 1980 since the rest of the country was under strict socialist ideological and structural control.

This strong government commitment and the unprecedented flexible approach sent positive messages across the border to Hong Kong. Later, a series of preferential policies on investment were issued. Labour costs were 20–30 times cheaper and land rents were also a fraction of the cost in Hong Kong. The business community there commented: 'Shen Zhen [one of the smallest counties in Guang Dong] is Deng Xiaoping's experiment. It must not fail. The value of land is bound to be quadrupled in the future.' The deeply held suspicion and prejudice had finally broken down.

In 1980 a few joint ventures were signed in clothing, handbags, small tools and handicrafts. These were quickly followed by contracts for hotels and other industries.

The follow-on

The focus for growth, originally in Guang Dong, spread to Fujian province, and then more widely still. Guang Dong (population 63 million, larger than the United Kingdom) has Hong Kong at the centre of its coastline, and Taiwan is off the coast of Fujian. Ethnic Chinese from Hong Kong, Taiwan, Singapore, Malaysia, Thailand and other places where they have settled, have provided the main thrust of this development. They have brought with them capital, business experience, energy and money-making skills (although in general not advanced technology).

Guang Dong has its own regulations, and enterprises within its jurisdiction are free from the central planning system. Moreover, they have been able to purchase materials from the market, although at a price higher than state-owned enterprises would pay. Their success has been remarkable.

Outside of these areas there have, however, been problems in achieving a balanced development between the state sector and the township sector. In the mid-1980s, many township enterprises moved out of their traditional agriculture-related, labour-intensive markets, duplicating the manufacturing capacities in the state sector and competing fiercely with it on key inputs and markets. In contrast to free competition where (the theory is that) the fittest survive, many ill-equipped, low-skilled and less efficient township enterprises have increased their market share at the expense of the more efficient state enterprises. This is due to the following reasons.

Firstly, the expansion of the market system and the preferential policy towards township enterprises in the 1980s provided unique opportunities for their rapid development.

Secondly, township enterprises are collectively owned by public authorities and/or groups of private individuals (like that of cooperatives in the urban areas). They have never been part of the state planning or allocation systems. This is the main reason why they found it hard to expand before 1979, when all inputs were allocated by the state. On the other hand, they have always operated in a more competitive environment for both inputs and outputs and so they have had tough budget constraints.

Moreover, they have had the full autonomy in decision-making on investment, finance, personnel, wages and bonuses, production and sales. They are able to pay competitive prices to suppliers and pass them on to consumers. Compared with state enterprises, they are more flexible, dynamic and more at ease with the market system.

Thirdly, in contrast to the township enterprises, the big state enterprises are still by and large under the state planning control, although some autonomy has been given to them. With more state allocations of inputs being replaced by market forces on the one hand, while the prices of their finished products remain fixed by the state on the other hand, state enterprises have been squeezed. The big enterprises are beginning to lose the advantages of cheap state-provided inputs and cannot take advantage of free market prices. They are suffering from increased costs and reduced profit.

This is particularly the case with the energy sector. To prevent the linked price increase in industrial inputs, coal and oil industries were not allowed to move their prices while the costs of all other raw materials have been increased. Being caught in between market imperfections and planning imperfections, some major state enterprises were on the verge of bankruptcy.[17]

The problem was how to make competition between state and non-state sectors constructive and not destructive. The government policy is:

1 to subsidize state enterprise losses caused by the dual system (policy losses), and to guarantee the key inputs at the state price;
2 to revive this sector through reform, both internally and externally, eliminating government interference; and
3 to bring about a rationalization programme of closing down, terminating production, merging and diversifying all loss-making enterprises (excluding those where the losses were the result of government policies).

In the authorities' view, the prosperity of the rural economy is very much dependent on the development of township enterprises. They are indispensable for the modernization of agriculture and the improvement of rural living standards. It is the government's long-term strategy to promote this sector. Its policies are that:

1 Township enterprises should aim for appropriate growth rates (not 'overexpansion'), with emphasis on the improvement of quality and economic efficiency.
2 The government will support and regulate this sector only through macro-planning, providing guidelines on its direction of development and thus preventing 'cut-throat' and wasteful competition with state enterprises.
3 Township enterprises are encouraged to develop labour-intensive, export-orientated and local resource-related sectors and are encouraged to work as subcontractors or to merge with state enterprises. Such coordinated developments in and around Shanghai have proved successful.

In the first quarter of 1992, the township sector achieved a 36 per cent increase in production. It now has fixed assets of Yuan 400 billion and contributes 30 per cent of total industrial value. The development of this sector has the following characteristics:

1 *Cooperatives* Throughout the Yantze Delta and the Jiao Tong Peninsula thousands of township enterprises subcontract or cooperate in production with state-owned enterprises. They have also set up numerous joint-research projects with state-research institutes and universities.
2 *Mergers and take-overs* In Je Jiang province, 80 per cent of 'township' enterprises merged with other enterprises to form corporate groups throughout the country. 40,000 such groups have been set up in the form of shareholding companies.
3 *Export orientation* About 60,000 'township' enterprises produce for export, contributing about one-quarter of total exports by value.
4 *A shift from labour-intensive to technology-intensive* As 'township' enterprises achieved economies of scale they have concentrated more and more on technical updating. Many have specialized in advanced technology.[18]

PRIVATE BUSINESS

In 1978 there were 150,000 households engaging in private business. By 1988 this had increased to 13 million. Now there are 14.5 million households, with 21 million people, in private business. These businesses have extended from restaurants and hairdressers to high-technology, consultancy, advertising, interior design, etc. The registered capital and the turnover has tripled. For example, in 1981, total registered capital in this sector was Yuan 460 million (average Yuan 250 per household). By 1990 this figure had increased to Yuan 39.7 billion, with an average household figure of Yuan 1,156. Total turnover has increased from Yuan 2.1 billion in 1981 to Yuan 14.9 billion in 1990. The private business sector has also contributed Yuan 14.7 billion or 5.1 per cent of the total tax revenue.[19]

ECONOMIES OF SCALE AND INDUSTRIAL ORGANISATION

In contrast to the Soviet economy, where huge state monopolies prevailed, Chinese industries and enterprises have been inherently fragmented. A lack of economies of scale is a common problem.

In China, all publicly owned enterprises are 'controlled' by either central or local government. The former are run by ministries and departments, the latter by bureaux and by sections of provincial, county and township governments in their own local interests. The resulting departmentalism and regionalism led to scattered and duplicated developments, isolated from each other administratively. As local budgets have expanded on the basis of local industry revenues, each town, county and province has endeavoured to be self-sufficient by setting up a comprehensive industrial structure not controlled from the centre.

There has also been underdevelopment. As new industries have been established they have had to be equipped with all-purpose machines and to carry out every process. Chinese economists refer to such developments as 'big and comprehensive' (such as the huge Nanjing Chemicals Complex mentioned earlier) or 'small and comprehensive'. A low degree of specialization, lack of inter-industry links and poor quality resulted. Here are some examples.

Washing machines

China started to produce twin-tub washing machines in 1978. By 1990 it reached a total capacity of 20 million. During the consumer boom in the mid-1980s, every province except Tibet invested in a washing machine plant, with more than 30 assembly lines. Sixty projects had cost US $240 million in foreign exchange (many assembly lines had imported parts and components) and Yuan 600 million.

In 1990, the washing machine industry suffered losses. Production fell from 12 million to 8 million units, and there was still a surplus. Facing over-capacity, all 30 washing machine plants switched to automatic washing machines. These required bigger capital layout and high technology. Some plants did not have the equipment or the skills. The total capacity of 30 plants at break-even level was 1.8 million units. The estimated total sales for the next three to five years were 300,000–500,000 units.[20]

The story of television

In the 1980s there was a shortage of colour televisions. At that time one could make a small fortune by selling a TV 'coupon' (an entitlement to purchase). By the end of 1991, there was a stockpile of 1.09 million sets. They are either unknown brand names or the wrong sizes. In China there are 57 television plants (two in the United States, seven in Japan), most of which are working well below their designed capacity.[21]

The ventilator war

Before 1991, the use and production of ventilators had been rigidly restricted by the government due to a shortage of electricity. In 1991, a new invention had reduced electricity consumption of ventilators by 50 per cent. In 1992 the number of ventilator plants had increased from 70 to 200. In Canton alone, 27 plants were set up. A small county invested Yuan 500 million. Ventilator production is facing the same future – overcapacity, small scale, huge waste at the macro-level.[22]

The lessons – and a solution

Since 1978 quality problems have been getting worse. Poor quality washing machines, televisions, ventilators and other goods have been continuously produced and have accumulated at retail outlets or warehouses at high storage costs. Such unmarketable products have been one of the reasons for large losses and the shortage of working capital. These goods should be sold at lower prices or be destroyed, but such measures have only been taken to a limited degree. Why?

Firstly, due to the reforms, enterprises are not really subject to market disciplines but are under 'soft budget constraints'. Loss-making enterprises will always be rescued by state subsidies or a state bank loan.

Secondly, the fixed retail price system made little difference between famous and lesser brands. There are few incentives and little autonomy for enterprises and retail outlets to lower the price or to reduce the supply of goods (retail outlets operate under the same system as that of enterprises). A market cannot function efficiently without a flexible price system.

Competition has not brought about better resource allocation in terms of investment. Since 1979, the authorities have decentralized investment control and have delegated much autonomy to the local government and (to a lesser degree) to the enterprise level. Driven by revenue needs, local governments and enterprises compete in investing in consumer durable goods. The socialist symptom of 'investment hunger' and the wasteful use of fixed assets has continued.

To address the issue, the government adopted the following policies:

(a) to organize industries on a more rational basis government policy decided to encourage mergers and take-overs, especially across regions and industrial branches; and
(b) to regulate new investment by reforming investment management systems.

Policies on mergers

Expansion of the market mechanism put pressure on enterprises to achieve economic efficiency. Some enterprises began to merge voluntarily. In 1984, the authorities of some big municipalities had incorporated this practice into their reform programme. In 1989, the State Economic Reform Commission, the State Planning Commission and the State Assets Management Bureau jointly issued 'temporary measures on mergers and take-overs'. By the end of 1989, some 7,000 enterprises had been taken over by 6,000 enterprises.

There have been three forms of mergers and take-overs: horizontal, vertical and conglomerate. The financial possibilities can be summarized as outright purchase, paying off debts, pawning (using state assets as security for finance, because they were not permitted to sell them, to be recovered later), controlling shares and loans.

Reorganization of the enterprise sector has proved to depend on other reforms such as public finance, ownership, the functions of government, financial markets and accounting systems. Given the complications and the importance of these issues, three special policy seminars were organized in January 1992, at which 12 policy measures relating to mergers and take-overs were put forward. These related to planning, budgeting, labour, personnel, sales, statistics, assets management, taxation and top management boardroom structure. Proposed by the State Planning Commission, the State Economic Reform Commission and the State Production Office, the State Council has now approved 'Proposals on the experiment of mergers and takeovers on a selective base'.[23]

Reorganizing existing enterprises: mergers in the automobile industry

Some 25 out of 29 provinces have automobile plants. In 1982 plants in only two provinces had reached minimum efficiency plant of around 50,000 units annually, the rest were under 10,000. Between 1980 and 1985 there had been an increase of 525 automobile plants, with very low specialization. Most of them just duplicated the existing production capacity. This increased unit costs. The small scale also made technology transfer difficult and wasteful.

It is not surprising that the earliest mergers and take-overs occurred in the automobile industry. In the period 1981–3, seven big automobile corporations were formed. In 1986, based on these corporations, four larger groups were formed, led by No. 1 Automobile Plant, No. 2 Automobile Plant, the Heavy Vehicle Plant and the NanJing Automobile Plant (the first three had achieved full autonomy from the central government). Now these four groups have merged with or taken over 494 factories and research institutes and units. They cover 27 provinces and municipalities and 14 government departments. There are also 33 formerly central-government-owned and 31 joint ventures and co-production firms. The reorganization has been based on an economic rationale which has broken the regional, departmental and industrial segregation. The four groups have encountered the following two major problems.

Firstly, there is incompatibility of the budgetary and investment management systems. As mentioned before, enterprises are owned by either central or local government. They allocate the investment budget and set the tax rate for enterprises. After the merger, ownership remained the same. The groups found themselves becoming tax collectors and investment allocators for government departments. There is no real economic bond between each group and its companies. Although each group as a whole has been given full autonomy on decision-making, the subsidiaries have not.

Secondly, most small firms were formerly owned by local government. After the merger, such governments still consider themselves the owner. Because they have control over finance and key inputs allocations, these small firms have to obey and pay tax to them. Ownership and management of the groups are therefore very muddled.[24]

What are the lessons?

The problem of ownership is the underlying cause of this investment behaviour. Under this system, nobody is held responsible for bad investment decisions and the consequent financial losses. To address this problem, under the Regulation issued in July 1992 enterprises and government agencies or departments will face financial and legal responsibilities for bad investment decisions. Enterprises have the right to lease and 'transfer' fixed assets at a price. The ownership will, however, remain with the people as a whole.

The 'Organization of Investment' programme has also been changed. Instead of the state alone directing investment for state-owned industries, the government will appoint a large company as the main investor which would then gather together other investors. The government itself would participate as an investor. This can be illustrated in the following example.

Video-recorder production – the new investment management system

To avoid chaos and wasteful investment in video-recorder production, a policy was formulated by the central government in April 1992. A detailed programme of technology transfer, absorption and localization targets has been issued. This investment programme is incorporated into the Eighth Five-Year Plan. According to this programme, China will construct only one video-recorder plant with a capacity of 3 million sets a year. The government has appointed the main assembly plant constructor and has decided the location. The leading plant will then invite other plants or institutions to invest in the form of shares. The leading plant will take the initiative to form the company and to organize production. Each investor will take the financial and production responsibility according to their shareholding in the company. The programme is the first of its kind in China's investment history.[25]

Problems of 'unfair' competition between sectors

Since 1979, the authorities have made great efforts to establish a market mechanism and to promote free competition. The advantages of a market mechanism and of free competition have been much advertised in the media. In order to promote competition, the authorities have liberalized the central planning control over resource allocation and price controls. The private and collective sectors have also been given favourable policy treatment. However, competition among the central-government-owned, the local-government-owned and the township enterprises has failed to bring the above-mentioned advantages.

Economic efficiency has declined and poor quality and unmarketable stockpiles have increased in both state and 'township' sectors. Energy consumption and the consumption of raw materials have also increased. Returns on investment have fallen. All these are the direct result of unfair competition, weakening state macro-control over pricing and over the direction of investment.

Throughout the 1980s township enterprises have had an average growth rate of 29 per cent a year. In 1984, it was as high as 47 per cent. In 1988, the labour force employed by this sector was 1.3 times that of the state sector. It contributed 25 per cent of total industrial value. It absorbed 46 per cent of the total working capital and 27 per cent of all total industrial loans. However, the tax contribution was only equivalent to 21 per cent that of the state sector. The asset/profit ratio was equivalent to 68 per cent of the same ratio in the state sector. These figures show that given all preferential treatments, the township enterprise sector combines higher raw material and financial consumption, lower efficiency and tax contribution.[26]

By comparison, state enterprises have obligations to pay much higher taxes to the state (55 per cent), in addition to donations to various government departments, associations and societies, as well as education, pensions, labour insurance, etc. (the 'township' sector is not obliged to provide such social welfare payments). State enterprises have less autonomy on investment, finance, sales and wages as the state has not yet released the resource allocation system for free transactions. Without power to decide selling prices and face the increasing costs of inputs, they have found it impossible to compete with the collective sector.

In short, the state sector is financially overburdened, with little autonomy in controlling its own fate. In contrast the 'township' sector has full autonomy, at least financially, with no social obligations, and can benefit most from liberalization. Hence competition between the state sector and the township enterprise sector is unfair.

Each state-owned enterprise has been under different allocation and price arrangements which made their profitability differ. These differences often have nothing to do with underlying competitiveness. Under the contract system, each enterprise negotiates the tax rate and profit quota with their owners in central or local government according to their conditions. Some pay 20 per cent tax and others 90 per cent.[27]

Central government ministries dictate what happens to state-owned enterprises and local governments dictate what happens at the local level. This means that local governments do not have jurisdiction over central-government-owned enterprises in their areas, and likewise the centrally owned enterprises cannot enjoy local support in tax relief and other preferential policies given to local enterprises. Hence within the public sector, enterprises are competing on an unequal basis.

The distorted price system, which does not reflect the scarcity and profitability of resources, has made free competition impossible. For example, the energy sector has been historically underinvested, with prices fixed at a very low level. The sector suffered most in the 1980s. On the other hand, the overpriced processing industries could always make a good profit without much effort. The dual pricing system is also prone to speculative activities. In the mid-1980s the rapid price rise in key industrial inputs made black market activities so profitable that enterprises made more money by selling state-allocated key inputs to the black market than through production. Some enterprises have more state allocations than others, some have more autonomy over the pricing and sale of the state production quotas. These differences destroyed the assumption of free-market competition.

What conclusions can we draw from these examples? If the market is imperfect under the market system, it is even more so under reforming socialism. There have been many market distortions. Enterprises have not yet become independent economic entities responsible for profits and losses. A complete and unified market framework needs to be established. The structural problems of regional isolation and protectionism need to be tackled. The government therefore has a key role in filling the gaps between the market and planning, providing macro-guidance and control.

In the 'Regulations' of 23 July 1992, the government has made a commitment to unify and promote markets throughout the country, eliminating unfair competition and combating protectionism.

THE SHAREHOLDING EXPERIMENT

The first joint-stock trading company emerged spontaneously in Shen Zhen in 1983. Since then there have been selective experiments in many enterprises. In October 1987, at the 13th Congress of the Communist Party of China, the authorities said that 'the shareholding system is another form of socialist ownership. The current experiment should continue.' By the end of 1991, there were 3,220 firms involved in it.

There are four types of shareholders: the state itself; state-owned and collectively owned enterprises; employees; and the general public. Among the 3,220 enterprises, only 2 per cent (89 firms) issued shares to the general public. The typical share distribution among these 89 firms is the following: state share (47 per cent), enterprises (29 per cent), private individuals (14 per cent), foreign ownership (9 per cent).[28]

The authorities defined the objectives of shareholding ownership as being:

(a) to transform enterprises into independent economic units accountable for their growth, profit and loss and management efficiency so that they can be separated from the government administration;
(b) to open up new sources of finance; and
(c) to promote a more rational resource allocation and the mobility of factors of production.

The authorities also emphasized the following:

1 State- or publicly owned enterprises must take the controlling majority of shares.
2 There must be no erosion of state assets. It is strictly forbidden to sell public assets to individuals in the form of shares (the obvious inconsistency with what is actually happening is not resolved).
3 Shareholding is subject to government approval. To become a shareholding company existing enterprises will change their ownership status.[29]

Scope of the experiment

Shareholding is not applicable in defence industries, scarce metal and mineral resources, banks, foreign trade corporations and other state-controlled monopolies.

The experiment can, however, be applied in the priority areas of energy, transport and telecommunications. However, the state itself must take the controlling majority. It is much encouraged in the highly competitive sectors and in capital- and technology-intensive industries.

Foreign shareholders are only allowed to purchase and trade 'B' shares. These are traded in the international market and among foreign firms and individuals.[30]

The shareholding system is more difficult and complicated to implement than the contract system. It depends on many factors such as the establishment of a stock market, the appropriate legal framework and a compatible accounting and auditing system. All these are just being set up in China, and they will take time.

According to the State Economic Reform Commission, the shareholding experiment throughout the country has experienced the following problems.[31]

Firstly, the lack of a legal framework which specifies property rights and the liability of a company makes it difficult for shareholders to know where they stand. Some experimenting companies had confused the concepts of debt and equity and guaranteed shareholders the initial investment, plus interest, plus dividends. Some enterprises had issued shares as bonuses, some had allowed withdrawal of shares and refunded shareholders and some even paid dividends at a higher rate to individuals than to the state.

Secondly, only Shanghai and Shen Zhen are officially designated as cities with stock markets, but several others set up their own stock exchanges. Without expertise and knowledge of a stock market, they created chaos. In June 1992 the authorities had to ban them. Without a proper financial market, enterprises tend to be undervalued on historic costs. Intangibles are generally not included (the concept does not exist).

Thirdly, the old accounting system is incompatible. Auditing, reporting and publishing systems are being set up. They are far from adequate to accommodate the shareholding experiment.

Fourthly, under the current dual price system there are major distortions in the performances of enterprises. This makes their evaluation even more difficult.

To sustain the experiments, a set of laws and regulations were enacted in May 1992. They include regulations on the shareholding practice (this has specified the objective, the main principles, the scope and the process of shareholding experiment). There is also a 'public limited company' law, a 'limited company' law, regulations on an accounting system for the experimenting enterprises and regulations on asset valuation (which proposed four methods of valuation).[32]

The Chinese shareholding system has the following features:

1 It is not designed to privatize the public ownership but to extend and share state ownership with collective enterprises and individuals.
2 It is used more as a policy vehicle to reinforce enterprise reform than as a way of redistributing wealth.
3 The experiment is strictly controlled (shareholding companies are subject to government approval), only two stock exchange markets are permitted, and there are restrictions on foreign shareholdings.

Ownership problems lie at the heart of the poor economic performance of state enterprises. The waste and underutilization of public assets are because there is no link between state assets and anyone's pocket. Without clearly defined property rights, neither state nor enterprise will be interested in the efficient use, maintenance and enhancement of enterprise assets. Enterprises will continue to pursue short-term gain, even de-capitalizing these assets (for example, using technical transformation funds and depreciation as bonuses). In the shareholding system experiment, the authorities emphasize public ownership. By doing so, the authorities assume that the performance of state enterprises can be improved without privatizing state enterprises. Therefore, the focus of shareholding reform is on autonomy and the separation of enterprise management from the 100 per cent state ownership and administration.

An 'investor's responsibility system' has now been implemented in which each institution will take financial responsibility according to its shareholding. But whether this will be an effective force remains to be seen.

A result of the experiment

To address this problem of ownership and control, on 23 July 1992 the 'Regulations on the Transformation of the Functions of State Enterprises' were issued by the State Council. They granted the following autonomies and rights:

1 Enterprises have full autonomy on investment decisions, profit distribution, pricing (except a few prices still fixed by the state), production, marketing, recruiting, personnel management, importing and exporting. They can decide on letting, leasing, transferring at a cost (though not selling) their fixed assets and equipment to other entities.
2 Enterprises have the right to refuse government mandatory production orders if they are not adequately supplied with the required state allocations. They have the right to refuse requests by government departments for 'donations' and 'fees'.
3 Enterprises must be responsible for losses due to poor management. In the first year of losses, the total salary and wage bill in the plant must be reduced. Management should reduce their salaries and have no bonuses. In the second year of losses, the plant manager could be dismissed. For

serious cases, enterprises would be ordered by government to stop production. Such enterprises would be given one year for reconstruction before bankruptcy would be declared.

THE CHANGING ROLE OF GOVERNMENT

There have been two main reform experiments at central government level, in 1981 and 1988. The content of the 1988 experiment includes the reorganization and reduction of the number of civil servants. Similar experiments have also been carried out at provincial level on a selective basis. From May 1992, reforms have spread to 200 counties. The contents of the reforms are:

1 To eliminate the direct management of enterprises by local governments.
2 To encourage mergers among industry, commerce, distribution outlets and agriculture.
3 To implement the new government functions of macro-policy control and supervision, service, information, coordination, construction of infrastructure.

At present the average employment in a county government is around 1,000–3,000 people in 50–60 sections, many of which have duplicated functions. This number will be greatly reduced and only key sections such as security, finance, auditing, industry, commerce and statistics will remain.[33]

The State Planning Commission controls all resource allocations and distribution, setting prices for everything from coal to a needle. After the reform, it now controls only 20 per cent of the total state assets, 16 per cent of the total industrial production and less than one-third of prices. The focus has been shifted to planning and coordination, formulating industrial policy on the growth rate, on structure, competition, macroeconomic control, promoting and regulating the markets, consultancy and information services. It has now set up four specialist teams: planning and investment; consultancy on economics and policies; information service; policy and research.[34]

The government will now be:

1 formulating economic development strategies, principles and industrial policies, controlling, planning and adjusting the industrial structure;
2 modifying enterprises' behaviour through interest rates, tax rates, exchange rates and price controls;
3 guiding enterprises in optimal resource allocation and structure according to the given industrial policy and the required scale;
4 helping enterprises to set up adequate personnel management, wage systems, financial systems, costing and accounting systems, depreciation provisions, etc;
5 promoting technical advances by providing training, market information and consultancy;

6 establishing and perfecting a unified, well-regulated market structure, by breaking regional isolation and allocations;
7 planning and coordinating capital, labour, financial, technology and information markets, and promoting completion of the establishment of a market system;
8 publishing market information, reinforcing market regulations and banning illegal activities and unfair competition.

The services to be provided by the government will include social services and infrastructure, law firms, auditing firms, job centres, accounting firms, assets valuation, consultancy and information services, training and re-employment services, setting up an arbitration system to safeguard the lawful rights of the labour force and to settle industrial disputes, and coordinating among enterprises and other institutions to sustain smooth production.

NEW INVESTMENT

China's first industrialization drive took place in the 1950s. Throughout the 1960s and 1970s, China tried to purchase technologies from the West but due to the political situation supply was very limited.

The planning system does not provide incentives for technical progress. As a result, by the end of the 1970s one-quarter of fixed assets in Chinese industries were well beyond their economic life. Many enterprises were equipped with antique facilities. For example, in metallurgy equipment was based on technology dating from the 1930s or 1950s. In textiles, some mills are still using Toyora looms made in the Meiji period (the 1860s).

Technological progress has become the key to the intensive development strategy. With large amounts of fixed assets to be updated and replaced, there has been a huge financial and technical gap. In the Chinese government's view, direct investment is the efficient means to help meet China's need for foreign capital, advanced technology and improved management. Starting from a low level in 1979, when six joint ventures were signed, direct foreign investment has increased rapidly. The net inflow increased eight-fold between 1980 and 1983. By May 1992, some 41,953 foreign-funded firms, with registered capital of US $49 billion, have been approved, among which direct investment totalled US $23 billion. Of these, 18,530 have commenced production.[35]

THE MANAGEMENT OF DIRECT FOREIGN INVESTMENT

Institutional development

In order to encourage foreign investment, a four-tier system was established in 1981. They are four special economic zones, 14 open coastal cities, open regions and development zones.

The special economic zones are designated to be built into platforms for export. These were initially in Guang Dong province close to Hong Kong, which provided abundant labour and space. One of these four zones in Shen Zhen exported on average US $10,000 worth of goods daily in 1992, with total exports US $3.4 billion.

The second tier (14 open cities in the coastal region) were introduced in 1984 and were characterized by advanced technology and skilled labour. Since 1984, these coastal cities have absorbed US $900 million through foreign investment. In 1987 alone they exported US $4.7 billion worth of exports, 12 per cent of the national total.

The third tier is the open regions of the Pearl River Delta, the Yangtze River Delta, Shangton Peninsula and Liaodong Peninsula. By comparison these regions are much bigger, with sound industrial structure. They are in the most prosperous and densely populated areas. In the Yangtze River Delta, for example, there are 11 cities and 50 million people. The area has the most comprehensive industrial structure. Occupying less than one per cent of China, the area has 7 per cent of the total population and contributes 7 per cent of total GDP.

The development strategies for the open regions are that they serve as a base for high-technology imports, for high value added exports, for absorbing and transferring advanced technologies to inland areas, for joint R & D projects and for the training of highly qualified scientists and technicians.

The fourth tier is the rest of the inland area, where economic conditions vary a great deal. These areas are rich in natural resources, with an abundance of labour resources, but less developed in technology, management skills and they lack capital. Later Hainan Island and Shanghai were designated special development zones. In August 1992 the government announced opening another 14 inland zones.

The macro- and the micro-control of direct foreign investment

In the authorities' view, Chinese economic development is not dependent on direct foreign investment but benefits from it. Therefore it must be integrated into the Chinese economic plan. All such projects are subject to the approval of central and local governments. Preference is given to the projects that fit into the investment priority areas of the economic development such as transport, telecommunications, energy, with the criteria of capital and technology intensity and projects with great export potential. In theory once the projects have been approved, they are automatically incorporated into the resource allocation system like other state enterprises. The resources include fuel, raw materials and hard currency. Up to the mid-1980s, the allocation also included the labour allocations. In the early 1980s, China also emphasized the majority share in joint ventures and that Chinese must be the chairmen not the deputies.

In the mid-1980s, problems arose in the following areas.

1 Some 60 per cent of such projects were in hotels and the service sector. Priority areas had attracted no more than 10 per cent of total investment. Very few projects had transferred technology, most of the projects met the criteria of small capital layout, low technology and quick return. By the end of 1986, 500 direct foreign investments had been terminated before their expiry date.
2 There has been a foreign exchange shortage. In 1986, 3,000 joint ventures could not balance their foreign exchange account. The authorities adopted various measures, such as investing in export companies, purchasing from Chinese producers for export, selling goods to Chinese firms possessing hard currency in order to obtain it for the government.[36] All measures proved to be difficult and complicated to implement, and they did not solve the problem. Later, the authorities made efforts to guarantee priority projects with hard currency and to extend the foreign exchange lending to all joint ventures. However, with the gradual development of a foreign exchange market, the problems have now been resolved.
3 The other problem has been the unreliability of supply. In theory, as soon as joint ventures have been approved they should enjoy the same rights of state allocations. In reality, they were looked upon as residual to the main economic activities and would be the last to receive the state supply. With the relevant transitional policy measures and the expansion of market allocations, these problems too have been resolved.

At the micro-level, labour disputes and quality have been the main problems. Chinese enterprises under the socialist system operate differently. There is little labour mobility. The units 'own' their employees. It was not uncommon to take a year or so to obtain a skilled person from a state unit. Joint ventures often had to pay compensation to the state units. Foreign management also found it hard to accept the Chinese practice of no dismissal, low disciplinary measures and promotion only. However, these problems are transitional.

Technology transfer

In terms of technology transfer, up to the mid-1980s, very few direct foreign investment projects transferred high technology. Except in some sectors such as oil and automobiles, most of the advanced technology had been transferred through purchase. Between 1978 and 1985, the Chinese government spent US $18.2 billion in purchasing technology. Between 1982 and 1985, 3,000 technology transfer projects involving US $3.7 billion were carried out. These have transformed the state enterprise sector.[37]

The major problems are duplicated transfer and low absorption and localization rate. In the mid-1980s, China had transferred 113 colour television assembly lines, 116 assembly lines for refrigerators and 108 assembly lines for washing machines. Most operated well below designed capacity. The utilization of TV facilities has been less than one-third of the total transferred capacity. In 1987 the transferred production lines for wallpaper could decorate all hotels and new buildings four times over. The transferred fast food production lines in 1987 could meet four years' demand.[38] These problems were rooted in the investment financing and management system of the planning model, and a lack of macro-planning and control.

Because of the poor quality and unavailability of domestic parts and components, many production lines have been supported by imports which intensified the foreign exchange shortages. During the reform, enterprises have become geared to short-term profit, with neither the incentive nor the ability to absorb the transferred technology.

There has not been a clear industrial policy towards absorption. Between 1985 and 1986, the State Economic Commission (SEC) issued mandatory directives:

1 To regulate technology transfer by tightening up the approval criteria, tax reliefs or tariffs on the needed or duplicated transfers, as well as customs controls.
2 To transfer equipment and facilities which are not available in China, to transfer production lines while making the best use of domestic parts and components and to transfer know-how and patents with the hardware.
3 To require each province and municipality to work out a technology transfer and absorption plan. The SEC would concentrate technical consultancy on the key technology transfer projects. Localization rates and targets have also been set.
4 To provide a special fund for technology absorption.[39]

LESSONS FROM PRACTICAL EXPERIENCE

It is not easy to change from one system to the other. It is even more difficult to change to an unknown and untried system. There are many economic models that one could learn from. However, each country has to work out a model to suit its own conditions and needs.

Economic reforms in socialist countries are not and should not be an academic exercise decided by a handful of intellectuals and academic economists, nor an ideological battlefield between planning and market systems. They must not serve the purpose and interests of a small group in society, either politically or economically.

Reform in China has been a democratic process in the sense that many of the ideas and practices started from the grass-roots level and became accepted as part of the reform programme.

The direction of such reforms should reflect these ideas and the demands of the people, to satisfy their needs. The economic reforms provided the first opportunities for ordinary people in China to speak their minds and to exercise their rights over political and economic matters. (Tienanmen Square was a big setback in this process.) The best indicators for success of the reforms are: (a) whether or not the living standards of the majority of the people have been improved, and (b) regardless of whether these improvements have come as a result of the people's own choice and from their own efforts, whether they represent the real democratic right, both politically and economically.

The primary needs of the country are stability and prosperity. The conditions that China has inherited from the past stemmed from the rigid planning system, which failed to provide incentives and initiatives for growth. What are the lessons from the past 14 years of change?

1 A coherent and well-coordinated approach is necessary Central planning is one complete system. China is moving away from that towards a new system, with many elements of a market system, whose characteristics are not yet clear. The move from one to the other should be carried out in a coherent and coordinated way, because so many parts of it are interconnected. In China the changes have been piecemeal and in consequence some have been self-defeating and counter-productive.

For example, when price controls on raw materials were relaxed and selling prices remained controlled, many enterprises turned from profit to loss. When the shareholding experiment started, financial and stock markets were not properly set up and the accounting and auditing systems were not compatible. As a result, reforms became chaotic or impossible. Even with well-coordinated reforms it still takes time for adjustments to work through the system. Originally the reforms were thought likely to take five years, then there was talk of 10 years. Deng Xiaoping has said that it would take about 30 years, and this is more realistic.

2 A cautious and controlled approach is desirable The Chinese economic reforms have been conducted as if in a series of laboratory experiments, although without any alternate structures to support them – a 'trial and error' approach. During these experiments, which are widely publicized, many modifications are made and lessons have been learnt until it is thought that the new system works. Then it is widely applied. This is a positive and pragmatic approach. It contrasts with the way in which changes have been occurring in eastern Europe and the CIS, and avoids large-scale chaos while minimizing the costs.

3 Strong government leadership is essential Government planning and macro-controls need to be strengthened during the transition period, not weakened. There will be gaps between planning and market systems which the government has to bridge. Until the new system is working well it is particularly important that the government holds the reins.

During the first part of the 1980s, up to 1986, decentralization and liberalization were carried out in a dramatic way. Market competition and liberalization were blindly followed. Macro-controls and the planning of major investments were neglected, as if the market system could automatically function perfectly. There was little evidence of industrial policies to keep a balance between different sectors and to regulate foreign investment, and little evidence either of control over growth rates. The economy became overheated in the mid-1980s. There was an assumption that the market, unregulated, would solve all problems. This was not the case.

4 State industries hold the key to success They should be supported not bankrupted. They need to be helped to reform. They are the mainstay of the economy. The large and medium-sized state-owned enterprises are the best legacy of 40 years of socialism in China. Over these years the state has invested and accumulated the country's best available equipment, technologies and human resources in these enterprises.

The support should not be through subsidies but through indicative planning, policy guidance and training until they can stand successfully on their own. Many have been inefficient in the past, producing low-quality output, but that should not be a reason for abandoning them now. They need time to adapt and change.

5 Private initiatives and incentives are a necessary but not sufficient factor for success Incentives to the private sector would not have succeeded without the strong commitment and full support of the Chinese government. It was the government not the private sector that built the first basic infrastructure of the special economic zones. Once the communist cadres and army engineers worked under the near-market situation, the outcome was completely different from what was expected. The success of the special economic zones is the result of a combination of government support and drive from the private sector.

Since 1979 the reforms initiated and nurtured by Deng Xiaoping have achieved remarkable progress. The prosperity of the people has sharply improved. Whole areas of the country are racing ahead economically. China aims to catch up with the middle-income countries by the year 2,000. Achieving this target looks more promising than ever before.

11

VIETNAM: IMAGE AND REALITY

Raymond L. Mallon

BACKGROUND

Historical introduction

For centuries Vietnam was mostly an independent state, though not always unified, until the French established colonial rule in the late nineteenth century. This was interrupted by Japanese occupation during the Second World War. Following their defeat, Ho Chi Minh proclaimed the Democratic Republic of Vietnam as an independent state on 2 September 1945. The French government attempted to reimpose colonial rule, but a growing resistance movement led to their defeat at Dien Bien Phu in 1954. An international conference in Geneva during that year provided for a temporary partitioning of the country at the 17th parallel until national elections could be held. The elections never took place. The country was divided into two states when the Republic of Vietnam was proclaimed in the south in 1956.

A protracted and destructive period of military conflict followed (the Vietnam War), until the overthrow of the Republic of Vietnam in 1975 and the reunification of the country in 1976 as the Socialist Republic of Vietnam. Communist regimes were also established in the neighbouring countries of Cambodia and Laos in 1975. Prior to 1975, very different economic systems had developed in the two states. Receiving technical and financial support from China and the USSR, the Democratic Republic in the north had adopted a socialist system of economic management. In the Republic of Vietnam to the south, which received extensive financial and direct military support from the United States and its allies, a capitalist economic system had developed.

Establishing a socialist system

The major drive to collectivize the agricultural sector in the north occurred between 1957 and 1960. The drive for 'socialist transformation' of non-agricultural industries began in late 1958, and most industrial and trading enterprises were under state control by the end of 1960. Village and handicraft industries were transformed into cooperative ownership at the same time. Rapid industrialization was an important development objective and, during the period 1960–75, a large proportion of state resources were allocated to the industrial sector. Despite the emphasis on industrial development, agriculture remained the dominant sector of the economy. The development of locally managed state enterprises, in addition to centrally managed state enterprises, was an important priority because of the imperatives of military conflict.[1] These imperatives included the need for regional self-sufficiency and a decentralized industrial base. Consequently the government deliberately aimed to decentralize many, but certainly not all, decisions concerning production and the provision of public services to provincial and district authorities. Thus, while Vietnam had a communist government, and many of the characteristics of a centrally planned economy, the system of economic management was quite different from that which existed in eastern Europe.[2]

Following reunification in 1976, the integration of the south into a national socialist economic system became an important priority. The negative impact on production incentives of attempts to collectivize agriculture, and nationalize industry and services, contributed to economic stagnation during the late 1970s. Following the Vietnamese invasion of Cambodia and the defeat of the Khmer Rouge regime in Phnom Penh in January 1979, economic difficulties were compounded because of the resultant increases in military expenditure, subsequent cutbacks in external assistance and destructive conflicts on the Chinese border.

Pressures for reforms

The emergence of major economic difficulties in the late 1970s led to a growing recognition of the need for administrative reforms to improve production incentives. Limited reforms were introduced on an experimental basis following the Fourth Party Congress in August 1979. The early 1980s were characterized by uncertainty about future policy directions, and grassroots moves towards the use of market mechanisms interacted with policy concessions and periodic clamp-downs (ADB 1989: 5–7).

The Sixth Communist Party Congress in December 1986 marked a turning point. Do Muoi, Chairman of the Council of Ministers, Vo Van Kiet, who soon became First Vice-Chairman (five years later he became Chairman and Prime Minister) and Nguyen van Linh (Party General Secretary) worked together to achieve change. The government, in response to increasing macroeconomic instability,[3] then unambiguously committed itself to *Doi moi* (renovation), and to a shift towards a more market-orientated economic system. During the Sixth Congress it was agreed also that there was a need to 'abolish the bureaucratically centralized management system based on state subsidies', and that production should be closely linked to the market (CPV 1987: 22–3).

A major change in policy towards state enterprises was initiated when the Council of Ministers issued a decree in November 1987[4] giving enterprises greater flexibility in production and financial decisions, and introducing a profit-based accounting system. These policy changes were reinforced in March 1988, when the 'Statute on State Industrial Enterprises' was promulgated. This marked the beginning of major changes to the system of economic management in Vietnam.

Resolutions passed in March 1988 recognized the legal status and rights of the family economy and the private sector. Agricultural reforms introduced in the following month returned the right of individual farmers to make production and marketing decisions. Following a series of price reforms beginning in 1987, official procurement prices of industrial and agricultural commodities were raised in July 1988, to reduce substantially the gap between free-market and official prices. These reforms were followed by banking and external trade reforms and, in March 1989, the adoption of a unified official exchange rate that has since been maintained close to the free-market rate.

Whereas there was a fairly rapid response to the policy reforms in terms of increased agricultural output and a rapid growth in small-scale service activities, the situation in the state enterprise sector has been mixed. While some enterprises have performed well under the market economy, others have not been able to adjust to reductions in subsidies, the lack of guaranteed markets for their output and increased domestic and import competition. The situation has been complicated by the almost complete cessation of exports to, and external assistance from, the former Comecon countries, which had previously been Vietnam's dominant trading partners, and the major source of its external assistance. This assistance from the former Comecon partners began to fall sharply from 1989 and stopped altogether in 1992. Trade with the former Comecon countries had fallen to a fraction of previous levels by 1991.

Many state enterprise workers lost their jobs, or were not paid, because of financial difficulties. This led to political pressures for renewed government support to the state sector and, by the latter half of 1989, the state banking system resumed supplying subsidized credit to state enterprises. This credit was generally provided with little assessment of the capability of the recipient enterprises to repay these loans. The rapid increase in domestic credit fuelled inflation and further compounded the already difficult financial situation of the banking system. It became increasingly apparent that further restructuring of state enterprises, including the state-run banking system, would be required if macroeconomic stability was to be realized.

It is important to note that while substantive economic reforms have been implemented, the new Constitution (approved April 1992) still recognizes that the Communist Party of Vietnam, 'acting upon the Marxist-Leninist doctrine and Ho Chi Minh's thought, is the force leading the state and society' (Article 4). The same Article also stresses that the Party must 'operate within the framework of the Constitution and the law'. On the other hand, Article 83 states that 'the National Assembly is the highest representative organ of the people and the highest organ of State power of the Socialist Republic of Vietnam...[and]...is the only organ with constitutional and legislative powers...[and]...shall exercise supreme control over all activities of the State'. Article 7 states that elections to the National Assembly should be 'held in accordance with principles of universal, equal, direct and secret suffrage'. The difficulties in classifying the political-economic system in Vietnam reflects the rapidly evolving nature of the system.

Economic environment for reform

Vietnam has been remarkably successful in implementing substantial economic policy reforms during a period when it was experiencing major external shocks. Moderate economic growth has been maintained during the adjustment process and macroeconomic stability has improved. Despite the loss of its former major export markets, Vietnam has achieved strong export growth and substantially diversified its export markets. The trade account has been almost balanced in recent years. The market exchange rate actually appreciated against the US dollar during 1992. Inflation has fallen drastically from pre-reform levels, but both inflation and unemployment remain important concerns. The large fiscal deficit and low levels of public and private investment are also important issues.

Now that the government has largely abandoned the instruments of central planning, it is important that the more indirect instruments required to manage monetary and fiscal policy in a market economy be developed. Monetary policy remains weak because of a poorly developed financial system, while fiscal policy is constrained because of a weak system of tax administration. The result has been high levels of inflation and inadequate government resources for maintaining and developing essential public infrastructure and services.

Poor fiscal performance has been aggravated by government support to loss-making state enterprises. Initially, subsidies were provided both directly by the government, and through cross-subsidies resulting from price regulations. More recently, subsidies have been provided in the form of cheap credit. Either way, the consequences have been to aggravate inflationary pressures. A major policy objective of the government now is to ensure greater macroeconomic stability, including low inflation. Improvements in the financial viability of state enterprise will be important in realizing this objective.

The recent improvements in economic performance cannot be sustained without increased investment. Given the limited budget revenue and limited external assistance, the government has barely enough resources to finance recurrent expenditure. It recognizes that the non-state sector, including foreign investment, will have to be an important source of investment growth and that further restructuring of the state sector, including liquidation and divestiture of non-viable, non-strategic enterprises, will be required to maintain economic growth and to improve macroeconomic stability.

There is also a growing recognition that state enterprises are often not efficient mechanisms for achieving social objectives, and that many social objectives would be better realized through direct measures. It is now government policy that state enterprises which are to remain under state ownership, to achieve social and other objectives, will have to operate on a more commercial basis. However, the process of implementing these policies is only just beginning.

Foreign investment approvals have grown strongly, from a small base, since the approval of a relatively liberal Foreign Investment Law in December 1987. Actual foreign investment inflows, however, remain low compared with inflows to the rapidly growing market economies in East and South-east Asia. Investment has been concentrated in service industries, oil exploration, agriculture and forestry. Chinese investors from Taiwan, Hong Kong and Singapore have been the dominant source of foreign investment. Major constraints to increased foreign investment include:

1 the impact that the US embargo is having on lending to Vietnam by the World Bank, the Asian Development Bank and commercial banks;
2 infrastructure problems;
3 bureaucratic delays; and
4 an inadequate legal and regulatory framework for investment.

Despite these constraints, foreign investors are preparing for investments in more substantive projects and further significant increases in foreign investment inflows are expected in the next few years. Significantly, a number of foreign banks were granted banking licences in 1992.

STATE ENTERPRISES IN THE VIETNAMESE ECONOMY

Overview

The share of state enterprises in national income has fluctuated between 22 and 29 per cent in recent years (see Table 11.1).[5] While this is high compared with most developing and OECD countries, it is considerably lower than that of most centrally planned economies. This reflects the fact that Vietnam remains a predominantly agricultural economy, and that the state accounts for only a very small proportion of agricultural output.

The share of the state in total employment is even less than its contribution to economic output, with state-sector employment accounting for less than 12 per cent of total employment in 1990. The proportion of labour employed by the state has declined since 1987, and this has been particularly pro-

Table 11.1 State enterprise sector in the Vietnamese economy 1987–91

	% shares of the total				
	1987	*1988*	*1989*	*1990 (prov.)*	*1991 (est.)*
National income	27	23	26	28	29
Employment (total)	15	14	13	12	na
agricultural	2.1	2.0	2.0	1.9	1.6
industrial	29.1	28.7	30.9	33.0	33.8
other	43.4	40.9	37.4	29.7	na
Government revenue*	67	55	48	50	na
Domestic trade	41	40	33	30	26

Sources: General Statistics Office (1991), *Statistical Data on the Socialist Republic of Vietnam: (1976–1990)*, and General Statistics Office (1992), *Economy of Vietnam – Review and Statistics*.
Note: * State enterprise contribution to total revenue (including external grants).

nounced in the service industries. The share of the state in domestic trade has fallen, from 41 per cent in 1987, to about 27.5 per cent in 1991.

The value of output per worker is much higher in the state industrial sector than the private sector (see Table 11.2). This higher labour productivity in state enterprises reflects both the capital-intensive nature of industries in which the state sector is most heavily involved (electricity, fossil fuels, metallurgy and the chemical industries), and previous policies that directed most investment capital to state enterprises, with little attention to assessing the economic viability of alternative technologies which may have made more effective use of relatively abundant labour.

The state sector still accounts for about 50 per cent of government revenue. Almost 90 per cent of budget revenue from state enterprises is obtained from centrally managed enterprises. Improvements in tax collection from the private sector will be increasingly important if the government is to maintain and increase budget revenues in an economy where the proportion of state enterprise output in national income is expected to decline.[6]

Structure of the state enterprise sector

There has been no centralized system for monitoring state enterprises in Vietnam. State enterprises have operated under the control of a wide range of central government ministries and agencies, as well as local and district authorities, and the central government does not know how many state enterprises are still operating. The latest official survey of state enterprises, undertaken in January 1990, found that there were 12,084 state enterprises operating in Vietnam. This survey also found that 4,584 of these enterprises were making substantial losses. The National Steering Committee on Debt Clearance has estimated that fewer than 8,000 enterprises are still operating.

Most state enterprises are very small. Sixty-seven per cent of industrial state enterprises employed fewer than 200 workers in 1991. Less than 5 per cent employed more than 1,000 workers. The largest 5 per cent of state enterprises account for about 50 per cent of total state enterprise output.

While only about 2,000 state enterprises are under the direct control of the central government, centrally managed state enterprises also account for about 50 per cent of total value added by the state sector, and they dominate output in many of the heavy industries, including electricity, oil and gas, coal mining, metallurgy, cement, chemical and fertilizer production. Most of the medium- to large-scale industrial enterprises are controlled by the central government.

The centrally managed state enterprises have enjoyed virtual monopolies in some sectors, including banking, coal mining, construction, electricity, fuel supply and sea, air and other long-distance transport. However, the private sector is providing increasing competition in transport and construction as well as in the manufacturing and service industries. In addition, many of the sectors where state enterprises have had monopoly powers are now being opened up to private foreign investment and to intra-provincial competition. During the last two years licences have been issued for foreign investment in sectors such as banking, coal mining and construction, which had previously been the sole domain of state enterprises.

Most of the 10,000 state enterprises under the control of provincial authorities are engaged in small- to medium-scale retail and commercial trading services. Others are engaged in light manufacturing industries, construction, transport, banking and tourism. Many of the locally managed state enterprises are already operating in an increasingly competitive environment, with competition from other state enterprises, the private sector and imports. Some 4,083 of the 4,854 loss-making state enterprises identified during the January 1990 survey were locally managed.

Many locally managed state enterprises are facing financial difficulties in adjusting to the market system, and a considerable number are effectively bankrupt. Some have already been liquidated. Other locally managed state enterprises, especially the better performing ones, have undergone 'spontaneous privatization'. That is, all or part of the assets have been transferred to alternative ownership structures on a fairly *ad hoc* basis at the discretion of local authorities. In some areas, the provincial authorities attempt to retain the monopoly powers previously enjoyed by local state enterprises. Locally managed state enterprises have often been an important source of economic power for provincial authorities.

Industrial sector state enterprises

While data on all state enterprises are limited, there is somewhat more information available on state enterprises operating in the industrial sector (see Table 11.2). The estimated 2,512 state enterprises in the industrial sector account for about one-half of total state enterprise output. State industrial enterprise employment in 1991 has fallen to less than 80 per cent of 1987 levels.[7] While the number of enterprises and their employment declined, gross production increased by nearly 20 per cent, with the rate of growth in output from the centrally managed state enterprises particularly strong. Labour productivity has increased dramatically, particularly in centrally managed enterprises.

Table 11.2 State-owned enterprises in the industrial sector of Vietnam 1987–91

	1987	*1988*	*1989*	*1990 (prov.)*	*1991 (est.)*
Total number	3,157	3,092	3,024	2,762	2,512
Centrally managed	1,579	1,449	1,459	1,384	1,252
Locally managed	1,578	1,643	1,565	1,378	1,260
Industrial output[(a)]			*% share*		
State sector	56	57	57	59	62
Non-state	44	44	43	41	38
Centrally managed	33	32	35	39	43
Locally managed[(b)]	67	68	65	61	57
Output per worker[(c)]			*Index*		
State sector	42	47	53	61	69
Non-state	26	29	33	38	39
Centrally managed	93	103	116	136	162
Locally managed[(b)]	34	37	41	45	47

Sources: General Statistics Office (1992), *Vietnam Industrial Statistics (1986-1991)*.
Notes: (a) percentage share of total industrial output in 1982 constant prices.
(b) Private, cooperative and provincial/district state enterprises.
(c) Index based on Dong '000 in constant 1982 prices.

The rapid improvement in productivity is indicative of the previous inefficiencies in the system. It indicates that the reforms implemented have already contributed to a substantial restructuring within the state enterprise sector. Despite this progress, there remains a substantial number of enterprises that are loss-making and represent a drain on the public sector budget.

Management control in state enterprises

Enterprises operating in the same industries were often associated together in unions of enterprises or general corporations. The extent of control exercised by these umbrella institutions varied, but the impact of the recent reforms has been to diminish their influence. Communist Party officials often held important positions in ministries, enterprise unions and enterprises. Actual lines of power and control were not easily discernible from organization charts. The extent of managerial autonomy varied considerably between enterprises.

With the exception of a limited number of 'strategic' state enterprises (mainly public utilities), the recent policy changes have resulted in the transfer of considerable decision-making authority to state enterprises. However, the rights and responsibilities of enterprise managers remain poorly defined. Some enterprise unions have begun to operate more like representative organizations for their industry, while others have developed as something more akin to a holding company for a group of enterprises.

During the initial phase of reform, managers and/or workers took complete control over the management of some state enterprises, and there were no clear mechanisms for ensuring accountability to the shareholder (the government). In other cases, government agencies continued to involve themselves in enterprise operations to an extent that ranged from a major role in day-to-day management decisions to something closer to that of a board of directors in a private corporation in a market economy. The extent of management control depended on the relative political power of central ministries, local governments, enterprise managers, enterprise unions and worker groups in individual enterprises. There was no systematic mechanism to ensure that the interests of the state, as owner of the enterprises, were protected.

While there is a clear commitment to reducing inefficiencies in the state sector, specific policy measures to deal with inefficiencies are still evolving. Various experiments have been made in terms of changing the management structure, and instituting a board of directors in some state enterprises. A law on the requirements for the establishment and divestiture of state enterprises was promulgated in November 1991. Since then, some provinces have acted quickly to transfer the ownership of some locally managed state enterprises. The authorities in Cuu Long province, in the Mekong Delta, have divested 145 state enterprises, or 78 per cent of the state enterprises managed by that province. The Central Institute for Economic Management has worked with a number of selected enterprises to establish boards of directors, but with only mixed success, as discussed later.

During recent restructuring, some individual enterprises have merged under the one management structure. In other cases, particularly in retail services, various units of a larger enterprise have been allowed to operate separately, often under some form of management contract. For instance, some state-owned restaurants and other service activities are now run as family businesses under management contracts.

Managing state enterprise reform

The process of developing a comprehensive programme for state enterprise restructuring has been complicated by the large number of central ministries and local government agencies responsible for the management and financial supervision of state enterprises. The government acted to overcome these difficulties by establishing two Steering Committees to deal with issues related to state enterprise reform.

The 'National Steering Committee on Enterprise Reform' was created to address policy and legal issues related to enterprise reform, to oversee experimentation with such reforms, and eventually to oversee implementation of these reforms throughout the country. This Committee is also responsible for the liquidation of indebted state enterprises which are not financially viable. The State Planning Committee acts as the secretariat for this Steering Committee. The National Steering Committee on Debt Clearance is responsible for clearing the overdue cross liabilities between state enterprises including the banking system. Progress has already been made in clearing a substantial value of cross-debts.

The State Planning Committee has overall responsibility for coordinating the formulation and implementation of the state enterprise reform programme. The Central Institute for Economic Management is responsible for drafting laws related to state enterprise reform for review by the Ministry of Justice. The Ministry of Finance has an increasingly important role in the financial supervision and performance monitoring of state enterprises.

As responsibility for the financial monitoring and supervision of state enterprises is transferred to the Ministry of Finance, it is envisaged that the role of line ministries will increasingly focus on the regulatory, advisory and information dissemination functions that such ministries would be expected to play in a market economy. This will be important in removing the previously inherent bias that resulted from ministries acting as both the regulator of a sector and as 'owner' of state enterprises in that sector. This bias inevitably led to situations where ministries responsible for the formulation and implementation of industry regulations favoured their 'own' state enterprises over private enterprises.

It is envisaged that the Ministry of Finance will increasingly play a role closer to that of a major shareholder on the board of directors of a corporation. However, as discussed later, considerable strengthening of accounting and auditing professional standards, and Ministry of Finance capability, will be required before the state can effectively protect its interest as the 'owner' of these enterprises. The actual situation concerning the different roles and responsibilities of the line ministries and the Ministry of Finance remain unclear, and these uncertainties are contributing to the delays in implementing many of the recent decisions concerning state enterprise reform.

THE CURRENT AGENDA FOR STATE ENTERPRISE REFORM

The future role of state enterprises

The preceding overview raises questions such as – what does the government see as the future role of state enterprises in Vietnam, and what is the intended outcome of the present restructuring? In the past, it has been difficult to find any clear statement concerning the eventual outcome of the reform process. The reforms have been justified as being necessary to meet economic and social objectives, but there have been only fairly vague public statements on what role state enterprises would play in the Vietnamese economy at the end of the reform process.

The vagueness about the final outcome of the reform process is a reflection of the fact that there was a large degree of uncertainty about how far the reform process should or could go. In addition, it was easier to 'market' limited economic reform to more conservative officials. During the initial stages of reform it was difficult to promote private property rights, when for years the Vietnamese public had been taught that public ownership was the basis of socialism. The term 'market economy' was avoided for many years, but is now acceptable. Private ownership of land is still not acceptable, but long-term transferable rights to land are now specifically recognized in Article 18 of the new Constitution, passed by the National Assembly in April 1992.

More recently, a somewhat clearer picture has begun to emerge as to the type of economic system which may be considered desirable by the country's leadership. Article 16 of the Constitution states that 'The aims of the State's economic policy are to make the people rich and the country strong.' While socialism remains a major stated goal of the government, the state-regulated market economies of East Asia are seen to provide lessons which could be useful in realizing the country's economic and social goals. The share of state enterprise output in total economic output is expected to continue to decline as private investment increases. The role of the state in economic activities is expected to focus increasingly on regulatory aspects and the promotion of private-sector investment. Parallels can be drawn with the present reforms being introduced in Vietnam and similar reforms introduced prior to periods of rapid economic growth in the Republic of Korea, Malaysia and Indonesia.

While the share of the state in total economic output is now expected to decline, there are areas where the state will continue to play a dominant role. Government policy clearly states that strategic state enterprises will remain state-owned. Strategic enterprises include those engaged in defence activities, public transport, public utilities, education, health services and key financial services. However, these enterprises will have to operate on a more commercial basis and, in many cases, will have to compete with the private sector.

The new Constitution recognizes the right of all economic sectors to engage in economic activities and to own and transfer resources including long-term rights to the use of land (Articles 16 and 18). The types of economic sectors specified in the Constitution are the state, collective, individual, private capitalist and state capitalist sectors. Article 19 specifies that state-run economic establishments shall enjoy autonomy in production and business decisions, and that the managers of state enterprise will be responsible for the efficient business operations of state enterprises.

Article 21 of the Constitution states that the private sector 'can adopt their own ways of organizing production and trading; they can set up enterprises of unrestricted scope in fields of activity which are beneficial to the country and the people'. Article 23 provides guarantees against nationalization. Articles 24 and 25 state that foreign investment and the expansion of external economic relations and foreign investment in Vietnam will be encouraged. These are extremely important indications for the future.

Policy, regulatory and legal framework

The government is in the process of formulating a comprehensive programme of state enterprise reform which will address the policy, regulatory and legal framework, the needs for improved management and financial supervision of state enterprises, the formulation of guidelines for the liquidation of bankrupt enterprises and the partial or complete divestiture of selected non-strategic state enterprises.

The government has stated that it is committed to a policy that state enterprises should operate on a commercial basis and compete on an equal basis with private enterprises. However, many state enterprises continue to be supported with subsidized credit, preferential access to contracts, and by institutional constraints to investment by potential competitors. Some government agencies continue to influence the management decisions of state enterprises on an *ad hoc* basis, but state involvement in strategic planning is generally limited to public utilities, such as the power companies. Some production targets continue to be set, but these are now really only projections and are not instruments of control.

The Ministry of Justice recognizes that the legal framework for state enterprise operations remains inadequate. Two laws being drafted at present and scheduled to be approved during 1992 will have important implications for future state enterprise reform. These are the Bankruptcy Law and the State Enterprise Law. There is still some debate about whether a separate State Enterprise Law is desirable, or whether state enterprises would be better included under a revised Company Law.

The Bankruptcy Law will be particularly important in enabling the banking system to lend to private enterprises on a commercial basis. Private enterprises, and other enterprises without government guarantees, face difficulties in obtaining access to bank financing because of the lack of adequate legal provisions for banks to liquidate collateral used for loans when borrowers do not meet scheduled repayments. The rights of lenders to liquidate mortgaged assets in the case of bankruptcy need to be clearly defined in order to provide potential private investors in state enterprises with increased access to credit for investment in divestiture programmes.

Land will be a potentially major asset of many state enterprises, but the value of this land will depend greatly on the length of the leasehold, the cost of any lease payments and the procedures for renewal of leasehold rights. The formulation of clear guidelines on this issue will be important to the success of any state enterprise reform programme. Proposals for changes in land laws to provide a more efficient basis for the functioning of a market, for transferring rights to the use of land, are presently being considered by the government.

Laws and regulations are also required to clarify the role of the state as enterprise owner, the rights and responsibilities of enterprise management and the legal power of the state in regulating enterprise activity. Recent years have been characterized by considerable uncertainty in this area, and this has caused major distortions in decision-making and has had a negative impact on investment.

Current plans envisage that state enterprises may operate under one of two distinct legal structures. Strategic enterprises will remain 100 per cent state-owned, but they will still be required to operate on a more commercial basis. Enterprises outside of these strategic sectors may be established as shareholding companies, and could be wholly or partly owned by either the state or private sector. In some cases, a minimum level of state and/or domestic ownership may be established, with the remaining shares freely tradeable. It is envisaged that these non-strategic enterprises will operate on a commercial basis, with the usual obligations to all its shareholders, including the state. However, any final decision will be dependent on the success or otherwise of trial state enterprise reform programmes that are currently being formulated. Changes will be required in the Foreign Investment Law to allow foreign investors directly to purchase shares in Vietnamese companies.

Anti-trust or competition laws are inadequate and many state enterprises are virtually guaranteed monopoly powers, without being subject to the price regulations which are usually imposed on monopolies in market economies. This has generated large profits to a few enterprises at the expense of the consumer and other enterprises. In some cases, provincial authorities act to protect the monopoly positions of local enterprises. This issue is becoming increasingly important as foreign investors entering joint ventures with state enterprises can be expected to try to negotiate to retain the monopoly positions now enjoyed by these enterprises. Where natural monopolies exist, general pricing regulations need to be developed to protect consumers and ensure economic efficiency.

Little attention has yet been given to the development of securities laws, despite the stated intention that shares in joint-stock companies will be tradeable. This need for a securities law will become more important as the number of shareholders in individual enterprises increases. The development of a formal stock market has a potentially important role to play in providing direct incentives for improved enterprise performance, and in mobilizing gold and US dollars presently held in large quantities in Vietnam as unproductive savings.

Improving management and financial supervision

The government has decided that the Ministry of Finance will be responsible for the financial monitoring and supervision of all centrally managed state enterprises. The finance department of the provincial authorities will have similar responsibilities for locally managed state enterprises. However, the implementation of an effective financial monitoring system remains a daunting task. The large number of enterprises involved, and the rudimentary level of development of accounting systems, mean that comprehensive financial monitoring will only be achieved in the longer term.

The government recognizes that it can monitor most of its assets by focusing its efforts on improving the financial monitoring of the largest 100–200 state enterprises. Some initial work has been undertaken, using a number of the larger state enterprises as case studies, in developing a computerized system of financial monitoring within the Ministry of Finance, but this system has not yet been implemented in a systematic manner. Individual enterprises can be expected to resist external monitoring, and a clear legal framework will be required to facilitate financial monitoring.

Improvements in accounting standards are required not only for external monitoring but also to improve internal management efficiency. New accounting standards were introduced in 1991, but these are not being implemented in a systematic manner. There are no professional associations of accountants and auditors, and no clear regulations on enterprise audits and the responsibilities and licensing of auditing companies. Training in basic accounting and management skills receive inadequate attention in education curricula.

Boards of directors have been introduced on an experimental basis in a limited number of state enterprises with the aim of improving management standards and accountability. These experiments have met with only limited success because of the lack of a clearly defined legal basis and definition of the power and authority of these boards. In particular, the rights and responsibilities of directors and managers were not clearly defined and were not enforceable. Consequently, existing power structures remained influential and often limit the effectiveness of the new management structures. The Company Law and the proposed State Enterprise Law should assist in clarifying these responsibilities.

Some progress has been made in improving management training in Vietnam. There has been an increase in the number of Vietnamese attending management training programmes in market economies. Increased foreign investment and a rapid increase in the number of expatriate managers resident in Vietnam has also been important in transferring skills. The capability of existing institutions to provide management training in Vietnam is being strengthened following cooperation arrangements with foreign institutions. The Bangkok-based Asian Institute of Technology (AIT) is establishing a campus in Hanoi to facilitate management training. The Swedish International Development Agency (SIDA) is also supporting the development of management training skills at the National Economics University. The United Nations Development Programme (UNDP), through its Management Development Programme, is supporting the government in its most urgent retraining needs. There is, however, still a major need for general training in basic office management skills to meet the changing needs of enterprises.

Liquidation and divestiture of state enterprises

A considerable number of enterprises are not viable and are not likely to become viable. Some of these have already been effectively liquidated. However, this has not been done in a systematic manner and the government and debtors have not always received adequate recompense from the liquidated assets. In addition, lenders to state and other enterprises have not been able to force these enterprises to sell assets, used as collateral, to meet outstanding loan repayments. It is intended that the Bankruptcy Law, which is presently being drafted and is expected to be submitted to the National Assembly in December 1992, will facilitate this process.

There are many small state enterprises engaged in the retail sector which the government now recognizes would be more efficiently operated if transferred to private ownership. Given the large number involved, it will not be possible for the central government to review each one. Proposals are being considered to develop guidelines for the divestiture of non-strategic enterprises and to delegate authority to make divestiture decisions concerning enterprises below a specified maximum size.

Medium- to large-scale enterprises will need to be reviewed more carefully. The government has recently selected a number of enterprises as candidates for transformation into joint-stock companies. On 6 June 1992, Prime Minister Vo Van Kiet announced a decision selecting seven state enterprises to be established as joint-stock companies. The enterprises selected involve a variety of manufacturing activities, presently controlled by a mixture of central ministries and provincial authorities, and are located in both the northern and southern regions of the country. In announcing the decision, the Ministry of Finance was requested to identify other enterprises which could be candidates for establishment as joint-stock companies. Following such changes, some or all of the shares in these companies may be sold to private domestic and foreign investors.

There has been some debate about the need for a formal stock market. The present policy is first to establish joint-stock companies, and then to consider the establishment of a stock market as the need arises. The government does not appear to have any ideological objections to establishing a stock market, and some preparatory work has been undertaken to determine what would be required to establish it in Vietnam and to lay the foundations for this possibility.

The scope and speed of restructuring is constrained by Vietnam's limited financial resources, in addition to political considerations. Government budget revenues are low, the financial system remains poorly developed and domestic savings in the formal financial system are minimal. While the US trade embargo is not critically important *per se*, the fact that this embargo has blocked that resumption of normal relations with the IMF, the Asian Development Bank and the World Bank has had a major adverse impact on Vietnam's access to capital. The lack of access to official capital flows from multilateral financing institutions has had flow-on effects which limit Vietnam's access to commercial credit.

The divestiture of smaller enterprises could be largely financed by domestic investors dependent on informal networks. Foreign investors may be an important source of financing for the larger enterprises. Most foreign joint-venture agreements so far have been with state enterprises. Partnerships already developed may provide an important basis for privatization.

The normalization of relations with the Asian Development Bank and the World Bank could also facilitate restructuring. These institutions have been increasingly active in the region providing loan and limited equity financing for privatization. They can also provide grant financing of technical assistance in the corporate and financial restructuring of state enterprises destined for privatization. Although it cannot finance technical assistance directly, the World Bank has begun executing UNDP and Japanese government-financed projects to assist in restructuring activities. The UNDP and the World Bank have been cooperating with the government to develop a major programme to support the government's efforts to restructure state enterprises, expected for approval in late 1992.

Social costs of adjustment

As discussed earlier, the number of people employed by state enterprises has declined substantially in recent years. The resulting increase in unemployment has been compounded by the partial demobilization of the army following the withdrawal from Cambodia, and the return of a larger number of overseas contract workers who had been working in the former Comecon countries and Iraq.

The fact that only a relatively small proportion of the population is employed in the state sector means that the unemployment problems, due to state enterprise reform, are not as severe as that experienced in the former Comecon countries. Nevertheless, the impact has been substantial in some areas and did contribute to temporary reversals of some reforms in 1990 and 1991. Access to structural adjustment or programme lending from the multilateral financial institutions could ease the adjustment costs and minimize the likelihood of any further reversals.

Some lessons

Vietnam has shown that a gradual shift away from a centrally planned economy to a more market-orientated economy can work. However, in drawing lessons from Vietnam's experience it is important to recognize the economic environment in which this reform took place. The country was facing major macroeconomic problems in a period of declining external assistance from, and trade with, the former Comecon countries. The government's fiscal situation was precarious and inflation was out of control. The state enterprise sector was a major contributing factor to these difficulties. In a situation of poor fiscal performance and very limited external assistance, the government simply could not afford to continue providing large subsidies to state enterprises if it was to realize its economic and social objectives. Moreover, it was becoming increasingly apparent that market systems and outward-looking policies were allowing neighbouring countries in East and South-east Asia to realize more quickly many of the economic and social objectives which were so important to the Vietnamese government. Pragmatic decisions to move to more market- and outward-orientated economic policies reflected these practical realities.

In marked contrast to other countries undertaking such reforms, Vietnam has received only very limited international support for its economic reform programme because of the US-led embargo. While most OECD countries have now broken ranks with the US government, Vietnam still does not have access to lending or direct technical assistance grants from the multilateral financing institutions. This has limited the choices available to the government and has also limited the scope to alleviate the social costs of adjustment.

Vietnam has moved cautiously in implementing economic reforms and in restructuring state enterprises. This has allowed the country largely to avoid the traumatic social adjustments that have taken place in some of the eastern European countries. The gradual approach has minimized social dislocation, and this has been an important factor in maintaining widespread support for the reform programme. The relatively small size of the state sector, the fact that the economy is predominantly agriculturally based, and the relatively small size and dispersed geographic location of individual enterprises, have also contributed to minimizing the social adjustment costs of reform.

The sequencing of reforms has been important to the success of the reform programme. Once the reform programme began to move in earnest in the late 1980s, the government moved fairly quickly to introduce market prices, including a largely market-determined exchange rate. The introduction of market prices and the decision to grant farmers long-term rights to the private use of land had an important positive impact in generating a fairly rapid supply response. This was important in improving macroeconomic stability and in absorbing some of the labour retrenched from the state sector. The resulting increases in rural incomes, plus a rapid expansion in service activities, also ensured that there were many more gainers than losers from the reform programme. This was important in ensuring continued support for the reform programme.

The early price reforms, followed by a reduction in direct subsidies to state enterprises and trade liberalization, were important in forcing state enterprises to adjust to the new economic system. The lack of clear guidelines concerning liquidation and/or divestiture of state enterprises resulted in some losses in state assets. Ideally the regulatory environment for state enterprises should have been better established before granting state enterprises management autonomy. *Ad hoc* decisions to deal with emerging bottlenecks are providing the impetus to develop a more systematic approach for restructuring state enterprises.

With the advantage of hindsight, it would have been preferable to have had a clear idea as to what sort of economic system would evolve at the end of the reform process. Plans could then have been made to address some of the legal, institutional, management skills and accountability issues at an earlier stage before they became such a bottleneck. However, even if decision-makers had a clear vision of the type of economic system that would evolve, the very enunciation of this vision could have reduced the likelihood of success of the reform process.

12

CUBA: CRISIS AND THE ROAD TO RECOVERY

Paul Collins

BACKGROUND

Cuba's socialist system was established in January 1959, after the forces of Fidel Castro ousted the Batista dictatorship. In contrast to its predecessor, the new government made great strides to improve the general standard of living in a socially equitable fashion (through increased expenditures on health, education and the provision of housing for all), and to develop indigenous scientific and technological capacities.[1]

The situation inherited by the Castro government was dire. In 1958 there was only one doctor per 960 inhabitants in Cuba, life expectancy was 62 years, infantile mortality 40 per 1,000, 40 per cent of the work-force had tuberculosis, 13 per cent had typhoid and 31 per cent had malaria. In 1992, there was one doctor per 272 inhabitants, life expectancy had risen to 75 years (equivalent to the United States) and infantile mortality at 10.7 per 1,000 was almost one-quarter of its previous level. In 1958, 23 per cent of the population over 10 years of age was illiterate; in 1992, 100 per cent of all children and 90 per cent of adults are literate.

In 1958, industrial employment was 279,000, with 90 per cent of factories employing 25 or fewer. In 1992, the industrial sector (excluding sugar) employed 750,000. Some 1.1 per cent of GNP goes on research and development, and there are 28,000 technicians in 143 research centres. In 1991 exports from the biotechnology sector exceeded the value of tobacco exports (US $200 million has been invested in the former). Finally, in 1958, two-thirds of the land was devoted to sugar. This has been reduced to 40 per cent today, with production increased from 5.6 million tons per annum to 7.6 million tons. There are 300 plants and installations in the sugar sector.[2]

EXTERNAL RELATIONS

The introduction of socialism triggered a dramatic break in Cuba's traditional international relations. The United States severed relations with Cuba in 1960 and imposed a trade embargo. This was a hard blow. For decades the island had relied most heavily on the US for needed raw materials, inputs and finished goods – products which were essential for Cuba's subsistence, growth and development. In fact, the US was by far the most important foreign partner, not only in terms of foreign trade, but also foreign investment, foreign credit and the transfer of technology.

Having lost its key provider of basic goods, Cuba had to find another partner. The Soviet Union was willing to fill the void.

From the 1960s until the mid-1980s, economic relationships between Cuba and the Soviet Union and its satellites became stronger. The closeness of this relationship is clearly illustrated by Cuba's foreign trade structure: by the mid-1970s, trade with the Soviet bloc accounted for about 60 per cent of Cuba's total foreign trade.

The deterioration of Cuba's terms of trade in the second half of the 1970s and early 1980s brought about an increasing shortage of hard currency. This was badly needed to buy basic raw materials and other inputs essential to the island's development. As the Soviet bloc could provide Cuba with the imports it needed through barter and other types of counter-trade agreements, the share of Cuba's foreign trade with those countries rose further, hitting about 85 per cent of total foreign trade – probably higher than any other socialist country outside of the Soviet Union (for example, it was around 60 per cent for North Korea).

Under agreements with the Soviet Union and eastern European countries, Cuba provided sugar, tobacco, nickel and citrus goods. All foreign trade operations were undertaken by the Ministry of Foreign Trade. In exchange the Soviet Union and its satellites provided Cuba with oil, capital goods and raw materials, transportation equipment and some production know-how.

Increasingly, Cuba's economy was becoming integrated with that of the Soviet bloc. Indeed, to a significant extent (especially in the production of some agricultural goods and machinery) Cuba became one more link in the Soviet Union's (planned) long-term production chain allocated widely among its network of republics. Furthermore, this trade was carried out at prices highly favourable to the island, often set without consideration of what price would be paid in international (competitive) markets. This favourable treatment was particularly marked in the exchange of oil for sugar: the Soviet Union was providing Cuba with more oil than it needed for domestic consumption at very low prices, in exchange for highly priced sugar. This was very important for Cuba, given its heavy reliance on oil for energy generation.

THE POST-1959 SYSTEM OF PLANNING AND ECONOMIC MANAGEMENT

President Castro believed that only through centralized planning and collective ownership of the means of production could a programme for equitable development succeed. Thus the emergent centrally planned system identified what goods would be produced by which state companies, with which production technologies, to whom these goods would be sold and at what price; and how many educational institutions would be located where, how many students/professionals would be trained in which fields of expertise to develop which scientific and technological capacities.

In 1977 Cuba introduced a modified system of planning, the SDPE (Sistema de Direccion y Planificacion de la Economia) based on the Soviet Union's 1965 reforms. Although there were problems in adapting the Soviet model to the culture of Cuba, the SDPE introduced self-financing of state enterprises, the criterion of profitability, incentives (both material in cash terms, and non-material), decentralization (which was the central theme) and organizational coherence. There was more worker participation in enterprise decision-making. However, prices were still set centrally every five years, investment was still determined by the Central Planning Board (Juceplan), and the key criterion remained 'meeting the planned output target'. President Castro himself played a part in the planning process.[3]

THE REVOLUTION'S ACHIEVEMENTS

Cuba's central planning has produced tremendous gains in social welfare over the past 30 years. As indicated above, this Caribbean island has the highest life expectancy of any developing country. The public health system, which is free, has eight times the number of doctors as 30 years ago, 65 times the number of nurses, 113 times the number of technicians and almost six times the number of doctors per person. The public health budget has risen 36-fold, while the population has increased by 50 per cent.

Cuba's educational system has soared in excellence. Between 1958 and 1988 the number of universities rose from three to 47, the number of professors from 203 to 23,487, the number of college graduates from 31 to 29,982. In addition, housing has been provided for basically the whole population.

Economic gains since the Revolution have also been significant. During the 1960s, the foundations for faster growth were laid. During the first half of the 1970s, the Global Social Product (which measures output of goods and services) grew at 7.5 per cent (average annual rate) and in the second half at 4 per cent. Growth continued at 7.3 per cent on average in 1981–5, with great reliance on imports. By comparison, population growth was near 1.5 per cent per year.

However, by 1986, a marked deterioration had set in. Growth rates have remained low or negative.

THE GROWING CRISIS

Thus until relatively recently, Cuba's 10.5 million inhabitants enjoyed a steadily increasing standard of living. However, since the early 1980s, and especially in the second half of the decade, the international situation has become very unfavourable to Cuba. The foreign debt crisis and the appreciation of the US dollar in the early 1980s demanded an even closer economic relationship with the Soviet bloc, at a time when the Soviet Union started to turn away from central planning.

In late 1985 Cuba introduced its 'rectification' programme to increase efficiency and alleviate shortages. New measures were introduced to streamline the government administration. Subsidies were cut and electricity prices were raised. In 1986 the Soviet Union launched *perestroika*. As it was clear that this would lead to a change in the Soviet Union's treatment of Cuba, changes under the 'rectification' programme were accelerated. Cuba started to look for ways to diversify foreign trade markets and products, and to promote foreign investment actively. Experiments at some enterprises started to link workers' remuneration to productivity, at the company (and not individual) level. These experiments continue.

The final shock came in 1989–90 with the events in eastern Europe and when the disintegration of the Soviet Union began. In late 1989, President Castro announced that the 'Special Period in Time of Peace' programme, launched at the beginning of the decade for military purposes, was to be expanded to economic considerations. Efforts to streamline Cuba's institutions were accelerated (for example, the professional apparatus of the Communist Party's Central Committee was reduced by 50 per cent); so was the search for new foreign trade relationships and foreign investments.

By December 1991, trade between Cuba and the Soviet Union had dropped by a reported 50 per cent. With the disintegration of the Soviet Union and the establishment of the CIS, it is unlikely that the former counter-trade-based relationship with Cuba will be restored. As a result, Cuba has lost access to needed inputs and finished products – most importantly oil needed to maintain economic activity.

This situation is not new to Cuba. As had happened years earlier with Cuba's relations with the United States, the island was losing its closest ally. Not surprisingly, Cuba searched for a development strategy which would reduce its dependence on foreign partners to a minimum.

This time, however, Cuba faces a significantly more difficult situation than in the early 1960s. On the *international front*, events in eastern Europe have left the country without an alternative major foreign partner; there are no signs of a re-establishment of relations with the United States in the foreseeable future. Competition in international markets, in foreign trade and investment, is much more fierce than in the 1960s. Cuba has made efforts to promote closer economic ties with other countries, particularly in Latin America, but results so far are limited. No other country, obviously, is in a position to fill in the void left by the United States in the 1960s and the Soviet Union in the 1990s.

On the *domestic front*, social unrest is expected to rise as unemployment increases and the economic situation deteriorates in the near term. However, the probability of this threatening social unrest is minimal since a large portion of the better-off, anti-Castro population left the country after the Castro administration was installed.

CUBA'S POLICY RESPONSES

Remarks made to the author by public officials in Cuba summarize the government's views on strategy: 'In Cuba we already knew what capitalism was 30 years ago. We have no interest in that kind of capitalism', and 'We want to improve our system, not to change it.'

The government recognizes that the improvements in the standard of living achieved by the Revolution cannot be maintained, much less improved, in the short term. In fact, during the Fourth Communist Party Congress held in October 1991, President Fidel Castro warned the audience of 1,300 delegates to prepare for tougher times in 1992, and Cuba is still operating under the 'Special Period in Time of Peace' plan.

Efforts to streamline the government apparatus at every level are continuing, and government ranks are being reduced. Some retraining is taking place to allocate resources according to today's priorities. For example, some government inspectors and advisers have been moved to posts with energy-efficiency-related responsibilities. The emphasis is on saving resources. Public investment programmes have been postponed, except for those with potential to generate foreign exchange. Accordingly, construction of new hospitals, housing and lower education facilities are being postponed, but construction of new hotels and other tourist facilities, as well as biotechnology laboratories, continues. The government budget is being reviewed. Authorities are reducing subsidies and defining prices according to production costs (production schedules remain in the hands of the Central Planning Board, however). But experiments with profit-sharing schemes at the company level continue. In addition, some measure of private entrepreneurship has been introduced – one-man service shops for carpentry, television and radio repair, etc. are now permitted.

Cuba's emergency measures are designed for both survival and development.[4] Resources are being concentrated on priorities such as the biotechnology sector and tourism. The latter now earns an annual income of US $400 million and is the largest earner of foreign exchange. In agriculture, where government measures to reintroduce animal traction to save fuel have been caricatured in some of the overseas press, the government is also ploughing back the results of its scientific research. Productivity is being increased through irrigation, locally produced fertilizers and high-yielding varieties of seeds. Acreage under sugar cultivation is being reduced to enable the planting of food crops.

Combining socialism and central planning with market-driven policies

Cuba's ideological foundation remains unchanged. In contrast with the ex-Soviet bloc, the ideological and methodological framework remains tied to socialism and central planning. But while the sectors strictly orientated to the domestic economy will continue to operate under the centrally planned system, those which have established, or have the potential to establish, economic relations with markets abroad are now being ruled under a more flexible system to allow them to respond to market forces, and thus have access to capital and products needed for domestic development.

Rather than shock treatment, officials have taken a gradual approach to planning, to be implemented through flexible policies and strategies and adapted as the domestic situation evolves. In fact, Cuban policy-makers believe that central planning has become even more important at this time. To them, adopting capitalism and free-market policies would lead to a non-optimal allocation of resources (production of non-essential consumer goods would rise at the expense of products needed for survival and growth), to non-equitable development and, as illustrated by the development in eastern Europe and the (former) Soviet republics, chaos. As explained by a central government official, 'introducing free-market policies at this time would be succumbing to the whims and trends of free markets, which could be disastrous'.

The new priorities

According to the 'Resolution on Economic Development of the Country' announced during the Fourth Communist Party Congress in October 1991, the priorities of the new economic plan have been defined to 'save the country, the Revolution and socialism'. State considerations continue to dominate over individual interests. Central planning is to be flexible, to provide room for adjustments, as needed and dictated by Cuba's internal conditions. These priorities include:

1 Attaining some reasonable level of self-sufficiency in the production of foodstuffs, through the more efficient use of resources and the application of new technologies.
2 Exporting as many Cuban-made, health-related products and services as possible, including those of the pharmaceutical, biotechnology and genetic engineering sectors.
3 Promoting the development of tourism as much as possible.
4 Reorientating scientific research and technology towards the alleviation of shortages.
5 Improving the foreign trade balance, by developing an export mentality and emphasizing import substitution. For export, the goal is to open new markets for traditional exports (i.e. sugar and related products, tobacco,

citrus, nickel, fisheries, coffee), and to develop new goods and services for exports, especially those which can generate foreign-exchange revenues in the short term.

6 Promoting foreign investment inflows (through equity joint ventures, co-manufacturing agreements, marketing agreements) which will contribute capital, technology and access to markets abroad. Emphasis is placed on granting preferential treatment to foreign investment from Latin America.
7 Increasing efficiency in production, and improving quality control systems. Production *per se* is to focus on spare parts and maximum use of raw materials.
8 Decentralizing secondary services, such as carpentry, radio and television repair, etc., which may now be provided by one-worker shops – thus permitting private entrepreneurship.
9 Reducing government expenditures, through increased production and diminished subsidies.
10 Reorganizing the state's central and territorial apparatus and foreign trade procedures, to look for solutions to the foreign debt, so as to reach a more efficient use of human and physical resources, and to reduce the bureaucracy.

Official policy statements made before and after the Fourth Communist Party Congress focus on the generation of hard currency via an improved foreign-trade-account balance and investment inflows, production of foodstuffs and increased efficiency in domestic production and management.

The external economy

The most significant changes are in foreign trade and investment at the macroeconomic level, and managerial changes at the company level.

In relation to foreign trade, the official goals are (a) re-establishment of traditional trade values at pre-crisis levels, (b) expansion of markets for traditional exports and (c) export product *and* market diversification.

Cuban sales abroad include traditional exports such as sugar and its by-products, tobacco, citrus products and nickel. Cuba is starting to market new goods and services, including tourism, health services, training of athletes, translation services, pharmaceuticals, biotechnology and genetically engineered products.

Cuba expects to continue to trade with the former Soviet bloc countries, although now on a foreign-exchange basis. To that end, Cuba is negotiating bilateral trade agreements with Estonia, Kazakhstan, Ukraine and Russia. Cuba has chosen to do so given already established ties, and the need for spare parts of machinery and equipment purchased from these countries.

In addition, Cuba is making advances to diversify its markets abroad, by sending missions to and inviting delegations from elsewhere. Apart from countries which are already trading with Cuba (such as Spain, Japan, Canada, China), special efforts are being channelled to establish and expand trade relations with Latin America.

Among the most radical changes in Cuba's public management system is the decentralization of foreign trade. Since the Revolution, the central government defined which products and services would be exported where, in which quantities, at what prices and in exchange for which products and services. These were defined according to Cuba's needs, more so than existing and potential capabilities. All imports and exports procedures were the responsibility of the Ministry of Foreign Trade. Until recently, procedures and processes to import and export were almost totally systematized: what worked for one enterprise would be applied to all others.

Now any company producing exportable goods may be granted the authorization to export directly – and several are already doing so (for example Suchel, which produces cosmetics). In fact, exporting companies have been given responsibility to become self-sufficient in hard currency and will use their export receipts to import needed inputs, such as oil and other raw materials. As a Cuban official explained, 'exporting companies are being granted financial autonomy'. Nevertheless, some support from the central government may be granted to purchase machinery and equipment needed to produce exportable goods.

Authorization to export and import directly is being granted on a case-by-case basis by the Ministry of Foreign Trade, whose new role is to assist and support foreign trade operations.

Decentralization of production is also taking place. For example, research centres previously devoted solely to research and development of new technologies have been given the responsibility to produce and sell their products abroad – after official authorization. Many have already started to do so, particularly in pharmaceuticals and health-related activities.

In answer to this new responsibility, exporting companies are redefining their operating structures along lines which allow them to respond more quickly and effectively to market opportunities. For example, marketing units are being created and personnel are being trained on international marketing strategies and techniques. These units are establishing systems to gather information on international markets and players and to survey those markets and study potential competitors, so as to identify marketing opportunities. Cuban sales forces in certain industries are now employing foreign salesmen who are nationals of the countries in which Cuba sells, or wants to sell, its products.

To increase productivity and stimulate creativity, incentives are being granted to workers and managers on a more widespread basis, permitting stronger links between productivity and remuneration. This change originated in the tourism industry, where foreign investment abounds. Until 1989, special incentives were strictly forbidden. After the government realized how such incentives could promote productivity and, in turn, foreign-exchange inflows, the ban on incentives was quickly eliminated.

Inward investment

Inward foreign investment is ruled by Decree 50 (1982). The process of foreign investment approval, authorization and administration is under the control of the State Committee for Economic Cooperation.

According to Decree 50, foreign investment is permitted through equity joint ventures, with foreign ownership permitted up to 49 per cent in joint ventures to be established with state enterprises, except for special cases for which the Executive Committee of the Council of Ministers authorizes greater participation. There are no restrictions on the remittances of profits and no taxes on shareholder dividends or executives' personal income. Exemptions can be granted on the 30 per cent profits tax and customs duties. Cuban personnel must be paid at officially established rates.

Although this Decree dates back to 1982, it was not until 1987 that the government started to promote inward foreign investment actively, and mainly in tourism. As a result, tourism has boomed. In fact, it is Cuba's fastest growing industry: in 1989, some 326,000 tourists visited Cuba, a 32 per cent rise on 1988. That pace is expected to continue, as new hotels rise along the beaches east of Havana.

Foreign investment in tourism is through equity joint ventures (mostly 50/50 ownership) with Cubanacan, a state company which operates very similarly to any market-led, competition-driven enterprise abroad. Under Decree Law 50, tourism has been granted special status, which has allowed Cubanacan more freedom in terms of its business conduct. Salaries are higher, incentives are prevalent.

In the past year the government has been strongly promoting foreign firms to come and invest in Cuba, to produce goods and services which will generate foreign exchange. The government has signed an oil exploration agreement with France's Total. An Italian telecommunications company is providing the infrastructure to improve telephone services. Investment is being sought actively in import substitution industries, such as textiles.

Although Decree Law 50 has not been changed, official efforts to promote foreign investment focus on the special allowances permitted under the law, and not on the general treatment. For example, foreign ownership may go up to 100 per cent now – and official statements are inviting specifically Latin American investors to take advantage of this ruling. Companies with foreign participation may grant special incentives to workers so as to encourage and reward higher productivity. In addition, the government has been active in organizing and receiving foreign missions of prospective investors.

ORGANIZATIONAL CHANGE AT THE MICRO-LEVEL

The status of enterprise management in Cuba

Managers of enterprises in Cuba's exporting sectors (such as biotechnology) generally agree with the government's commitment to attempt to alter the macroeconomic strategy by adjusting rather than radically changing internal economic and political structures and processes. In the words of one, 'we need to develop rapidly a capacity to understand, negotiate with outsiders, produce for and enter world markets'. Cuba thus needs negotiating and legal skills to develop better marketing agreements and structures to protect its interests. Finally, Cuba needs promotion and public relations skills to tell its story effectively to the rest of the world. It needs to establish international credibility for its products and trust and confidence on the part of its joint-venture partners.

At the same time, any further increase in the marketing success of the potentially lucrative biotechnology industry, for example, could depend on broader economic, social and political changes – or on permission for the industry to act as an exception to what has been the normal practice.

Conceptually, marketing in Cuba has been closely identified with promotion and sales. Lack of a comprehensive marketing strategy has been evident on the means to determine how to package, price, distribute and advertise products, to organize a marketing effort, to protect intellectual property and systematically and effectively to develop markets.

For the biotechnology sector, at the root of Cuba's problem is the lack of a coordinated effort to market products and respond to opportunities. It is not clear if any individual entity has both the responsibility and the authority to coordinate Cuba's market strategy, and to respond to opportunities in biotechnology. Financial incentives to reward workers have also been rare in Cuba. Too much of the time only negative incentives are used in industry. This sometimes motivates people out of fear, but it deadens creativity and does not encourage people to excel – only to meet targets. Up until now, Cuba would choose what products to develop based on the island's needs. To compete abroad effectively, market research should lead product development, and not the other way around. There does not appear to be any entity capable of surveying world markets, for example.

Like pharmaceuticals, the biotechnology industry in Cuba was developed to provide the population with better health care. It has been extremely successful in meeting that goal. However, to compete abroad, a reorganization of the industry is needed along market-orientated lines. This will permit the industry to respond more quickly and effectively to (the fierce) competition among biotechnology firms in the international markets. A major problem appears to be the production and marketing apparatus geared to the long lead times and stable economic environment of a centrally planned economy. For three decades, this kind of planning served Cuba well. However, faster-responding, more nimble and more flexible organizations are needed to compete in today's global economy.

Management training needs

UNDP-sponsored training requires assessments among sectoral and unit directors and staff. These indicate that marketing, advertising and industry analysis are the highest priority areas if their managers are to compete in world markets. While some lumped these three areas together, others saw them as separate. Those who made the distinction saw industry analysis as the study of where a product might fit into world production systems, who were the competitors, buyers and suppliers, what substitutes existed and what specific strategy might be developed for Cuban products based on comparative advantage. They saw marketing as a separate but related effort of analysis which included the ability to construct and use surveys which would identify specific groups of consumers and their tastes and preferences. Finally, they saw promotion more as the effort of developing and producing advertising. Often comments were made about problems in specific product areas. For example, pharmaceutical and biotechnology producers noted that they were at a great disadvantage because they did not fully understand how this international business functioned and how to break in.

The second most important priority was quality control in production. Most saw this as an effort of linking international consumer tastes and product specifications to the actual production process. This also included the generation of internal systems and processes to guarantee that quality production could be maintained. In some product areas, such as drugs and biotechnology, interest was expressed about learning how to comply with international protocol.

The third priority was greater exposure to the techniques and practices of negotiation. Most felt that Cuban managers had little experience negotiating internationally and that their abilities to negotiate internally might be improved as well. They expressed great interest in workshops on negotiating styles and methods.

Many interviewees noted that most Cuban managers had no experience at all in dynamic market-orientated firms since the Revolution. They felt that training courses might help prepare them for production in world markets but that this training needed to be complemented by short internships in overseas firms where they could see how production, marketing and quality control were managed. Thus, internships after managers completed their courses became the fourth priority area.

The fifth priority was to acquire up-to-date information about world prices, market and product trends. Those who expressed this opinion felt that it would be difficult for Cuban enterprises to compete in world markets without this information. They rated improved information sources above the sixth priority, more general skills for managers in the area of management information systems.

Other areas mentioned were better understanding of market economics, international trade and finance. Better language abilities were considered essential. Finally, respondents referred to the need for more analysis of internal legal, institutional, procedural and inter-organizational bottlenecks to export production.

Management development strategy

Recognizing the foregoing, the Cuban government has taken new initiatives in management education and capacity building with respect to (a) education for public managers, (b) training of management teachers and trainers and (c) improving the capacities of public managers in areas such as international trade, market economics and foreign investment.

The government believes that efforts to build management capacity can best be coordinated through SUTCER, Cuba's Unified System for the Development and Training of State Managers. SUTCER was created in 1988 to 'plan, coordinate, develop, organize and control the efforts of training and development of public functionaries in Cuba'.

It has a high-level director, a coordinating commission made up of top officials from each sector and a technical staff committee. It has the responsibility to supervise six centres of higher education, 23 branch centres and 15 regional and provincial centres. It has a staff of 18 teachers, trainers, managers and analysts. SUTCER's target group is the more than 190,000 Cuban enterprise managers (directors, general managers, area managers, brigade chiefs and others).

Its staff recognize that this large target group cannot be reached directly. Thus, its emphasis is on the development and communication of policies and strategies and of sector supervision by its technical staff (each staff member has supervisory responsibility for a sector). In addition, SUTCER attempts to reach its base through the development of new general course modules that can be widely disseminated through offering courses to train teachers from each of the centres who can then engage in mass dissemination.

The best way to understand SUTCER's work style is through an example. In the past year SUTCER has offered a highly popular course module on general management techniques which has been disseminated throughout the system. The module focuses on leadership styles, communication and participative group-based problem-solving. Some of the initial ideas for the module were generated before SUTCER existed. These ideas began to be articulated when staff from different training centres invited professionals in international management from many countries to come to Cuba to offer courses and to give their ideas. A core group of Cuban professionals began to experiment with these ideas and adapt them to local circumstances. Many of these professionals now form part of SUTCER's current technical committee as full-time staff. The design of the module on general management techniques emerged from this process after SUTCER was created. Its dissemination through training trainers has its parallels in other earlier efforts in the Cuban literacy campaign and mass education.

Because of SUTCER's function and its work style, it has been designated by the government to spearhead the new efforts to prepare managers for the changes in the world economy and to implement the new national objectives of product and market diversification.

International support

In the context of the government's objective to promote exports and to increase its international competitiveness, Cuba's continuing UNDP Management Development Programme aims to strengthen the foundations for the development of a new management culture that will meet the requirements of Cuba's adaptation to changes in the global economic environment. To these ends, project activities over two years have been directed firstly, towards strengthening national institutional capacities and financing for management training relative to the above, and secondly, towards enhancing the management skills of managers of selected export sectors/enterprises (citrus, sugar derivatives, biotechnology and pharmaceutical products).

Since April 1991, project activities have included five principal activities: study tours to the United States, Canada and Europe; two two-week training modules on international marketing and industry analysis; two two-week training modules on negotiations; two two-week training modules on international trade and economics; and a one-week module on intellectual property protection. The project has generated important new learning and a high level of enthusiasm within the Cuba pilot group of managers and professors. Exciting new training modules have developed materials which can later be disseminated more widely to Cuban managers.

Policy changes are making the Cuban enterprise environment more conducive to international trade. As a result of general guidelines set in the recent Communist Party Congress, more enterprises are permitted to participate directly in international trade without intermediation through the Ministry of Foreign Trade. In other cases enterprises are now conducting their foreign commerce through trading companies, whose number more than doubled during 1991. Since 1990 the number of enterprises and economic entities permitted to engage in foreign trade directly has increased from 300 to 500.

Policy-makers are also becoming increasingly willing to move beyond management training to actual enterprise reform experiments. SUTCER initially considered its mandate as primarily the training and education of managers. Today it shows great willingness to link training to changes in enterprise and environmental structures and processes to make its enterprises competitive.

CONCLUSIONS

Conclusions presented below range over a number of issues bearing on the nature, problems and prospects of Cuba's efforts to find a way out of its current crisis.

Firstly, in contrast with nearly all of its former socialist bloc partners – except North Korea and perhaps Turkmenistan – Cuba is pursuing a path of economic adjustment in which it is striving to maintain the basic social achievements of its Revolution. Although state ownership remains the preferred and major mode, significant decentralization of economic management is taking place and an apparently autonomous enclave of exporting enterprises is emerging.

Secondly, in pursuing a selective strategy of this kind, Cuba's resource endowments are considerable: abundant human capital and investment in scientific and technological research and development, especially in the fields of biotechnology, pharmaceuticals and health care products; natural resources (e.g. nickel); location advantageous to tourism; and stability and determination. On the negative side may be the ability of the population to tolerate the adjustment costs and deprivations in the short term. In this sense, continued US hostility will only provide further political support for the Castro government, which has already been helped by the United States in accepting exiled Cuban dissidents.

Thirdly, Cuba's survival strategy also faces challenges internationally. It is competing with a number of other countries for foreign investment while some of its export products – particularly pharmaceuticals – are also in highly competitive sectors globally.

Fourthly, there are also strategic risks: can the selective and gradualist approach of Cuba turn the economy around in time to enable it to survive without external, ex-USSR support?

Fifthly, as Cuba attempts to do so, how can Cuba's planning system manage some of the emerging contradictions within its overall strategy, particularly the split between the centrally planned and controlled domestic market and the much freer exporting and foreign-exchange-earning sectors? How is it dealing with the same products sold both domestically and overseas?

Finally, in terms of institutional capacity and its adaptability, Cuban managers have shown themselves highly retrainable to play new roles in the global economy. The question that remains, however, is the ability of the overall system to move quickly forward from basic management training to structural change in what might be the enabling policy and institutional environment. Individually, none of these problems is insuperable and none lies beyond the known capacities of the Cubans to deal with. Under an optimistic scenario therefore, and assuming Cuba can continue to take strides in protecting its intellectual property and to emulate its political aggressiveness with ruthless economic bargaining, Cuba could become a model for other less industrialized countries.

13

NORTH KOREA: 'SCIENTIFIC MANAGEMENT' TO THE RESCUE?

Paul Collins

BACKGROUND

The Democratic People's Republic of Korea (North Korea) has two northern borders, the longer one (1,041 km) with China (Manchuria), and the other (16 km) with Russia. The Republic of Korea is to the south. North Korea has a land mass of 123,000 sq km, about the size of New York State and almost as large as England, with a population of 22 million. Its GNP per capita was estimated at US $1,273 in 1990 (one-fifth of that in the Republic of Korea), with an aggregate of about US $27 billion.[1]

The peninsula of Korea has only been open to the West for little more than a century, and after 1905 the whole country was virtually run by the Japanese. In 1945 the Russians entered Korea from the north, the Americans entered from the south, and the Japanese left. After abortive attempts to reach agreement for the whole country, the border between north and south settled down at the 38th Parallel, the first time that the country had been divided in almost 1,200 years.

The Democratic People's Republic was set up in 1948, and Kim Il Sung became Premier. In 1950 the north invaded the south, which a force under a United Nations flag repulsed, and in the truce of 1953 the battle line – mostly just to the north of the 38th Parallel – became the new border. Both the Soviet Union and China gave North Korea substantial aid after 1953.

President Kim Il Sung, whose 80th birthday was in April 1992, remains the leader while his son, Kim Jong Il, is also very powerful. The two dominate the three-man Supreme Presidium of the Korean Workers' Party, which controls all aspects of the state government (the third member is O Jin U, the Armed Forces Minister). In a major speech in February 1992, Kim Jong Il said that 'socialist society, when the state develops techniques in a coordinated way according to plans as required by the socialist economic law, is superior to capitalist society'.[2] The one-party rule in North Korea is based on and influenced by the ideology of *Juche*, or self-reliance.

The development of a nuclear industry in North Korea, with, it is believed, weapons capability, has been a stumbling block in the normalization of relationships with the West, and with Japan and South Korea. In recent years there have been seven rounds of discussions between the prime ministers of the north and the south, with some progress. However, the opening up of diplomatic relations between China and the Republic of Korea, together with increasing trade difficulties, especially since the disintegration of the Soviet Union (which was its main trading partner), is tending to leave the Democratic People's Republic in North Korea rather isolated and in increasing difficulty.

THE ECONOMY

Heavy industry was introduced into North Korea by the Japanese in the 1930s, and, in spite of much destruction in the wars, it remains dominant and still receives high priority. Chemicals, cement, iron and steel, textiles, machinery and electric power are the most important (including an installed capacity for hydroelectric power in 1986 of 8,700 MW). The development of heavy industry is seen as an essential aspect of the philosophy of *Juche*.

North Korea is also rich in minerals – coal, iron ore, magnesium, graphite, lead, zinc, tungsten, cadmium, gold and silver. President Kim Il Sung wrote in 1988 that:

> Our Party's aim was to create our own solid base of heavy industry which would be able to produce at home most of the raw materials, fuel, power, machines and equipment needed for the development of the national economy by relying on the rich natural resources and sources of raw materials in our country.[3]

The Third Seven Year Plan (1987–93) aims at 'placing the national economy on a scientific basis and making it more Juche-orientated'.[4] Higher priority is now given to advancing light industry and agriculture 'to produce larger quantities of good quality daily necessities and foodstuffs which cater for the tastes of the people'.

Economically, however, the country is in considerable difficulty. Up to 1990 the trade balance had been steadily deteriorating, especially with the Soviet Union/CIS, its predominant trading partner (Table 13.1). Since that time there have been three significant developments. The first was the disintegration of the Soviet Union and the subsequent Russian requirement in 1991 for 'real prices' in hard currency for its exports to North Korea. That trade has virtually ceased. (North Korea was never a full member of Comecon, but had observer status.)

Secondly, early in 1992 the Chinese also required hard currency for their exports, and North Korea imposed similar conditions on its exports to both China and Russia.[5]

Thirdly, trade with the Republic of Korea has suddenly sprung to life, from

Table 13.1 North Korean foreign trade 1986–90 (three largest trading partners)

	US $ million				
	1986	*1987*	*1988*	*1989*	*1990*
CIS/USSR					
Exports	642	683	887	891	1,047
Imports	1,187	1,391	1,922	1,641	1,688
Balance	–545	–708	–1,035	–750	–641
China					
Exports	255	215	212	167	142
Imports	281	305	380	399	403
Balance	–26	–90	–168	–232	–261
Japan					
Exports	154	218	293	268	271
Imports	204	238	263	216	194
Balance	–50	–20	30	52	77

Source: *Economist Intelligence Unit Report* on 'China and North Korea', No. 2, 1992.

almost zero, reaching some US $190 million in 1991. This is very significant, especially for the future development of the Democratic People's Republic.

There are, however, growing food shortages. North Korea has diverted some of its domestic consumption of rice into exports to earn hard currency (and is importing significant quantities of lower-quality, cheaper rice), while wheat imports were over 750,000 tons in 1991.

Developments have occurred in many advanced industries, precision instruments, machinery, turning lathes, presses, large electric generators and transformers. While their traditional heavy sectors have also expanded, the poor state of some roads and chronic problems of the railways are holding back the whole economy.

The development of trade has been hampered, however, by several other factors, including failure to meet debt repayment obligations (estimates vary of North Korea's foreign debt, but is probably in the region of US $3 billion), the low quality and lack of diversity of exportable goods and the failure to adhere to delivery dates and other contractual obligations. There are sometimes difficulties in foreigners obtaining payment for North Korean imports.

North Korea's development strategy has been essentially inward looking, with trade policy emphasizing import substitution, within the overall framework of 'self-reliance'. Its achievements have been considerable, in the development of a heavy industry base, in the engineering sector and especially in health and education. However, the changed relationships with Russia and China, and the continuing reluctance of other countries to engage fully with the country, in part because of the economic matters mentioned and the unresolved nuclear situation, have resulted in the North Korean economy reaching a watershed.

Yet the economic conditions for a substantial expansion of trade exist – abundant high-grade raw materials, a broad industrial base, engineering capabilities, a highly skilled and disciplined labour force and competitive labour costs. Selective export promotion may be an effective way forward.

Apart from Soviet and Chinese economic aid following the end of the Korean War in 1953, there has been very little wider international support to the economy. However, some modest aid has been given by the United Nations Development Programme (UNDP), in three phases. In 1980–6 US $20 million was spent on 20 projects; in 1987–91 US $22 million was spread over 45 projects; and in 1992–6 US $26 million has been allocated – for energy, environmental protection, for promoting international business links and for management development.

Inflation may now become a problem. For the February 1992 birthday of Kim Jong Il, all workers received a 43.4 per cent increase in their wages, and all pensions were increased by 50.7 per cent. The state purchase price of rice from the farmers was increased by 26 per cent, although official retail prices were unaffected (the official retail price of rice was 0.08 won, while the free market price was about 9.5 won). The army received a 50 per cent pay increase. For President Kim Il Sung's 80th birthday in April, there were mass promotions in the army, and huge and elaborate celebrations (over 3,000 dancers and other artists were brought in from 80 countries).

MANAGEMENT OF THE STATE

The economy has been driven by a series of three-, five- and seven-year plans, associated with an almost total reliance on a highly centralized Soviet-type state planning system. All industry is state-owned, and most retail stores are administered by the People's Services Committee. Enterprises have annual and monthly quotas, and may even be set targets on a 10-day basis. All prices are controlled (except in the 'black market').

In 1961 the Taean management system was established for setting targets and budgets (observed by the President when he visited the Taean heavy engineering works in that year). It is a three-stage process:

1 Government targets are issued as part of a seven-year plan.
2 Proposals are made by management on the basis of available capacity. A process of consultation then ensues between the State Planning Commission and individual enterprises.
3 There is agreement on production targets after collective discussions with the workers, the secretary and the factory manager. These result in a finally agreed production plan. Enterprises are then allocated resources on that basis.

The overall system is complex. There are many inherent challenges, such as the need to reconcile central directives with local enterprise initiatives. A number of smaller enterprises report to provincial planning bodies and have a degree of autonomy. Other larger provincial enterprises report to their ministry or commission.

Between enterprises an equally complex system of relationships operates, rather along the lines of the *Kombinats* in eastern Germany in which groups of enterprises create vertically and horizontally integrated units, with common domestic and foreign marketing.[6]

Moreover, under the Independent Cost Accounting System, enterprises are allowed to buy and sell goods among themselves (at centrally approved prices). Profits are retained and distributed among the workers.

Economic plan and budget documents suggest some official dissatisfaction with managerial performance. To recapture earlier growth rates, especially to improve exports, stress is now being placed on increased productivity. The key to this is seen in enhancing management technology and 'placing production and management practices on an improved scientific basis'. The inward-looking aspect of the Korean economy has meant that it has not kept pace with modern management techniques in production. Surveys by the UNDP concluded that considerable improvements in resource use and output could be achieved by introducing decision-support systems into strategically placed enterprises for more effective management control over production activities, and other techniques.

THE NATIONAL POLICY FRAMEWORK FOR CHANGE

The government has thus embarked on a series of far-reaching measures. These are:

1 Putting production and management on a more scientific basis, through automation and computerization.
2 Diversification of external economic relations through state and local authority foreign trade with market economies. This has highlighted the need for improved marketing understanding in the Ministry of Foreign Trade and in enterprises.
3 The intention to press ahead with joint ventures with foreign enterprises under its 1986 Joint Venture Law, to which there has been little international response so far. This also highlights the need to strengthen government institutions and management capabilities.

Automation, computerization and management development

The government's strategic approach to management development, and the driving force of its programme to improve productivity, is computerization. The overall benefits of modern management methods, based on scientific and analytical management techniques involving computerization, have been seen to offer better management control over production, accelerated work flow, enhanced strategic planning and management capabilities, and the optimal use of installed production capacities, investment, people and materials.

Trade liberalization

The objectives of trade liberalization are:

1 the creation of a more open economic environment in which trade is made more efficient and competitive;
2 a more diversified export structure, both products and markets; and
3 an accelerated growth in export earnings.

Any anti-trade bias in the system of controls and incentives will be eliminated, the exchange rate needs to be realistic, and complementary measures need to be taken to reduce costs (and thus improve profitability) in both import-competing and exporting sectors.

Strategy for inward foreign investment

The number and magnitude of foreign investments in North Korea have been small, and have not brought with them the high technologies and export capacities which had been expected – in spite of a relatively liberal joint-venture law, advantageous tax legislation in 1985–6 and efforts to improve the infrastructural and support facilities for joint ventures.

A Ministry of Foreign Trade official explained to the writer that the following approaches were being adopted:

(a) to give political security to foreign investors;
(b) to develop an economic policy which is clear, decisive and stable;
(c) to improve management systems;
(d) to improve the quality and standards of manpower; and
(e) to resolve the market problem in a socialist economy.

The obstacles are seen as being the credit standing of domestic enterprises, the still incomplete legal, institutional and regulatory framework for joint ventures, and limited capabilities to negotiate deals on the policy as well as the project level. Also, the dominance of state-owned enterprises reduces the possibilities for joint ventures, and the scope for flexible decision-making. There is also the lack of an overall promotional strategy.

In December 1991 the first 'zone of free economy and trade' of 621 sq km was set up in the north-east of the country. It is centred on the port of Nanjin, close to the larger city of Chongjin and within the Tumen Delta area, where further large developments are being considered. There is clearly a lot to be done, however. The port of Nanjin has not been modernized for 60 years and has a capacity to take ships no larger than 15,000 tons. Other infrastructure is very inadequate.[7]

Perhaps the main problem to overcome is one of attitudes and awareness of experience elsewhere. Technical improvements can be made, in installing computers and in introducing advanced management production planning and control techniques in businesses, but observing China's experience, state-provided infrastructure beforehand (the best that could be provided), with freedom from state control, were key factors initially. Such circumstances, and the demonstration that the government meant what it said, attracted foreign interest in inward investment. China benefited from having Hong Kong on its doorstep, with many ethnic Chinese from there and other countries willing to bring in new investment. North Korea has close neighbours, too, which are highly successful – the Republic of Korea (with its historic ties), Japan and an increasingly prosperous China.

THE UNDP MANAGEMENT DEVELOPMENT PROGRAMME

In addition to support for numerous projects (mentioned earlier) and for the promotion of joint ventures, the UNDP is assisting in the area of scientific management. The present management in many enterprises, while very enthusiastic to improve, for example, the utilization of installed capacities, investments, manpower, raw material consumption, power and energy efficiency, do not know how to do so.

In three of the leading enterprises – the Taean Heavy Machine Complex, the Pyongyang Textile Combine and the Anjou Coal Mine – lists have been drawn up of the management and operational areas where new techniques can significantly improve performance. By way of example, for the Pyongyang Textile Combine the list reads:

(a) analysis of production activities and reporting on production, units, departments, articles, plans, targets and quality;
(b) consumption and supply of raw materials;
(c) utilization of production capacities;
(d) monitoring of progress in the production of fabric;
(e) deployment, utilization and productivity of weavers/operators;
(f) personnel data and administrative functions related to personnel;
(g) financing and budgeting.

To improve the capabilities of management and operations in such areas, the aim of UNDP is to achieve the following:

1 *One national workshop* in modern management methods for senior management of industries and in government to be set up and operating.
2 *Five 'Management Analysis Groups'* (MAGS), one each in the Pyonyang Information Centre, the University of National Economy, the Taean

Heavy Machine Complex, the Pyongyang Textile Combine and the Anjou Coal Mine – all to become fully established and functioning.

3 *Five computing facilities*, one in each of the above organizations, to be procured, installed and operational, with likewise an additional computer system for the General Bureau of Cooperation with International Organizations.

4 *A core group of personnel of the five MAGS to be well trained* in management information systems, operational research and decision optimization, production scheduling and control, decision-support systems, and transport and distribution systems.

5 *Three pilot demonstration software packages* in management in each of the immediately above five systems areas, one in each of the three firms mentioned, fully developed, installed and operational.

6 *Future computerization plans in each of the three companies*, prepared and available.

7 *Four workshops/training courses* conducted by national project personnel in the several areas of management systems above (management information systems, etc.).

8 *A quarterly newsletter to disseminate information* about the activities of the five MAGS for the benefit of other enterprises.

CONCLUDING COMMENTS

In conventional economics, the policy of self-sufficiency might be considered as inhibiting and distorting to the economy. The benefits of trade on the basis of comparative advantage could be lost. But in the new thinking on economic development the idea of 'self-sustainable communities', especially ones that use mostly locally available indigenous materials and little fossil fuel, are looked on with favour.

Unlike most other centrally planned economies, North Korea is contemplating neither radical political and economic reform (as, for example, in Mongolia), nor radical economic reform without political change (Vietnam). The government does not appear to accept that any form of broad economic change is either necessary or desirable. It is a cautious reformer, with limited objectives in clearly defined sectors and activities.

Whether this approach will yield the benefits which the government is seeking must remain for the present an open question. Global economic conditions at this time are not in their favour. However, the reform processes already started (described above) may generate a dynamic of their own which, combined with possible future political change, may well prove difficult to control.

The risks are many. In the sphere of international trade and joint ventures, potential investors may be unwilling to turn to North Korea because of political conditions, or the government's credit standing. Greater awareness of what will attract foreign investors, for example in special economic zones, is a prime need.

In management development, the knowledge of the English language by project personnel is extremely important. Without this, the acquisition of understanding through training and consultant experts will be minimal. This in turn would adversely affect the success of projects.

Further questions remain. There are implementation risks associated with the specific projects mentioned earlier. For example, what will the responses be in practice, and how effective will their communication be to other enterprises?

The nature of the change strategy and policies by comparison with other countries with which North Korea may be in competition will be a key factor. Much can be learnt, for example, from the Chinese reform programme – a country which is not abandoning socialism but is nevertheless changing fundamentally in its economic and industrial policies – and from developments in the south.

There may also be divergencies between the outcomes of formal planning and the reality of foreign markets. North Korea is a secretive country which needs clear windows onto the outside world.

The capacity of the economy to undertake reforms is also in doubt, given the interdependence of so many of them (the problem of the railways, for example). There are dangers in piecemeal reforms not connecting.

There is the role of macroeconomic stability and policy. To increase money incomes by 40–50 per cent overnight, albeit towards the end of a planning period, is bound to have serious – and probably unplanned – consequences.

Finally there is the fundamental question about the causes of business success. Up-to-date management skills and practices, together with widespread computerization, are necessary in practically every kind of manufacturing activity, and in many services, but they are not sufficient. Business leadership is also crucial and the formulation of a winning strategy, swift responses to changing circumstances, the willingness to take risks, awareness of what is happening elsewhere in the world are among the other factors which will prove also to be necessary in a tough competitive environment. The forthcoming UNDP seminars notwithstanding, it is difficult to see how these can be developed within the present structure of planning in North Korea, and – one may be tempted to think – within the politics, culture and habits of its people. Yet there is clear evidence that the ethnic people of Korea can be very successful on a global scale. The task is well within their reach.

NOTES AND REFERENCES

1 SURVEY OF CONTRIBUTIONS

Notes

1 M. Gorbachev, *Perestroika*, London, Fontana/Collins, 1987, pp. 30–4.
2 There has, for example, been a large spontaneous growth of small unincorporated businesses, especially in Czechoslovakia and Poland. See S. Johnson (NBER unpublished), in *The Economist*, 4 April 1992.
3 *Goskomstat*, 1987, quoted in J. Lloyd, 'The October Revolution', *Financial Times*, 2 October 1992.
4 W. Carlin and C. Mayer, 'Restructuring Enterprises in Eastern Europe', CEPR Discussion Paper no. 700; *Economic Policy* 15, October 1992.
5 See Lloyd, *op. cit.*
6 N.A. Nazarbayev, *Strategy for Establishment of Kazakhstan as a Sovereign State*, Kazakhstan Pravda (undated but issued in 1991). By comparison, President Yeltsin's autobiography *Against the Grain, An Autobiography*, London, Jonathan Cape, 1990, is unclear about his vision of the future.
7 D. Fraser, *Financial Times*, 14 July 1992.
8 'The Castro interview', *Euromoney*, July 1992.
9 Yeltsin, *op. cit.*, pp. 138, 176.
10 G.D.N. Worswick and P.H. Ady, *The British Economy in the Nineteen-fifties*, Oxford, Clarendon Press, 1962, p. 230.
11 Ian Jeffries, *A Guide to the Socialist Economies*, London, Routledge, 1990, pp. 61–72.
12 See also Carlin and Mayer, *op. cit.*
13 This proposal is rather similar to that put forward by the UK *Select Committee on the Nationalized Industries* (Chairman Ian Mikardo MP), 'Ministerial Control of the Nationalized Industries', Session 1967–8 (three volumes). In the White Paper, 'Ministerial Control of the Nationalized Industries' (Cmnd 4027, May 1969) the Committee's recommendation for a Ministry of Nationalized Industries separate from the 'sponsoring departments' was rejected largely because of the interdependence of efficiency and the 'public interest' and fears about contradictory policies.

References

Gorbachev, M. (1987) *Perestroika*, London: Fontana/Collins.
Heath, J. (ed.) (1990) *Public Enterprise at the Crossroads*, London: Routledge.

Jeffries, I. (1990) *A Guide to the Socialist Economies*, London: Routledge.
Nazarbayev, N.A. (undated but issued in 1991) *Strategy for Establishment of Kazakhstan as a Sovereign State*, Kazakhstan Pravda.
Schumacher, E.F. (1973) *Small is Beautiful*, London: Blong & Briggs Ltd.
Select Committee on the Nationalized Industries (in the UK), 'Ministerial Control of the Nationalized Industries', Session 1967–8, (3 vols).
Worswick, G.D.N. and Ady, P.H. (1962) *The British Economy in the Nineteen-fifties*, Oxford: Clarendon Press.
Yeltsin, B. (1990) *Against the Grain, An Autobiography*, London: Jonathan Cape.

3 REVITALIZING THE RUSSIAN ECONOMY – CATCHING UP

Notes

1 I am deeply indebted to Marjorie Nicholson and George Miller for their collaboration in writing this chapter. The copyright for Figures 3.1, 3.2, 3.3 and 3.4 is with Russian Consultancy Ltd.

5 POLAND – THE 'BIG BANG'

Notes

1 P. Bozyk, *Droga donikad? Polska i Jej Sasiedzi na Rozdrozu* (Poland and its neighbours at a crossroads), Warsaw, BGW, 1991, pp. 34–5.
2 See J. Kornai, *The Road to a Free Economy: Shifting From a Socialist System: The Example of Hungary*, New York, Norton, 1990, p. 20.
3 The programme was twice presented in Poland by World Bank officials. See *Seminar on Managing Inflation in Socialist Economies*, Warsaw, EDI, World Bank, 12–13 March 1990; *Conference on Adjustment and Growth: Lessons for Eastern Europe*, Macroeconomic Adjustment and Growth Division of the World Bank, in association with the World Economy Research Institute, Warsaw School of Economics, Pultusk, Poland, 4–5 October 1990.
4 *Paport o Stanie Gospodarki* (Report on the state of the economy), Warsaw, Council of Ministers, 3 December 1991, pp. 39–40.
5 See J. Sachs, D. Lipton, 'Poland's economic reform', *Foreign Affairs*, summer 1990, p. 55.
6 See P. Bozyk, 'Scenarios of transformation to a market economy in central and eastern Europe', World Economy Research Institute, Centre for International Comparative Studies, Working Paper No. 57, January 1992, pp. 11–31.
7 See *Ustawa Budzetowa na rok 1992. Uzasadnienie* (Budget Bill for 1992), Warsaw, Council of Ministers, March 1992, pp. 60–2.
8 At mid-1992 the following stocks were being traded on the stock exchange: Tonsil, Prochnik, Krosno, Exbud, Kable, Swaredz, Wolczanka, Zywiec, Irena, Okocim and Elektrim. See J. Szekaj, Z. Duda, 'Co slychac na gieldzie' (What's new on the stock market?), *Zycie Gospodarcze*, No. 14, 5 April 1992; 'Podzial zyskow' (Division of Profits), *Nowa Europea*, No. 54, 16 April 1992.
9 See *Raport o Stanie Gospodarki*, *op. cit.*, pp. 38–9.
10 See P. Bozyk, *Kto winien*? (Who's to blame?), Warsaw, Wydawnictwo Polskiej Agencji Ekologicznei, 1992.
11 See *Paport o Stanie Gospodarki*, *op. cit.*, pp. 42–4.

12 At mid-1992 the highest-rated private business schools in Poland were: International School of Managers, Gdansk; Polish International Management School, Warsaw; International Management Centre, Warsaw; Poznan School of Managers, Poznan; International Business School, Ryni, Warsaw; International School of Managers, Klodzienko, Warsaw. See 'Polskie szkoly biznessu' (Polish Business Schools), *Nowa Europa*, No. 57, 22 April 1992.

References

Bozyk, P. (1991) *Droga Donikad? Polska i Jej Sasiedzi na Rozdrozu*, (Poland and its neighbours at a crossroads), Warsaw: BGW.

—— (1992a) *Kto Winien*? (Who's to blame?), Warsaw: Wydawnictwo Polskiej Agencji Ekologicznei.

—— (1992b) *Scenarios of Transformation to a Market Economy in Central and Eastern Europe*, World Economy Research Institute, Centre for International Comparative Studies, Working Paper No. 57, January.

Council of Ministers (1991) *Paport o Stanie Gospodarki* (Report on the state of the economy), Warsaw: 3 December.

—— (1992) *Ustawa Buzetowa na rok 1992. Uzasadnienie* (Budget Bill for 1992), Warsaw: March.

Kornai, J. (1990) *The Road to a Free Economy: Shifting From a Socialist System: the Example of Hungary*, New York: Norton.

Sachs, J. and Lipton, D. (1990) 'Poland's economic reform', *Foreign Affairs*, summer.

World Bank (Economic Development Institute) in collaboration with the World Economy Research Institute (WERI), Central School of Planning and Statistics (1990) *Seminar on Managing Inflation in Socialist Economies*, Warsaw: World Bank, 12–13 March.

World Bank (Macroeconomic Adjustment and Growth Division) in association with the World Economy Research Institute (1990) *Conference on Adjustment and Growth: Lessons for Eastern Europe*, Pultusk, Poland: Warsaw School of Economics, 4–5 October.

6 THE CZECHOSLOVAK 'LARGE PRIVATIZATION'

Notes

1 The first draft of this paper was supported by a grant from the International Center for Economic Growth within the Reform Round Table working group series, for which we are very grateful. We would like to thank everyone who has given us useful comments, especially Mr George Truitt of ICEG. Any errors or inconsistencies in the text are solely the responsibility of the authors. We are grateful also to Michael Allen of Price Waterhouse for his comments on the shortfalls of voucher privatization.

References

Bohm, A. and Kreacic, V. (eds) (1991) *Privatization in Eastern Europe: Current Implementation Issues*, San Francisco: The International Center for Public Enterprises in Developing Countries.

CERGE UK (1991–2) *Privatization Newsletter*, Prague: Issues 1–7, October 1991–June 1992.

Conte, M. and Svejnar, J. (1990) 'The Performance Effect of Employee Ownership Plans', in A. Blinder (ed.), *Paying for Productivity*, Washington: The Brookings Institution.

Dornbusch, R. and Edwards, S. (1990) *The Economic Populism Paradigm*, NBER working paper, May.

Gati, C. (1990) *After Communism, What? The Political Agenda in Central and Eastern Europe in the 1990s*, Washington: Third U.S.–Czechoslovak Roundtable on Economic Relations.

Grosfeld, I. (1990) *Privatization of State Enterprises in Eastern Europe: The Search for Environment*, Paris: Delta, Doc. no. 90–17.

Hanke, S.H. (ed.) (1987) *Privatization and Development*, San Francisco: International Center for Economic Growth, ICS Press, Institute for Contemporary Studies.

Hinds, M. (1990) *Issues in the Introduction of Market Forces in Eastern European Socialist Economies*, Washington: World Bank, Report No. IDP/0057.

Hlavacek, J. and Mejstrík, M. (1992) 'Precondition for Privatization in Czechoslovakia in 1991/1992', in J. Earle, R. Frydman and J. Rapaczynski (eds) *Studies of Privatization in Eastern Europe*, New York: St. Martin's Press.

Klvacova, E. (1992) 'Privatizace v Mezicase', *Ekonom* 8.

Kornai, J. (1990) *The Road to a Free Economy, Shifting from a Socialist System*, New York: Norton.

McDermott, G. and Mejstrík, M. (1990) *Czechoslovak Competitiveness and the Role of Small Firms*, Berlin: Paper for the conference at the WZB.

Mejstrík, M. (1990a) *Innovation and Technology Transfer* (Proceedings of conference), Prague: Institute of Economics, Prague.

—— (1990b) *The Transformation of Czechoslovakia to a Market Economy. The Possibilities and Problems*, Warsaw: UNDP Seminar on Privatization.

—— (1992) 'Where are We Headed: The Case of Czechoslovakia', in M. Claudon and T.L. Gutner (eds) *Comrades Go Private (Strategies for Eastern European Privatization)*, New York: New York University Press.

Milanovic, B. (1989) *Liberalization and Entrepreneurship Dynamics of Reform in Socialism and Capitalism*, New York: Armonk, M.E. Sharpe.

Mizsei, K. (1990) *Experiences with Privatization in Hungary*, Washington: World Bank Conference.

Mlcoch, L. (1989) *Behavior of Czechoslovak Enterprises*, Prague: Institute of Economics, Research Paper No. 348.

Nellis, J. (1990) *Privatization in Reforming Socialist Economies*, Ljubljana: Conference on Privatization in Eastern Europe, ICPE/EDI World Bank/UNDP.

Ramanadham, V.V. (ed.) (1990) *Privatization in Developing Countries*, New York: Routledge, Chapman and Hall.

Sachs, J. and Lipton, D. (1990) 'Creating a Market Economy in Eastern Europe, The Case of Poland', *BPEA*, 1.

Shliefer, A. and Summers, L. (1988) 'Breach of Trust in Hostile Takeovers', in A. Shliefer and L. Summers (eds) *Corporate Takeover: Causes and Consequences*, Chicago: University of Chicago Press.

Svejnar, J. (1989) 'A Framework For the Economic Transformation of Czechoslovakia', *Plan Econ Report*, V, 52.

Vuylsteke, C. (1989) *Techniques of Privatization of State-Owned Enterprises* (Volume I: Methods and Implementation), Washington: World Bank Technical Paper Number 88.

Young, S.D. (1990) *Business Valuation and the Privatization Process in Eastern Europe: Challenges, Issues and Solutions*, Fontainebleau: INSEAD.
Zamrazilova, E. (1990) 'International Comparisons of Economic Development Levels Between East and West European Countries', *Jahrbuch des Ost-Europa Wirtsschaft*, November.

7 EAST GERMANY – SCALING DOWN

Notes

Comments on the drafting of this chapter from Andrew Glyn and Peter von Richthofen have been especially helpful.

1 A more detailed treatment of the Treuhand's method of privatization, and a theoretical framework within which it can be compared to eastern European approaches to privatization, can be found in Carlin and Mayer (1992).
2 For a discussion of the economic issues involved see Carlin and Mayer (forthcoming).
3 For examples of cases where this has occurred, see Hartel *et al.* (1991).
4 Descriptions of the early stages of restructuring this Kombinat can be found in Carlin and Mayer (forthcoming) and Carlin (1992).

References

Akerlof, A., Rose, A.K., Yellen, J. and Hessenius, H. (1991) 'East Germany in from the cold: the economic aftermath of currency union', *Brookings Papers on Economic Activity*.
Carlin, W. (1992) 'Privatization in East Germany: 1990–1992', *German History*, 10, 2.
Carlin, W. and Mayer, C. (1992) 'Restructuring enterprises in Eastern Europe' (CEPR Discussion Paper No. 700), *Economic Policy*, 15, October.
—— (forthcoming) 'The Treuhandanstalt: privatization by state and market', in O. Blanchard, K. Froot and J. Sachs (eds) *Transition in Eastern Europe*, Chicago: Chicago University Press and NBER.
Härtel, H-.H., Krüger, R., Seeler, J. and Weinhold, M. (1991), 'Institutionelle Ursachen von Wettbewerbsverzerrungen in den neuen Bundesländern', *HWWA-Report*, 92.

8 REFORMING 'SELF-MANAGED' ENTERPRISES IN SLOVENIA

Notes

1 S. Estrin, *Self-Management: Economic Theory and Yugoslav Practice*, Cambridge, Cambridge University Press, 1983.
2 E.T. Comisso, *Workers' Control under Plan and Market*, New Haven, Yale University Press, 1979.
3 S. Grozdanic, *Workers' Self-Management and Participation* (National Report, Vol. 1), International Center for Public Enterprises, 1980.
4 *Joint Ventures and Acquisitions in Slovenia*, Ljubljana, Agency for Privatization and Development Fund, 1992.
5 U. Korze and M. Simonetti, 'Privatization in Yugoslavia', in A. Bohm and V. Kreacic (eds) *Privatization in Eastern Europe*, Ljubljana, International Center for Public Enterprises, 1991.

6 U. Korze and M. Simonetti, *Privatization of Tobacco Company Ljubljana*, International Private Enterprise Development Research Centre, 1992.
7 E. Pirkmajer, 'Denationalization in Slovenia: The former owner's point of view', in *Reprivatization in Central and Eastern Europe*, Central and Eastern European Privatization Network, 1992.
8 The most critical factor which triggered the final countdown to Slovenia's independence was when Slovenia was required by the Federal Central Bank – the National Bank of Yugoslavia – to advance inflationary credits to Serbia.
9 R. Jayashankar, *Development of Management Support Systems for Slovene Enterprises*, Paper for the International Workshop on Strategic Information Planning, International Center for Public Enterprises, 1992.
10 M. Warner, 'Management vs. Self Management in Yugoslavia', *General Management*, 1990, 16, 2.

10 THE PEOPLE'S REPUBLIC OF CHINA: SOCIALISM WITH A DIFFERENCE

Notes

1 *Economic Daily*, 31 January 1992.
2 Since 1982 government departments have issued *Development Plans on Key Research Areas of Science, 863* (high-technology development plan), and the *Torch* plan.
3 *People's Daily*, 1 January 1992. Speech by Mr Rong Yi Ren, Chairman of China International Investment Corporation, on his visit to London.
4 Gao Shangquan, *The Process and Basic Experience of China's Economic System Reforms*, delivered at the conference organized by the Overseas Development Institute in London, April 1992.
5 *People's Daily*, 27 November 1990.
6 *Economic Daily*, 14 June 1992.
7 *People's Daily*, 19 June 1992.
8 *Economic Daily*, 6 May 1992.
9 *Economic Daily*, 5 June 1992.
10 *Regulations on the Transformation of the Function of State Owned Enterprises*, 23 July 1992.
11 *Economic Daily*, 10 March 1992.
12 *People's Daily*, 22 April 1992.
13 *Economic Daily*, 10, 11 March 1992.
14 *Economic Reference*, June 1992, p. 14.
15 *People's Daily*, 15 May 1992.
16 *Economic Daily*, 14 June 1992.
17 In 1989 the Da Tong Coal Mine, which supplied 10 per cent of China's total coal consumption for industry, plunged from 306 million yuan profit to 83 million yuan loss. The profits of No. 2 Automobile Corporation (the second largest in China) were reduced by 28 per cent between January–April 1989.
18 *People's Daily*, 24 May 1992.
19 *People's Daily*, 1 June 1992.
20 *People's Daily*, 27 November 1990.
21 *Economic Daily*, 28 February 1992.
22 *Economic Daily*, 6 May 1992.
23 *Economic Reference*, 1992 (internal).

24 *Economic Reference*, 1989, no. 27.
25 *Economic Daily*, 18 June 1992.
26 Zhou Shu Lian, Pa Shu Ping and Chen Shu Xien (eds) *Research on China's Industrial Policy*, p. 511.
27 *Economic Daily*, 30 March 1992.
28 Liu Hong Ru, 'Issues on the Shareholder Experiment', *People's Daily*, 23 June 1992.
29 *Measures on the Shareholding Experiment*, issued by the State Council 15 May 1992.
30 *Ibid.*
31 *Economic Daily*, 21 May 1992, spokesman from the State Economic Reform Commission.
32 *People's Daily*, 29 June 1992.
33 Chen Beng-Zhu, 'Thoughts on the Reform of Government Functions', *People's Daily*, 8 June 1992.
34 *People's Daily*, 7 June 1992.
35 Rong Y. Ren, *People's Daily*, 1 June 1992.
36 *Problems of Foreign Investment*, Ministry of Trade 1988 (internal document).
37 *People's Daily*, 15 April 1987.
38 Chang Shu Je (ed.), *Asset Restructure – a Study on Enterprise Merger*, Shaanxi: Shaanxi publishing house, January 1992, p. 93.
39 Interview with Huang Wen Pao, Chief Engineer in the State Planning Commission, 1987.

References

Chang Shu Je (ed.) (1992) *Asset Restructure – a Study on Enterprise Merger*, Shaanxi publishing house.

Chen Bingan, Hu Ge and Liang Zhaosong (1991) *The Mystery Success of Shen Zhen*, Shen Zhen: Hai Tien publishing house.

Gao Shangquan (1992) *The Process and Basic Experience of China's Economic System Reforms* delivered at the conference organized by the Overseas Development Institute in London, April 1992.

Measures on the Shareholding Experiment, issued by the State Council 15 May 1992.

Regulations on the Transformation of the Function of State Owned Enterprises, 23 July 1992.

Zhou Shu Lian, Pa Shu Ping and Chen Shu Xien (eds) (1992) *Research on China's Industrial Policy*.

11 VIETNAM: IMAGE AND REALITY

Notes

The author, Senior Economist, UNDP, Hanoi, has benefited greatly from numerous discussions with Vietnamese officials and other specialists working in Vietnam. The views expressed are personal, and do not represent that of any organization.

1 The consequences of the war, and US bombing of the north, on central planning is reviewed briefly in Lang (1985: 6–8).
2 See B. Ljunggren, *Market Economies under Communist Regimes; Reform in Vietnam, Laos and Cambodia*, Stockholm, SIDA, forthcoming, for a more detailed discussion of this issue.
3 Inflation reached more than 700 per cent, exports were stagnant, the current-ac-

count deficit was increasing rapidly and international reserves were desperately low.

4 Decree No. 217-HDBT, On Renovating the Planning, Economic, Accounting and Socialist Business of State Enterprises.

5 Data collection systems in Vietnam are poorly developed and are only just beginning to be adapted to the new system of economic management. Figures quoted should be treated with caution.

6 Surprisingly, government revenue in Vietnam, as a percentage of GDP, is considerably lower than in most market economies in Asia.

7 A micro-level study by Mitsui (1992) found similar declines in employment between 1985 and 1990, with the rate of decline higher in Hanoi than in Ho Chi Minh City.

References

Asian Development Bank (1989) *Economic Report on the Socialist Republic of Viet Nam*, Manila.

Beresford, M. (1988) *Vietnam: Politics, Economics, and Society*, New York: Pinter.

Communist Party of Vietnam (CPV) (1987) *6th National Congress Documents*, Hanoi: Foreign Languages Publishing House.

—— (1991a) *7th National Congress Documents*, Hanoi: Foreign Languages Publishing House.

—— (1991b) *To Understand the 7th National Congress of the Communist Party of Vietnam*, Hanoi: Foreign Languages Publishing House.

Foreign Languages Publishing House (1992) *Socialist Republic of Vietnam: Constitution (1992)*, Hanoi.

General Statistics Office (1991) *Statistical Data on the Socialist Republic of Vietnam (1976–1990)*, Hanoi.

—— (1992a) *Economy of Vietnam – Review and Statistics*, Hanoi.

—— (1992b) *Vietnam Industrial Statistics (1986–1991)*, Hanoi.

Hisaak Mitsui (1992) *Effects of the Recent Industrial Reforms in Viet Nam: Remarkable Transformation to the Market Economy*, Tokyo: International Development Centre of Japan.

Nguyen Khac Vien (1987) *Vietnam: A Long History*, Hanoi: Foreign Languages Publishing House.

SPC/UNDP (1990) *Report on the Economy of Vietnam*, Hanoi.

Tan Teng Lang (1985) *Economic Debates in Vietnam*, Singapore: Institute for South East Asian Studies.

Vylder, S.D. and Fforde, A. (1988) *Vietnam: An Economy in Transition*, Stockholm: SIDA.

World Bank (1992) *Vietnam: Restructuring Public Finance and Public Enterprises*, Washington.

12 CUBA: CRISIS AND THE ROAD TO RECOVERY

Notes

1 This chapter draws upon work undertaken by Susan Brandwayn of the UN Department of Economic and Social Development (formerly the UN Centre on Transnational Corporations) and work undertaken jointly for UNDP with Marc Lindenberg (Harvard University) and Andrew Zimbalist (Smith College).

2 This section draws from the presentation of Raul Taladrid Suarez, Vice-President, State Committee for Economic Co-operation, Havana to the UNDP Colloquium on Management Development in Centrally-planned Economies, London, 1–3 April, 1992.

3 See A. Zimbalist (1985) 'Cuba's Economic Planning: Organisation and Performance', in S.Halebsky and J.Kirk (eds) *Cuba: Twenty-five Years of Revolution 1959–1984*, Praegar, New York; and (1989) 'Incentives and Planning in Cuba', *Latin American Research Review*, 24, 1, January. See also the controversy surrounding planning in Cuba in *Cuban Studies*, vol. 17, 1987 and vol. 18, 1988.

4 Raul Taladrid Suarez, *op. cit.*

References

Zimbalist, A. (1985) 'Cuban Economic Planning: Organisation and Performance', in S. Halebsky and J. Kirk (eds) *Cuba: Twenty-five Years of Revolution*, New York: Praegar.

—— (ed.) (1987a) 'Cuba's Socialist Economy Toward the 1990s', *World Development*, 15, 1 (special issue), January 1987. Book version (1987), Boulder, Colorado: Lynne Rienner.

—— (1987b) 'Analyzing Cuban Planning: A Response to Roca', *Cuban Studies*, 17.

—— (ed.) (1988) *Cuban Political Economy: Controversies in Cubanology*, Boulder, Colorado: Westview Press.

—— (1989a) 'Incentives and Planning in Cuba', *Latin American Research Review*, 24, 1.

—— (forthcoming) 'Reform in Cuba', in I. Kim (ed.) *Reform in Communist Systems: Comparative Perspectives*, Washington: Washington Institute.

—— (forthcoming) 'Industrial Management Reform in Cuba', in I. Jeffries (ed.) *Industrial Reform in Socialist Countries*, Cheltenham: Edward Elgar.

Zimbalist, A. and Bruydenius, C. (1989) *The Cuban Economy: Measurement and Analysis of Socialist Performance*, Baltimore: Johns Hopkins University Press.

13 NORTH KOREA: 'SCIENTIFIC MANAGEMENT' TO THE RESCUE?

Notes

1 *Economist Intelligence Unit*, 'China and North Korea', No. 2, 1992. Up-to-date official published statistics about North Korea are almost non-existent. Reliance has to be placed largely on unofficial sources.

2 *Economist Intelligence Unit*, *op. cit.*

3 *Korean Review*, 1988, p. 114.

4 *Korean Review*, *op. cit.*

5 It is possible that the agreement refers simply to pricing goods at world prices, but it should in any event probably be seen as a diplomatic move not unconnected with China's relationships with the Republic of Korea.

6 W. Carlin and C. Mayer, 'Restructuring Enterprises in Eastern Europe', (CEPR Discussion Paper No. 700), *Economic Policy*, 15, October.

7 *Economist Intelligence Unit*, *op. cit.*

INDEX

accounting 28; China 195; Czechoslovakia 104; North Korea 241; Russia 59; Vietnam 206, 217
Agency for Privatization *see* Slovenia
agriculture: Cuba 226; Poland 90, 95; Russia 49, 59; Vietnam 204, 205, 206, 208, 220
aid 34; to Kazakhstan 83; to Mozambique 162, 163, 164; to North Korea 240; to Russia 50, 74; to Vietnam 208, 219, 220; *see also* technical assistance
Anisinov, S. 70
armaments expenditure in Russia 49, 50, 58
Asian Development Bank 219
Asian Institute of Technology 218
auction methods of privatization 109, 116, 117, 128, 153
Austrian state sector 104
automobile industry of China 190–1
autonomy: Russian republics/regions 68, 69, 71; USSR republics 56
Aven, P. 70
Azeev, A.A. 72

balance of trade: Cuba 228; Poland 98; Vietnam 207
Baltic states: and Cuba 228; currency 56; independence 56
bankruptcy: China 184, 197; Czechoslovakia 121, 123, 124; East Germany 128; Vietnam 210, 215, 218
banks and banking: Czechoslovakia 118, 124; Kazakhstan 86, 88; Mozambique 166, 168; Poland 92, 99; Russia 52, 53, 57, 58; Slovenia 148, 150, 154–6, 157; Vietnam 206, 208, 215–16
Barannikov, V. 70
Barchuk, V. 70
barter 25; Cuba 223; Czechoslovakia 104; Russia 50, 59
baukema 127, 129–36
big bang *see* shock transformation
biotechnology in Cuba 226, 227, 228, 231, 232
bonds and securities: Mozambique 168; Slovenia 157
Brezhnev, L. 43, 46, 47
budget deficit: Kazakhstan 76, 77, 82–3; Poland 91–2; Vietnam 207
budgeting: China 186; Slovenia 159
Bulgak, V. 70
bureaucracy: Cuba 226, 228; Mozambique 167; Russia 49–50; USSR 45; Vietnam 205, 208
business plans (Czechoslovakia)120

Cambodia and Vietnam 205
capital market *see* stock market
Castro, F. 20, 21, 23, 222, 223, 224, 225, 226
centralization 8, 32–3; China 176, 188, 193, 202; Cuba 223–4, 227; Mozambique 165, 166, 167; North Korea 240–1; Russia 51, 63; USSR 39–43; Vietnam 205, 207, 209, 210, 211
Chernomyrdin, V. 70, 75
China 16–18, 22, 175–203; investment in Kazakhstan 87; and Korea 238, 239, 240, 243; and performance contracts 31; state sector 104; Vietnam 205
Chinese emigrants, impact on China 17,

33, 185
Chissano, J. 163, 167, 168, 170, 171
Chou En-lai 175
Chubais, A. 69, 70
ChunChing 179
CIS 44, 49; coordination within 53–4, 77, 87; and Cuba 225, 228; foreign exchange 56–7; industry 43; and Kazakhstan 77–8; and North Korea 238; and Russia 56; trade within 47, 56, 77–8, 88
Civic Unity (Russia) 74
civil war in Mozambique 162–71
CMEA *see* Comecon
co-manufacturing agreements in Cuba 228
collectives: China 178, 184–7; privatization 61; Vietnam 205
colonial rule in Mozambique 163, 164, 169, 170, 171
Comecon (CMEA): and Cuba 223, 228; and Czechoslovakia 105; and Kazakhstan 78; and North Korea 238; and Russia 56; trade with 23, 25–6; trade within 105; and Vietnam 206, 220
command economy 6, 8, 18, 33, 39–43, 104
commercialization 24; Poland 11, 95, 97
Commonwealth of Independent States *see* CIS
Communist Party: China 175, 183, 194; Cuba 225, 226, 227, 234; Czechoslovakia 106; Poland 96; Russia 66, 72; Slovenia 152; USSR 50, 66, 67; Vietnam 205, 206, 211
competition 29–30; China 186, 190, 192–4; Germany 129; Poland 92; Vietnam 206, 216
computer systems: North Korea 241–2, 243, 244, 245; USSR 44, 46
consumers/consumer sector: China 188–9; Cuba 227; Kazakhstan 76, 78; Poland 91, 93; Russia 52, 59; USSR 41, 42, 44
contracting-out: China 184, 187; Russia 59
cooperatives: China 184–7; Russia 47; Vietnam 205
corporate governance 30; East Germany 128; Poland 97–9
corruption 31–2; China 179; Czechoslovakia 109; Russia 73; USSR 45, 48, 63
Council for Mutual Economic Assistance *see* Comecon
coupons *see* vouchers
credit 25; Kazakhstan 9, 85–6; Mozambique 170; North Korea 242, 244; Poland 91, 95; Russia 5, 50, 57, 59; Slovenia 148; Vietnam 206, 207, 215–16, 219
crime 31–2; USSR 48; *see also* corruption
Cuba 20–1, 22, 222–36; aid to Mozambique 164; and CIS 225, 228; and Comecon 223, 228; and Russia 57, 228
cultural differences 5, 23, 33
currency: Baltic states 56; CIS 56; Russia 52–3; USSR 45; *see also* foreign exchange; money
Czechoslovakia/Czech and Slovak republics 12–13, 24, 103–25; foreign investment 100; Funds of National Property 12, 13, 120, 121, 123; Investment Privatization Funds (IPFs) 13, 110–11, 117–21, 124, 125; privatization 63, 105–25; state sector 104

Danilov-Danilyan, E. 70
debt (and inter-enterprise debt) 25; Cuba 225, 228; Czechoslovakia 120, 123–4; Kazakhstan 77; Mozambique 168, 170; North Korea 239; Russia 50, 57, 74; Slovenia 155; Vietnam 206, 209, 218
decentralization: China 190, 203; Cuba 228, 229, 235; East Germany 128; Poland 90; Russia 48–9; USSR 43–4; Vietnam 205
decision-support systems 241
defence *see* armaments
democracy 35
denationalization in Mozambique 166
Deng Xiaoping 16, 18, 23, 33, 35, 175, 178, 185, 202, 203
devaluation in Poland 91, 92
Development Fund *see* Slovenia
development socialism 46
development zones: in China 199; *see also* special economic zones
direct sale methods of privatization

110, 116, 135–6, 151, 153
distribution: China 183; Russia 48; *see also* service sector
dividends: China 195; Czechoslovakia 121
Dneprov, E. 70
Do Muoi 205

East Germany *see* Germany, East
EC *see* European Community
economic reform 24, 25; Kazakhstan 76–89; Poland 90–102; Russia 47–54, 55–75; Slovenia 144–61; Vietnam 207–8
education and training 28; China 197; Cuba 222, 224, 232–4, 235; Kazakhstan 83; Mozambique 163; Poland 100–1; Slovenia 160; Vietnam 218
efficiency: China 180, 192; Cuba 225, 228; Poland 95, 96; Vietnam 212, 217
egalitarianism 5, 33; in China 182
electrical goods industries in Mozambique 169
embargoes: against Cuba 222–3; against Vietnam 204, 208, 219, 220
employment: China 182, 200; Cuba 222; Vietnam 208–9; *see also* unemployment
energy resources: China 186; Cuba 226; Kazakhstan 81, 88
environmental concerns in privatization 65
equity joint ventures *see* joint ventures
Erin, V. 70
Estonia: and Cuba 228; *see also* Baltic states
ethnic differences *see* cultural differences
European Community: and Kazakhstan 83; and Slovenia 161
exchange rate 24; Czechoslovakia 197; Poland 92, 96, 98; Vietnam 206, 207, 221; *see also* foreign exchange
exports: China 187; Cuba 227, 228, 229, 235; Kazakhstan 88; Poland 96, 98; Vietnam 206, 207
extensive development in China 176

family enterprises: in China 178, 188; in Vietnam 206, 212
Fedorov, N. 70
financial policy: Kazakhstan 85–6; Slovenia 159
financial supervision in Vietnam 217–18
financial system: Poland 102; Vietnam 207, 217, 219
fiscal policy: Mozambique 168; Russia 57; Vietnam 207, 220
food: Cuba 226, 227, 228; Mozambique 162, 165, 168; North Korea 239, 240; Russia 48, 50
foreign exchange 34, 200; CIS 56–7; Cuba 223, 226, 228, 230; North Korea 238, 241; Poland 91, 96; Russia 53, 54, 74; Slovenia 156; *see also* exchange rate
foreign investment 33–4; China 176, 178, 195, 198–201, 203; Cuba 225, 228, 229, 230, 235; Czechoslovakia 100, 106, 108, 120, 122; Hungary 100; Kazakhstan 87–8; Mozambique 167, 168–9, 170; North Korea 242–3, 244–5; Poland 99–100; Russia 62, 65, 74; Slovenia 145, 157–9; Vietnam 208, 210, 215, 216, 219
foreign trade 5; within CIS 47, 56; with Comecon 23, 25–6; within Comecon 105; Cuba 223, 225, 227, 228–9, 234; Czechoslovakia 105; Kazakhstan 83; North Korea 238–40, 244; Poland 96; Slovenia 145–6; Vietnam 206, 215
Frelimo 162, 164, 165, 167, 168, 170
fuel *see* energy
Fujian 178, 185
Funds of National Property *see* Czechoslovakia
Furnznov, B. 70

Gaidar, Y. 57, 74, 75
Gang of Four (China) 175
Gao Shangquan 177
Gerashchenko, V. 74
Germany: economic and monetary union (GEMU) 127–8, 141; Federal Finance Ministry 140–1; investment in Kazakhstan 87
Germany, East 4–5, 13–14, 126–43; aid to Mozambique 164; privatization 126–43; state sector 104
Germany, West 104
Gisag AG 130
Gorbachev, M. 3, 44–5, 46, 47
Gosplan 5–6, 40, 41, 42, 46, 47, 55, 59, 67

Grachev, P. 70
gradualism 23–4, 105, 202
grass roots privatization 62, 63
Group of Seven and Kazakhstan 77
Guang Dong 22, 178, 185–6, 199

hard currency *see* foreign exchange
health care: China 183; Cuba 222, 224, 231; Mozambique 163; Poland 95
heavy industry: China 176; North Korea 238; Russia 58; USSR 41, 42; Vietnam 210
Ho Chi Minh 204, 206
Hong Kong: and China 17, 178, 185, 199; and Vietnam 208
housing: Cuba 222, 224; Kazakhstan 79
Hua Guofeng 175
Hungary: foreign investment 100; privatization 62; state sector 104

illiteracy *see* literacy
import quotas: Kazakhstan 87; Russia 56
import substitution in Cuba 230
imports: Kazakhstan 78; North Korea 239; Poland 93, 96, 98; Vietnam 206
incentives: China 182, 203; Cuba 229–30, 231
income tax in Russia 52
incomes: Cuba 225, 229; Poland 92, 93; Slovenia 147–8; *see also* pay
independence of Baltic states 56
industrial output: Kazakhstan 76; North Korea 241; Poland 93; Russia 50, 74; USSR 41, 43
industrial relations in China 200
industrialization in Vietnam 205
industry: China 176–203; Cuba 222; East Germany 126–43; North Korea 238; Poland 90, 92–3, 94–6, 97–8; Russia 46–7, 59–60, 71–3; Slovenia 145–6; Vietnam 209–11
infant mortality in Cuba 222
inflation: Kazakhstan 76–7, 81, 86; North Korea 240; Poland 92; Russia 48–9, 57, 74, 75; Vietnam 207, 220
information flows: China 198; Cuba 232; Czechoslovakia 120; North Korea 244; Slovenia 155; USSR 46; Vietnam 213
infrastructure: China 176; East Germany 135; North Korea 242–3; Vietnam 208
inputs *see* resources
insurance sector in Poland 99
intensive development in China 176
interest rates: China 197; Kazakhstan 86; Poland 91, 92, 98; Russia 57, 75; Slovenia 148
International Center for Public Enterprises (Slovenia) 160
International Monetary Fund (IMF): and Kazakhstan 83; and Mozambique 163, 166, 167, 170; and Poland 91, 92, 97; and Russia 74; and Vietnam 219
international trade *see* foreign trade
investment: China 176, 180, 185, 190, 191–2, 193, 196, 198–201, 203; Cuba 224, 227, 228; Kazakhstan 76, 77, 84–5, 87; Poland 93, 96, 97; Russia 57, 58; Slovenia 148, 155; USSR 43; Vietnam 207–8, 209, 215, 219; *see also* foreign investment
Investment Privatization Funds (IPFs) in Czechoslovakia 13, 110–11, 117–21, 124, 125 *see also* mutual funds
investment tax in Russia 52

Japan: and Korea 237, 238, 243; and Vietnam 219
Jezek, T. 112
jobs for life in China 182, 200
joint stock companies: China 194; Czechoslovakia 108, 114, 116; Kazakhstan 78, 80; Russia 47, 62; Vietnam 218–19
joint ventures: China 178, 181, 185, 200; Cuba 228, 230; Kazakhstan 79, 87; North Korea 241, 242, 244; Poland 99–100; Russia 47; Slovenia 150, 157; Vietnam 219

Kazakhstan 9–10, 22, 76–89; amortization in 85; and CIS 77–8; and Cuba 228; political structure 88–9; privatization 78–83
Khaldadze, V. 70
Khizha, G. 70, 75
Khlystun, V. 70
Khmer Rouge 205
Kim Il Sung 237, 238, 240
Kim Jong Il 237

Klaus, V. 108
Kluchnikov, V.A. 72
Kohl, H. 4–5
Kombinats 13, 126–7, 128
Korea 237
Korea, North 21–2, 237–45
Korea, South 237, 238; and China 238
Kozyrev, A. 70

labour insurance in China 183–4
land tenure: East Germany 128; Kazakhstan 79; Russia 49, 65–6; Vietnam 216, 221
land values: China 185; Vietnam 216
language skills 233, 245
Latin America and Cuba 225, 228, 229, 230
Latvia *see* Baltic states
leadership 22–3
leasing *see* rental/leasing
legislation: China 195–6; North Korea 241, 242; Vietnam 208, 212, 215–17
legislation for privatization: Czechoslovakia 106–7, 112, 120, 121; Mozambique 167; Russia 65–6; Slovenia 149, 152–3
lending *see* credit
liberalization of trade 24–5; North Korea 242; Russia 55–7
life expectancy: Cuba 222, 224; Mozambique 162
lifetime job security in China 182, 200
liquidation of enterprises: Poland 98, 99; Vietnam 208, 216, 218–19, 221
liquidity: Czechoslovakia 124; East Germany 128; Slovenia 146
literacy: Cuba 222; Mozambique 162, 170
Lithuania *see* Baltic states
loans *see* credit
local government *see* municipal
locally managed enterprises: China 179, 188, 190, 191, 193; North Korea 240; Vietnam 205, 209, 210, 217
location of industry in USSR 43
loss-making enterprises: China 196–7; Poland 95; Vietnam 209

management 27–9; China 181, 183, 197, 200; Cuba 228, 231–4, 235; Kazakhstan 80–1, 83; Mozambique 170; North Korea 240, 241, 242–4; Poland 100–1; Russia 72–3; Slovenia 160; Vietnam 211–12, 215, 217–18
management buy-outs (MBOs): East Germany 133; Russia 61, 62
management development: Cuba 233–4, 235; North Korea 243–4, 245; *see also* management
Mao Zedong 175
market access in Poland 96
market economy 35; China 176, 180–1, 186, 189, 192–4, 203; Cuba 227; Czechoslovakia 105; Kazakhstan 84, 89; Mozambique 168; Poland 90, 91–2, 97; Russia 47, 54; Slovenia 147–8; USSR 46; Vietnam 205, 206, 210, 213, 214, 220
market socialism 46
marketing: Cuba 228, 229, 231; North Korea 241
materials *see* resources
Matyukhin, G. 57
Mencinger, J. 153, 154
mergers: China 180, 187, 190–1; Vietnam 212
microelectronics industry in East Germany 127, 136–41, 142
Mikroelektronik Erfurt 127, 136–41
military expenditure *see* armaments expenditure
minerals: Kazakhstan 87; North Korea 238
ministries: China 193; Czechoslovakia 108, 120; Mozambique 166; North Korea 241; Poland 96, 100; Russia 46, 47–8, 49–50; USSR 67; Vietnam 209, 213
money/monetary system: Czechoslovakia 104; Kazakhstan 76, 77, 86; Mozambique 168; North Korea 245; Poland 91; Russia 51; Slovenia 156; USSR 42–3, 48; *see also* currency; foreign exchange
monopolies 29–30; Czechoslovakia 104; East Germany 129; Kazakhstan 9, 79, 81, 83–4; Poland 90, 94, 97; Russia 54, 60; USSR 39, 43, 48; Vietnam 210, 216
Moscow City Council 50
Mozambique 15–16, 162–71
municipal enterprises in China 179, 188, 190, 191, 193
municipal government in Russia 68, 69

mutual funds 7; Czechoslovakia 13, 109, 110, 117–19; Slovenia 154

Nanjin 242
nationalization in Vietnam 205, 215
natural revenues 104
Nazarbayer, N. 10, 22, 23
Nechayev, A. 58, 70
negotiation practices 232
Nguyen van Linh 205
Nizhny Novgorod 7, 59
North Korea *see* Korea, North
nuclear industry in North Korea 237–8, 239

O Jin U 237
OECD countries and Vietnam 220
oil: Cuba 223, 225, 230; prices 56; Russia 56; *see also* energy
oligopolies in Czechoslovakia 104
Olszewski, J. 95
open cities/regions in China 199
output *see* industrial output
ownership and control of industry 59–60, 71–3; China 177–8, 196; Cuba 223; Germany 141; Poland 98; Russia 59–60, 62, 65; Slovenia 146–8; Vietnam 214, 216; *see also* private sector; privatization; state sector

Pamfilova, E. 70
Pavlov, V. 48
pay: China 181–2; Cuba 230; East Germany 128; Kazakhstan 82; Mozambique 166; North Korea 240; Poland 92; Russia 52; Slovenia 147–8; USSR 42; *see also* incomes

pensions: China 183–4; North Korea 240; Russia 50
perestroika: Russia 49; USSR 3, 22, 44, 45, 46, 48, 225
Performance contracts 30, 31; Kazakhstan 81
personality cults in USSR 46
pharmaceuticals in Cuba 227, 228, 229, 231, 232, 235
Planning Ministry, USSR *see* Gosplan
Poland 10–12, 23–4, 90–102; privatization 62; Property Board 102; state sector 104
political structure: Kazakhstan 88–9; Russia 66–71; USSR 67
pollution damage in East Germany 135–6
Portuguese in Mozambique 163, 164, 169
poverty: Poland 98; Russia 49, 50, 51; USSR 48
prices: China 186, 189, 193, 195, 196, 197, 202; CIS intra-trade 56; Cuba 223, 224, 226; Czechoslovakia 104, 105; Kazakhstan 77, 81–2; Mozambique 165, 168, 170; North Korea 240; oil 56; Poland 97–8; Russia 50, 51, 58, 75; Slovenia 148; USSR 41, 42, 44; Vietnam 206, 216, 221
primary sector in Poland 92–3
private sector 34; China 178, 188, 203; Cuba 226, 228; Poland 90; Vietnam 206, 210, 214, 215, 218
privatization 24, 34–5; from above 62–3; of collectives 61; Czech Republic 113–18, 120, 121–2, 123; Czechoslovakia 63, 105–25; East Germany 126–43; environmental concerns 65; from grass roots 62, 63; Hungary 62; Kazakhstan 78–83; management of 26–7; Mozambique 169; Poland 62, 92, 95, 98, 99, 101; Russia 39, 47–51, 59–66, 69, 71–5; Slovak Republic 113–16, 120, 121–2, 123; Slovenia 148–61; small enterprises 63; USSR 45, 47; Vietnam 210; *see also* legislation for privatization
privilege in USSR 46, 48
productivity: China 182; Cuba 225, 229–30; East Germany 128; North Korea 241; USSR 45; Vietnam 209, 211
profits: China 179, 180, 186, 196; Cuba 226; Czechoslovakia 104; Mozambique 167, 168; North Korea 241; Poland 95; Russia 48, 74; USSR 43, 45, 59; Vietnam 206
public sector: China 177, 180; Mozambique 165–7; Poland 90, 95; Russia 59; *see also* state sector

quality control: China 180, 189, 192, 200; Cuba 228, 232

raw materials *see* resources
regional government in Russia 68, 69
Renamo 162, 166
rental/leasing: Czechoslovakia 120; Poland 99
research in Cuba 227, 229
resources: China 186, 190, 191, 196, 197, 200, 202; Cuba 226, 227; Kazakhstan 81, 88; North Korea 241; Poland 91, 96; Russia 47, 50, 58, 73; USSR 42, 43, 45
restitution of enterprises: Czechoslovakia 106–7, 116; East Germany 126, 135; Slovenia 152
retail sector: China 189; Mozambique 165; North Korea 240; Russia 59; Vietnam 212, 218
revitalizing 3–4, 33–6, 90
rewards *see* incentives
rural economy of China 187
Russia 5–8, 22, 39–54, 55–75; autonomous republics/regions 68, 69, 71; Cabinet 66, 68, 69, 70; and CIS republics 56; Committee for State Property 61, 69, 71; Congress 39, 49, 50, 51, 66, 68, 69, 74; and Cuba 57, 228; Federal Property Fund 71–2; and Kazakhstan 78; liberalization of trade 55–7; and North Korea 238, 239; political structure 66–71; President 66, 67; privatization 24, 39, 47–51, 59–66; Security Council 66, 68, 69; State Property Committee 61, 69; Supreme Soviet 50, 57, 58, 60, 66, 68, 69; US aid 50, 74
Russian Democratic Party 74
Russian Union of Industrialists 74
Rutskoi, A. 74
Ryzhkov, N. 47

Sachs, J. 50, 154
salaries *see* pay
sale methods of privatization 110, 116, 135–6, 151, 153
Saltykov, B. 70
savings in Vietnam 219
scale economies 29, 43; China 188
scientific management in North Korea 241–2
scientific research in Cuba 227, 229
sectorial privatization, Poland 11; Russia 62, 63–4
securities and bonds: Slovenia 157; Vietnam 216–17
self-management systems in Slovenia 146–8, 155
self-reliance of North Korea 239, 244
separation of powers in Russia 63, 66, 69
service sector 7; China 183, 200; Poland 90, 91; Vietnam 206, 209, 210, 212
shares/share holding: China 194–7; Czechoslovakia 110, 121; Kazakhstan 80–1; Poland 98–9; Russia 62; Slovenia 153, 157; Vietnam 216–17
shock transformation 23–4, 36; Cuba 227; Poland 92, 101; Slovenia 154
Shokhin, A. 70
shortages: China 183; Cuba 225, 227; Russia 48; USSR 45, 48
Shumeiko, V. 70, 75
Sidorov, E. 70
Singapore and Vietnam 208
size of enterprise 6, 29–30; China 188, 191, 192; Czechoslovakia 103, 104, 110; East Germany 126; Kazakhstan 29, 79; Poland 11, 94; Russia 54; Slovenia 145; Soviet Union 43; Vietnam 210, 218, 221; *see also* small enterprises
skilled workers in Mozambique 171
Slovak Republic: privatization 113–16; *see also* Czechoslovakia
Slovenia 14–15, 144–61; Agency for Privatization 148–61; Development Fund 14, 148, 151; and Yugoslavia 144
small enterprises: Cuba 222, 226, 228; Czechoslovakia 116, 119; East Germany 126, 127; Mozambique 166, 167; North Korea 241; Poland 11, 98; privatization 63; Russia 47, 63; Slovenia 145; Vietnam 206, 210, 221
social issues in reform: Cuba 225–6, 235; Kazakhstan 82–3; Poland 95, 98, 101; Russia 64; Vietnam 208, 219–20
social services: China 183–4; Cuba 224; Mozambique 167; Poland 95; Russia 49
socialism: Cuba 227, 235; Vietnam 214

Solidarity (Poland) 91
South Korea *see* Korea, South
special economic zones: China 185, 199, 203; North Korea 21, 242, 245
specialization in production in China 188
speculation in USSR 45, 48
spontaneous privatization in Vietnam 210
Stalin, J./Stalinism 39, 53
standard of living in Cuba 222, 224
state enterprises 30–1; China 177, 178, 179–84, 186, 193–4, 196, 203; Cuba 223–4, 227, 235; Mozambique 164–5, 166, 170, 171; North Korea 240–1, 242; Slovenia 147; USSR 45; Vietnam 205–21
state intervention 32, 214; China 177, 179–80, 187, 197–8, 202–3; Cuba 228; Mozambique 164; Poland 95–6; USSR 44; Vietnam 215
state orders: Kazakhstan 78, 81, 84, 85; Russia 46, 47
state regulation in Kazakhstan 84–9
state sector: proportion of economy 104; *see also* public sector
statistical data in USSR 42
stock market: China 195; Czechoslovakia 121; Poland 91, 99; Slovenia 156–7; Vietnam 217, 219
strategic aims of governments 22–3
student grants in Russia 50
subsidies: China 189; Cuba 225, 226, 228; Kazakhstan 82; Mozambique 167, 168; Poland 95; Russia 49; Vietnam 205, 206, 207, 215, 220, 221
sugar: Cuba 222, 223, 226, 227, 228; Mozambique 169; Russia 56, 57
super-monopolies: Russia 54; USSR 39, 43, 48
supervisory boards 30; East Germany 128, 141; Poland 97, 98, 102
supply *see* resources
Supreme Soviet (Russia) 50, 57, 58, 60, 66, 68, 69
Supreme Soviet (USSR) 40, 41, 67
SUTCER 233–4
Swedish aid to Mozambique 164
Swedish International Development Agency 218

Tabeev, F.A. 72
Taean management system (North Korea) 240
Taiwan: and China 178, 185; and Vietnam 208
take-overs *see* mergers
Tarasov, O.N. 72
tariffs: Poland 96; Russia 56
taxation: China 197; Cuba 230; Kazakhstan 86, 87; Mozambique 167; North Korea 242; Poland 91, 92, 95, 96, 98; Russia 50, 52; Slovenia 159; Vietnam 207, 209
technical assistance: to Kazakhstan 83; to Vietnam 219, 220; *see also* aid
technological innovation: China 176, 187, 198; Czechoslovakia 108; North Korea 242–3; Poland 97; Slovenia 148
technology transfer: China 176, 200–1; North Korea 242
television manufacture in China 188–9
tender methods of privatization 116, 117
Titkin, A. 70
Tobacco Company of Ljubljana 150–2
tourism in Cuba 226, 227, 228, 229, 230
township sector in China 16, 178, 184–7, 192–3
trade: within CIS 47, 56, 77–8, 88; *see also* embargoes; foreign trade; liberalization of trade
trade agreements in Russia 56; *see also* Comecon
trade unions in Poland 96
training *see* education and training
Travkin, V. 72
Treuhand-Zentral 128, 143
Treuhandanstalt (THA) 13, 126, 127–9, 143
Turkish investment in Kazakhstan 87

Ukraine: and Cuba 228; and Russia 56
Umek model of privatization (Slovenia) 154
unemployment: China 184; Cuba 225–6; East Germany 126, 128, 129, 137, 141; Kazakhstan 76, 82; Russia 57; Vietnam 206, 207, 219–20; *see also* employment
unit trusts *see* mutual funds
United Nations Development Programme (UNDP): Cuba 232, 234; Mozambique 170; North Korea

240, 241, 243–4, 245; Vietnam 218, 219
US: aid to Russia 50, 74; and Cuba 222–3, 225, 235; investment in Kazakhstan 87; and Korea 237; and Vietnam 204, 208, 219, 220
USSR: aid to Mozambique 164; autonomy of republics 56; Congress 67; coup attempt (Aug 1991) 48, 56; and Cuba 223, 225; economic system 39–46; Gosplan 5–6, 40, 41, 42, 46, 47, 55, 59, 67; and Korea 237, 238, 240; political structure 67; President 67; republics 55–6; *see also* CIS state sector 104; Supreme Soviet 40, 41, 67

Valuation Commission: Slovenia 15, 149; *see also* valuation for privatization
valuation for privatization: China 195; Czechoslovakia 119, 120; East Germany 129, 135; Russia 64; Slovenia 15, 149, 151, 153
value-added tax: Kazakhstan 86; Russia 50
ventilator manufacture in China 188–9
video-recorder manufacture in China 192
Vietnam 18–19, 204–21
village industries in Vietnam 204–5
Vo Van Kiet 19, 23, 205, 218
Volsky, A. 74
vouchers for privatization 7, 26; Czechoslovakia 12, 108–18, 122–3; Kazakhstan 79; Poland 11; Russia 61, 74; Slovenia 154

wages *see* pay
war: Mozambique 162–71; Vietnam 204, 205
washing machine manufacture in China 188–9
West Germany *see* Germany, West
Western influences on Russia 50, 51, 53, 56
worker ownership: Poland 97, 99; Russia 61; Vietnam 212
works councils: Czechoslovakia 107; Poland 96, 97; Slovenia 146–8, 150, 153
World Bank: and Kazakhstan 83; and Mozambique 163, 166, 167, 170; and Poland 97; and Vietnam 208, 219

Yefimov, V. 70
Yeltsin, B. 22, 39, 46, 49, 51, 56, 60, 65, 66, 70
Yoroblev, A. 70
Yugoslavia and Slovenia 144, 145, 155, 160

zones for development *see* development zones; open cities; special economic zones